THE INTENTIONS OF INTENTIONALITY

AND OTHER NEW MODELS FOR MODALITIES

SYNTHESE LIBRARY

JAAKKO HINTIKKA

THE INTENTIONS
OF INTENTIONALITY
AND OTHER NEW MODELS
FOR MODALITIES

D. REIDEL PUBLISHING COMPANY

DORDRECHT-HOLLAND / BOSTON-U.S.A.

Library of Congress Cataloging in Publication Data

Hintikka, Kaarlo Jaakko Juhani, 1929–

The intentions of intentionality and other new models
for modalities.

(Synthese library ; v. 90)
Includes bibliographical references and indexes.
1. Logic—Addresses, essays, lectures. 2. Semantics
(Philosophy)—Addresses, essays, lectures. 3. Modality
(Logic)—Addresses, essays, lectures. 4. Knowledge, Theory
of—Addresses, essays, lectures. I. Title.
BC50.H55   160   75–31698
ISBN 90–277–0583–6

Published by D. Reidel Publishing Company
P.O. Box 17, Dordrecht, Holland

Sold and distributed in the U.S.A., Canada, and Mexico
by D. Reidel Publishing Company, Inc.
306 Dartmouth Street, Boston,
Mass. 02116, U.S.A.

Printed in The Netherlands by D. Reidel, Dordrecht

CONTENTS

PREFACE

The leisure to do the thinking whose results are gathered here has largely been provided by the Academy of Finland, whose support has also made possible the help and co-operation of a group of younger logicians and philosophers.

Less tangible support and help is unfortunately harder to record and to thank for. Once again, in working on the many themes I have tried to weave together in this book I have incurred more intellectual and moral debts I can in so many words acknowledge here. Let me only say that the closer to home I get the greater they become. I have especially in mind my colleagues and students at Stanford; my colleagues in Helsinki; the past and present members of my research group in Helsinki; and incomparably more than anybody else my wife Soili.

Helsinki, April 1975

JAAKKO HINTIKKA

INTRODUCTION

A literal-minded reader might easily object to the (sub)title of this volume. What is to be found here, he might allege, are neither models, nor modalities *stricto sensu*, nor yet any completely new applications of modal logic. Even though the purpose of the title is only to signal the continuity between the present volume and its predecessor, *Models for Modalities* (D. Reidel Publishing Co., Dordrecht, 1969), the objection is sufficiently well taken to serve as an excuse for an attempt to put my enterprise in a wider perspective.

The main working assumption on which both this book and its predecessor are predicated is the usefulness of what is often referred to by the far too grandious and metaphysically charged term 'possible-worlds semantics'. It is essentially a generalization of the semantics (model theory) for modal logics developed in 1955–63 by several logicians working largely independently of each other. This is the ultimate source of the word 'modalities' in my subtitle. Some of the main features of the transition from earlier views – particularly from Carnap's semantical treatments of modality – to full-fledged possible-worlds semantics are discussed below in Chapter 5. There (and partly also in Chapter 6) the reader will also find a brief survey of some of the main insights made possible by possible-worlds semantics.

Even though possible-worlds semantics still is not being appreciated by all philosophers of language and of logic, it has since 1957 developed from a revolutionary novelty into a well-established part of contemporary philosophical logic. This breakthrough is probably due to Richard Montague more than anyone else. He emphasized especially vigorously the importance of possible-worlds semantics both as a cornerstone of a general theory of language and as a tool of philosophical analysis.

Accordingly, I do not feel any longer the same need to argue for the value of semantical methods in the study of language and in philosophy as I did in several chapters of *Models for Modalities*. However, other general problems have largely replaced the old task of convincing my audience of the importance of semantical methods. The problem now is: What is the wave of the future within possible-worlds semantics itself? What are the directions into which it will have to be developed? What are the important applications by means of which it can prove its mettle? The several essays collected together here are as many arguments for one kind of answer to these questions. What is new in them is thus not the basic techniques of modal logic (and its semantics), but the fresh applications of these techniques. Strictly speaking, I am not presenting new *models*, either, but rather new interpretations and applications of model-theoretic conceptualizations. The novelty is not complete when compared with *Models for Modalities*, but sufficient to justify the subtitle, it seems to me.

A good deal of philosophers' attention has been directed to applications of possible-worlds semantics to logical (analytical) modalities and to related problems. Much of the recent discussion in this direction has nevertheless been inconclusive and sometimes quite shallow. If I am right, this is not particularly surprising, for it seems to me that Quine's objections to quantified modal logic are in the last analysis conclusive against the unlimited use of logical (analytical) modalities. This is argued below in Chapters 2 and 6. Even though we can in fact do incomparably more both in the semantics of modalities in the narrower sense and in the semantics of propositional attitudes than Quine admits, I have come around to thinking that his basic point against logical modalities is essentially correct.

This does not by any means show the futility of quantified modal logic or its pragmatic inapplicability. What it shows is the dependence of this applicability on further assumptions which are logically speaking merely contingent. Before such 'transcendental' assumptions are examined carefully, I do not see much hope in applications of possible-worlds semantics to some of the most cherished metaphysical questions which have figured prominently in recent discussion.

Thus the main prospect of possible-worlds semantics is in the direction of propositional attitudes. And it is indeed here that possible-worlds semantics has in my opinion achieved its greatest successes. One of these is the quantifier-analysis of subordinate questions with an epistemic main verb, mentioned and used repeatedly in the bulk of this book. Its earlier, cruder form has been substantially improved on by the discovery of the need of an alternative universal-quantifier reading besides the earlier existential-quantifier one. (Cf. Chapters 1 and 7 below for a brief explanation of this new observation.) Even more striking is the discovery of two different cross-identification methods, the descriptive method and the 'acquaintance' method, right in the middle of our own conceptual system. (By cross-identification one of course means telling whether a member of one possible world is or is not identical with a member of another one.) This duality of cross-identification (individuation) methods was expounded already in *Models for Modalities*. It is discussed in several passages of this volume, most prominently in Chapters 3 and 4. Perhaps the most important feature of this contrast between two different methods of (as it were) drawing cross-world identification lines ('world lines') is that neither is any more or any less fundamental *sub specie logicae*.

The implications of this discovery still do not seem to be sufficiently understood by contemporary philosophers. Hence a few indications of these implications (as I perceive them) may be in order.

For one thing, this duality shows that we just cannot take the identity of an individual in different possible worlds for granted. Individuals, unlike logic according to Wittgenstein, just cannot take care of themselves. (See the first aphorism of Wittgenstein's *Notebooks 1914–16*.) And this in turn implies *inter alia* that the unanalyzed idea of 'rigid designator' does not cut any epistemological ice.

Admittedly the sets of possible worlds which serve to illustrate my duality of world lines are different from the ones which are typically considered in discussions of rigid designators. The latter are postulated counterfactual situations, the former sets of possible worlds compatible with someone's knowledge, belief, or some other propositional attitude. However, this does not reduce the impact of the discovery of the relativity of cross-identifications. It shows, once and for all, that cross-identification is not to be taken for granted. As I put it in my Quine paper, even an allegedly rigid designator can be bent by epistemic considerations.

The whole complex of problems about names and other more or less rigid designators cries out for a deeper analysis in terms of the two methods of cross-identification. An essential ingredient of any such analysis will probably be an insight into the role of causal chains in the semantics of several epistemic concepts. This insight is expounded in

Chapter 4 below. It seems to explain partly the seductiveness of the 'rigid designator' idea. (An individual surely takes care of its own causal connections, we might say.) However, this seductiveness is dispelled as soon as it is seen that causal connections serve to establish only one very special kind of link in the world lines of our individuals.

Although this restricted role of causality in the semantics of perceptual concepts spoils the rigid designator idea, it does not spoil the possibility of vindicating some of the most characteristic theses of the so-called causal theories of perception as a part of the logical analysis of these concepts. Since I have earlier shown how to make the best of sense-datum theories of perception within the same approach (cf. Chapter 3 below), we seem to have here a truly remarkable consilience of different-looking viewpoints in the semantics of perceptual concepts.

The differences between traditional sense-datum theories and my 'informational' analysis of perception have nevertheless turned out to be much more difficult to diagnose than I formerly supposed. Some remarks on this matter are presented in Chapter 4 and in Sections 7–11 of Chapter 10 below. As a rather bold generalization of this insight into the propositional and informational nature of perception, I shall put forward in Chapter 10 a thesis connecting with each other the basic idea of possible-world semantics and the nature of intentionality (in Husserl's sense) at large. Even though this generalization undoubtedly needs further development and further discussion, maybe even further qualifications, already in its present form it seems to me to bring to light many interesting connections – some of them surprisingly detailed – between possible-worlds semantics and Husserl's phenomenology. How general our problems become on this level is illustrated in the final essay of the volume, where some of the problems of linguistic representation highlighted by possible-worlds semantics are argued to have counterparts in the field of pictorial representation – counterparts which have been operative in the development of modern painting. Even though much remains to be done in the field staked out by these two last essays, I hope that they already serve to show to what a tremendous extent the most promising philosophical applications of possible-worlds semantics lie in the direction of 'intentional' concepts, especially propositional attitudes.

But how can I be so sure of the duality of cross-identification methods on which I have been relying? The best large-scale evidence I can refer to here turns on the insight that this duality has a striking linguistic counterpart in the contrast between two ubiquitous grammatical constructions in English. The logic of descriptive cross-identification is largely that of subordinate wh-questions with an epistemic main verb, while the logic of individuation by acquaintance is that of the grammatical direct-object construction (e.g., seeing someone, remembering somebody, knowing him, etc.) Although there are marginal exceptions to this parallelism, it works surprisingly well and can in fact be developed much further than I have done in the present book. (See nevertheless Chapter 3 below.) It follows that the grammatical direct-object construction admits of a quantifier reconstruction similar to the existential-quantifier analysis of certain subordinate wh-questions.

This is philosophically significant, for the direct-object construction has traditionally presented a *prima facie* counterexample to propositional and informational interpretations of concepts like perception and memory. The 'reduction' (paraphrase preserving logical force) of the direct-object construction to the obviously propositional that-construction (*via* quantifiers) thus removes a major obstacle to the recognition of the intentionality of perception.

However, the greatest interest of this analysis of the direct-object construction is the promise it gives of successful uses of possible-worlds semantics for linguistic purposes. Beside their own intrinsic interest, such uses have the merit of providing independent tests of the success or failure of one's logical semantics. Again, it seems to me that much recent work in (and on) possible-worlds semantics has missed a wide field of potential applications – and of potential evidence. For instance, I would go as far as to suggest for instance that the best large-scale evidence for my quantifier analysis of subordinate questions (proposed originally in my book *Knowledge and Belief* in 1962) is to be found in the logico-linguistic theory of direct questions into which this analysis can be generalized. The generalization is still in progress, but Chapter 7 below illustrates what can be done in this direction. It is especially gratifying to see how the controversial uniqueness premises of epistemic logic yield at once an interesting answer to the much-debated question: What is an answer to a given question? Further illustrations are found in my recent paper, 'Questions about Questions' in *Semantics and Philosophy*, Milton K. Munitz and Peter K. Unger (eds.), The New York University Press, New York, 1974.

This is not the only promising direction for linguistic applications, however. A few others, closely geared to the interests of contemporary linguists, are tentatively discussed in Chapter 8 of the present volume. Several of the possibilities foreshadowed there can be pushed much further. A large number of potential applications in the direction of language theory likewise come briefly up in the survey presented in Chapter 1 below. What is said there nevertheless remains within the sphere of logical and philosophical rather than grammatical theory. Although I there (and elsewhere) discuss the logical and semantical force of many natural-language expressions, the question as to how this force is connected with the purely grammatical properties of the expressions in question is not raised.

An especially interesting question – illustrating some of the points made in the programmatic opening chapter of *Models for Modalities* – comes up repeatedly in Chapter 1. It is the possible use of pragmatic and conversational factors in explaining the logic of natural-language expressions. In direction, too, we seem to have excellent possibilities for further work.

There is an interesting line of argument for Montague's thesis that possible-worlds semantics can serve as a general framework of meaning analysis which has recently occurred to me. It is briefly discussed in Chapters 5, 6, and 10 below. It takes off from Frege's and Husserl's idea that the meaning of an expression is the way in which its extension is given to us. If we interpret this 'way of being given' functionally and if we most liberally allow whole worlds to be the arguments on which these functions depend, we obtain precisely Montague's idea of meanings as functions from possible worlds to extensions. When looked upon in this light, the step from Frege and Husserl to possible-worlds semantics thus appears surprisingly short.

This 'transcendental deduction' of possible-worlds semantics is at the same time useful in bringing out some of the shortcomings of possible-worlds semantics so far. For what people actually traffic in are not meaning functions as abstract mathematical entities (infinite classes of pairs of correlated argument-values and function-values), but suitable 'algorithms' or 'recipes' for as it were actually finding the function value. Even more importantly, the meaning functions seldom depend as their argument on the *whole* possible world, fully analyzed, in which the reference (the value of the function) is located. The relevant arguments must somehow be only certain 'parts' or 'aspects' of the world in question. But if so, some of the 'parts' we have to take into account here may be impossible to extend to a consistent 'whole world'. Thus we obtain at once also a way out of the paradox of 'logical omniscience', i.e., the assumption that everybody knows all the logical consequences of what he knows (and likewise for other propositional attitudes). This way out is briefly explained and motivated in Chapter 9. Once again, I am only scratching the surface of highly interesting-looking possibilities which are in the process of being investigated more deeply. In this book, the talk of 'parts' or 'aspects' in which I just indulged must be left merely metaphoric. However, Dr. Veikko Rantala is in the process of working out a simple and elegant treatment which makes honest model-theoretic sense of these loose locutions.

I am uncomfortably aware of the shortness and abruptness of these hints at the common problems and common themes that tie together the different parts of this work. I can only hope that they nevertheless serve to bring to light some of the problems and potentialities which otherwise could easily remain hidden.

A NOTE ON THE ORIGIN OF
THE DIFFERENT ESSAYS

Chapter 1 first appeared under a slightly different title ('Terms' instead of 'Verbs') in *Contemporary Philosophy in Scandinavia*, Raymond E. Olson and Anthony M. Paul (eds.), The John Hopkins Press, Baltimore, 1972, pp. 105–122. It is reprinted here with the kind permission of The Johns Hopkins Press. I have revised this chapter more thoroughly than any other one here. Not only have I tried to cover in this survey several observations made since it was originally written. I have also changed my mind on more than one point made there.

Chapter 2 is reprinted almost intact from *Synthese* **21** (1970) 408–424. It has meanwhile appeared (like the rest of this number of *Synthese*) also in *Semantics of Natural Language*, Donald Davidson and Gilbert Harman (eds.), D. Reidel Publishing Co., Dordrecht, 1972.

Chapter 3 was originally published in the *Journal of Philosophy* **67** (1970) 869–883. It appears here with the permission of the Managing Editor of the *Journal*. It was written as my contribution to the APA Symposium on 'the Logic of Belief' on 28 December, 1970.

Chapter 4 is scheduled to appear also in *Ajatus* **36** (scheduled for 1974, appears in 1975). This volume of *Ajatus* comprises the proceedings of the 1973 International Symposium on Perception in Helsinki. My essay is reprinted here with the permission of the publisher of *Ajatus*, the Philosophical Society of Finland.

Chapter 5 appeared originally in the Carnap number of *Synthese*, that is, in *Synthese* **25** (1973) 372–397. Virtually no changes have been made in it. Neither the editor's nor the publisher's reprint permission has presented any problems in this case.

I wrote Chapter 6 as an intended contribution to the Library of Living Philosophers volume on W. V. Quine. When I found out how long it will probably take to see that volume in print, I switched it to the present collection. Its literary format seems to me to reflect the development of its subject, which has progressed almost literally by dialogue. Each new development has solved some of the earlier problems but also led to new questions – or at least to the reappearance of the old ones in a new form.

Chapter 7 will also appear in an anthology of papers on questions, to be edited by Henry Hiż.

Chapter 8 is reprinted from *Approaches to Natural Language: Proceedings of the 1970 Stanford Workshop on Grammar and Semantics*, K. J. J. Hintikka, J. M. E. Moravcsik, and P. Suppes (eds.), D. Reidel Publishing Co., Dordrecht, 1973, pp. 197–214. I have corrected an embarrassingly large number of slips and infelicities and made several additions and changes, including one fairly major one.

Chapter 9 first saw the light of day as my reply in *Ajatus* **32** (1970) 32–47 to two critical notes by Richard L. Purtill and Kathleen G. Johnson Wu, respectively. I have here omitted the part which discusses Mrs. Wu's note and made a number of small changes. It appears here with the permission of the Philosophical Society of Finland.

Chapter 10 is also appearing in *Essays on Explanation and Understanding*, Juha Manninen and Raimo Tuomela (eds.), D. Reidel Publishing Co., Dordrecht, 1975.

Chapter 11 was originally presented as a lecture under the auspices of the Van Leer Foundation of Jerusalem in March 1974. A Hebrew translation is due to appear in *Iyyun* in Israel. It is partly based on an essay in Finnish which appeared in *Aika* in 1972 (pp. 133–146).

All the reprint permissions are gratefully acknowledged.

CHAPTER 1

DIFFERENT CONSTRUCTIONS IN TERMS OF THE BASIC EPISTEMOLOGICAL VERBS

A Survey of Some Problems and Proposals

In studying the conceptual problems connected with any logically or philosophically interesting term, one of the very first questions we encounter concerns the different grammatical constructions in which it normally occurs (insofar as there is a non-trivial difference in meaning between them). Some distinctions between such constructions have figured prominently in recent philosophical literature. A case in point is Ryle's emphasis on the distinction between *knowing that* and *knowing how*, to which I shall soon return. However, in most cases surprisingly little systematic work has been done to clear up the precise relations between the different constructions and their relative priorities. For instance, even though there are a great many books and articles on the concept of goodness and on the meaning of the word 'good' it seems to me that the interrelations of the different grammatical constructions in which it can occur are but imperfectly understood. Some of the most acute discussions of the meaning of 'good', for example those by Paul Ziff in *Semantic Analysis* and by Jerrold J. Katz in *Philosophy of Language*, concentrate almost exclusively on the use of the word 'good' in the construction 'a good X'.[1] These authors do not ask whether this is a basic and irreducible construction for the relevant logical and philosophical purposes, or whether it can be analyzed in terms of other uses of 'good', for instance, the one exemplified by 'It is good that'. I suspect that the latter is more fundamental than the use in the form 'a good X'.

In the case of the different constructions which involve the verb 'know', a number of results, some very interesting, are scattered about in the literature. Several observations that I have made elsewhere (in print or informally) can be regarded as answers to questions concerning the relation of these different constructions to each other or can be illustrated in terms of such answers. A survey of these interrelations will therefore amount to a quick survey of a part of my recent work in epistemology. In order to formulate the answers I am trying to give now, however, it is first necessary to develop a way of raising the questions to be addressed.

What different types of constructions are there involving the verb
'know'? The following distinctions between different kinds of constructions are found in the literature or are for other reasons relevant to
epistemological discussion:

(1)   Knowing that versus knowing how

(2)   Knowing that versus knowing whether

(3)   Knowing that versus such constructions as
         knowing what, knowing who, knowing when,
         knowing where, etc.

(4)   Knowing that, or some construction which is like the second
         part of either (2) or (3) in that it involves a subordinate clause,
         versus knowing plus a (grammatical) direct object (e.g.,
         knowing someone). We might call these the that-construc-
         tion, the interrogative constructions (or *oratio obliqua* con-
         structions), and the direct object construction, respectively.[2]

(5)   Knowing that ... *a* ... (where '*a*' is a singular term) versus
         such constructions as knowing of *a* that ... he (she, it)....
         There is a related contrast between the constructions 'it is
         known that...' and 'someone is known to...', for instance:
                  it is known that... *a* ...
         and
                  a is known to be such that... he (she, it)....

Instead of speaking impersonally of what is known we could of course
speak here of what some particular person knows.

The last two distinctions, (4) and (5), concern the ways in which
singular terms can enter into a construction governed by the verb 'know'.

It is not claimed that the above list exhausts all of the interesting
distinctions or even all of the distinctions to be met with in contemporary
philosophical literature.

I have a definite thesis to put forward concerning these different constructions. I suggest that, as far as the basic logical force of the different
constructions is concerned, they can all be characterized or 'defined'
in terms of the construction *knowing that*, with the exception of one
somewhat dubious sense of the construction *knowing how*.

Some of the arguments I can give for this thesis have been or will be presented elsewhere. Here I shall first indicate what interest this thesis would have, supposing that it can be established. One reason why it is interesting is that it would show that knowing is in a very strong sense a *propositional attitude*. This is shown (or at least suggested) by the fact that all of the different constructions in terms of the verb 'know' can be reduced (if I am right) to the sense in which the nature of knowledge as a propositional attitude is most explicit, for the 'knowing that' construction quite obviously does not involve a relation of a person (the knower) to any individual object (any individual in the general logical sense of the word). Insofar as the concept of knowledge can be conceived of as a relation, it obtains between a person and an entity or set of entities of an entirely different logical type. Philosophers have sometimes spoken of a proposition as the second term of this relation. I have proposed that the semantics of such 'propositional attitudes' as knowledge, belief, etc., be discussed, not in terms of unanalyzable propositions, but in terms of what I have ventured to call 'possible worlds' or 'possible states of affairs'.[3] The basic idea is that every attribution of a 'propositional attitude' such as knowing to a person can be paraphrased by speaking of the totality of possible worlds compatible with the presence of this attitude in the person in question (at the time about which we are talking). For instance, to say that p is known by a to be true is nothing more – or less – than to say that p is true in all of the possible worlds compatible with a's knowing what he in fact knows. The plausibility of this idea is probably much more obvious than is its great usefulness for a satisfactory semantical (model-theoretical) theory of propositional attitudes.

A reduction of the direct object construction to the *knowing that* construction would be especially interesting in connection with the problem of the nature of the objects of knowledge. Such a reduction would reinforce the suggestion that in the last analysis individual objects can figure as objects of knowledge only in the sense of occurring as members of the possible worlds or possible states of affairs specified by the subordinate clause in 'a knows that p'.

Further interest is lent to the general thesis of this chapter by its virtually being a special case of a much more general thesis concerning the nature of all intentional concepts. For this thesis, see Chapter 10 below.

The construction whose reduction to 'knowing that' is easiest to explain is the 'knowing whether' construction in distinction (2) above.[4] Clearly,

(6) a knows whether p

is equivalent to

(7)   (a knows that p) $\vee$ (a knows that not-p).

This gives us a clue as to the analysis of the other constructions of the type *knows + an interrogative clause* (cf. (3)).[5] In these constructions we are not confronted by a yes-or-no alternative but a choice of the right (and known) answer from a wider selection of candidates. For instance, 'a knowns who b is' might from this point of view be thought of as a disjunction comparable to (7):

(8) a knows that $(b=x_1)$ $\vee$
         a knows that $(b=x_2)$ $\vee$
         ....

where $x_1, x_2, \ldots$ are all the individuals there are. The intended logical force is presumably captured by

(8)* (Ex) a knows that $(b=x)$

or perhaps by

(8)** (Ex) (x is a person $\wedge$ a knows that $(b=x)$).

This suggestion is reinforced by other considerations. One trouble with such disjunctions as (8) is that the range of singular terms one can substitute for the x_i's has to be restricted somehow. (For instance, substituting 'b' for one of the terms 'x' would spoil the game.)

We have no such trouble in (8)* or (8)** if we insist that one's bound (bindable) variables have to range over genuine individuals. Eloquent reasons for so insisting have in fact been voiced by Quine, and elsewhere I have tried to explore some of the implications of such a course.[6] Here they serve to reinforce the merits of (8)* or (8)**. Knowing of *some definite individual* that it is identical with b is surely sufficient for knowing who b is, however insufficient merely knowing the truth of some identity of the form '$b=c$' may be. (To know of some actual person that he is the author of *Under the Volcano* is to know who this author is, whereas merely to

know that this author is identical with the author of *Ultramarine* is not.)
It should be clear, however, that (8)* and (8)** capture only half of
the force of 'knows who' statements. If someone says,

(9)   Doctor Welby knows who has pneumonia and who only has
       common cold

he is asserting more than the good doctor's ability to make the right
diagnosis in (at least) *one* case. Rather, what is being asserted is that
Dr. Welby can *always* tell the difference. This means that we have to
keep in mind a reading of subordinate wh-questions (*knows + interrogative clause*) different from the one exemplified by (8)* or (8)**. On
this reading, the first half of (9) has the force of

(9)* (x) $(x$ has pneumonia $\supset$
       Dr. Welby knows that x has pneumonia).

In more general terms, the difference between the two readings can be
said to be the same as the difference between

(10)* (Ex) $(F(x) \wedge a$ knows that $F(x))$

and

(10)** (x) $(F(x) \supset a$ knows that $F(x))$.

In principle, we always have to heed both these potential readings of a
wh-question, although collateral information and pragmatic pressures
often filter out one of them.

Sometimes there is also a presumption present to the effect that the
difference between the two readings does not matter, which amounts to
the assumption that there is exactly one individual x satisfying $F(x)$. I
think that we can see here how this presumption naturally comes about
through conversational expectations. *Ceteris paribus*, we feel entitled to
assume that speakers do not multiply readings beyond necessity.

The unmistakable presence of two different readings of wh-questions
poses many interesting theoretical problems concerning the relation of
such questions to the notion of ambiguity. I will discuss these problems
elsewhere. What is already clear, however, is that the only construction
with 'knows' needed on either reading is the 'knows that' construction.

Other constructions involving interrogative clauses admit of a parallel treatment. For instance, '*a* knows when *s* occurred' can be paraphrased (roughly) by

> (*Ex*) (*x* is a moment or period of time ∧ *a* knows that *s* occurred at or during *x*),

or (somewhat less plausibly) by

> (*x*) ((*x* is a moment or period of time ∧ *s* occurred at or during *x*) ⊃ *a* knows that *s* occurred at or during *x*).

In all paraphrases of this sort, the verb 'knows' occurs only in the construction 'knows that', exactly as I have suggested. From these paraphrases it can also be seen that the meaning of the constructions thus reduced the 'knowing that' construction turns on a rather subtle interplay between epistemic notions and quantifiers. It seems to me that such interplay also underlies distinctions (4) and (5).

From the above discussion, one can perhaps gather what the trouble with (8) is. In order to spell it out, the vocabulary and imagery of 'possible worlds' foreshadowed in my earlier remarks is especially useful. (It also has the deeper merit of admitting of a development into an explicit and precise semantical theory). A free singular term cannot always be used in (8), for it need not specify a unique individual. The reason can perhaps be seen as follows: A free singular term may refer to different individuals in the different possible worlds compatible with *a*'s knowledge. (If *a* does not know who the author of *Ultramarine* is, then in some of the different possible worlds compatible with what he knows the term 'the author of *Ultramarine*' refers to different persons.) But if these possible worlds are (as I have suggested) part and parcel of all talk about what *a* knows or does not know, then in the context of such talk some singular terms will fail to pick out a unique individual, simply because the individual referred to varies from one relevant possible world to another. For this reason, not all free singular terms can be used as substitution instances of bound (bindable) variables (whose function is precisely to range over individuals) in (8), for this would make nonsense of the usual interpretation of quantification theory.[7]

It can be seen, however, that any free singular term can be used to make statements about a definite individual, namely, about the individual to which it as a matter of fact refers (in the 'actual world'). Thus there is a highly important ambiguity in many statements made in ordinary discourse in terms of a free singular term, for example, 'b', in contexts which, like epistemic contexts, involve implicit consideration of several 'possible worlds'. Such a statement may be taken as being (so to speak) about the different individuals which are b (i.e., different in different possible worlds of the relevant sort). However, it may also be taken as being about the individual who in fact is b. The two interpretations yield logically independent propositions. For instance, someone might know a lot about the author of *Ultramarine* (e.g., about his stylistic and moral peculiarities) without knowing anything about Malcolm Lowry the individual (for he might fail to know who this author is). On the other hand, an acquaintance of Lowry's might know a few things about him without knowing that they were true of the author of *Ultramarine*. Precisely this distinction, it seems to me, is what is signaled by such differences in construction as are listed in (5). These grammatical constructions do not constitute infallible evidence as to how a statement is intended to be taken, but quite often they give us helpful clues in this respect.

In order to spell out the difference, it is again useful to recall that bindable variables range over genuine individuals. If '$F(b)$' is a statement about b, 'whoever he is or may be', we can turn it into a statement about the individual who in fact is b by replacing 'b' with a bindable variable (e.g., 'x') in '$F(b)$' and specifying this individual by saying that he must (actually) satisfy the condition '$x = b$'. If we presuppose that such an individual exists, we obtain

$$(Ex) [x = b \land F(x)].$$

If not, that is, if we are merely speaking of such an individual 'should it exist', we can use formulation

$$(x) [x = b \supset F(x)].$$

For instance, such constructions as

> 'a knows of b that he is rich'

or

> 'b is known by a to be rich'

will thus be paraphrased either by

$$(Ex) (x = b \land a \text{ knows that } x \text{ is rich})$$

or

$$(x)\,(x=b \supset a \text{ knows that } x \text{ is rich}).$$

Again, in these paraphrases 'knows' occurs solely in the construction 'knows that'.

Thus we have obtained what seems to me a viable explication of distinction (5).[8] Again, we can witness an interesting interplay of propositional attitudes and quantification.

The distinction is perhaps especially clear in the case of such statements as

> The king believes the impostor to be the prince who disappeared.

Here the king would not express his belief by saying,

> I believe that the impostor is the prince who disappeared.

Rather, what is intended is that the king believes of the individual who in fact is an impostor that he is the prince. It seems to me that both the need for distinction (5) and the naturalness of our explication of it can be seen especially clearly in this example.

This leaves only distinctions (1) and (4) to be analyzed. Since (4) is by far the subtlest of our distinctions, and since its import turns out to be clearest in the case of the analogous constructions in terms of certain other epistemologically interesting verbs, I shall postpone my discussion of it to a later stage of this chapter. Likewise, (1) will be commented on later.

It is to be noted that our being able to capture the distinctions (5) in terms of our simple logical apparatus does not yet amount to an explanation why the natural-language expressions in question come to express these distinctions. Such an explanation can be given by means of the semantics for quantifiers and questions in English which I am in the process of developing.

Here I can only offer a number of supplementary remarks and general comments on the different constructions with the verb 'know' and their interrelations.

First of all, the actual usage is somewhat variable, and often one construction can be made to do what is easily seen to be the job of another. In some cases this may even be philosophically misleading.

J. L. Austin has pointed out that the direct object construction (cf. (4)) is often used to express what also could be expressed by means of the second construction distinguished in (3): 'knowing the winner of the Derby' may mean simply 'knowing what won the Derby' (i.e., 'knowing which horse won the Derby') although there is no grammatical reason why it could not mean being acquainted with the horse in question, by analogy with, for example, 'knowing last year's Miss California'.[9]

More subtly, Austin points out that even the 'knowing what' construction is occasionally taken in different ways:

When… Mr. Wisdom speaks generally of 'knowing his sensations' he presumably means this to be equivalent to 'knowing *what* he is seeing, smelling, etc.', just as 'knowing the winner of the Derby' means 'knowing what won the Derby'. But here again, the expression 'know what' seems sometimes to be taken, unconsciously and erroneously, to lend support to the practice of putting a direct object after *know*: for 'what' is liable to be understood as a relative 'that which'. This is a grammatical mistake: 'what' can of course be a relative, but in 'know what you feel' and 'know what won' it is an interrogative (Latin *quid*, not *quod*). In this respect, 'I can smell what he is smelling' differs from 'I can know what he is smelling'. 'I know what he is feeling' is not 'There is an *x* which both I know and he is feeling', but 'I know the answer to the question "What is he feeling?"' And similarly with 'I know what I am feeling': this does *not* mean that there is something which I am both *feeling* and *knowing*…. Uncritical use of the direct object after *know* seems to be one thing that leads to the view that… sensa, that is things like colours, noises and the rest, speak or are labelled by nature, so that I can *literally* say what (that which) I see: it pipes up, or I read it off. It is as if sensa were *literally* to 'announce themselves' or 'identify themselves'….

Austin's remarks illustrate the great philosophical interest of many distinctions one can make here. Needless to say, in the remainder of this paper we shall assume that in the construction, 'knowing what', 'what' is to be taken as an interrogative and not as a relative, unless the contrary is explicitly stated.

Again it would be of interest to ask the further question as to how the English expression 'knowing what' comes to have its two meanings. Again, an answer is forthcoming only on the basis of an extended separate investigation.

Those uses of the grammatical direct object construction which are easily and trivially paraphrased in terms of the other constructions may be called its elliptical uses (or senses). Cases in point are, e.g., the phrases 'knowing the winner of the Derby' and 'knowing the Cramér-Rao theorem', which, respectively, mean simply knowing which horse won the Derby and knowing what the Cramér-Rao theorem expresses (i.e., knowing that the variance of an estimate and differential information are related inversely).

The non-elliptical uses of the direct object construction are those which do not obviously reduce to the other constructions, e.g., knowing a person. It is only the relation of these to the 'knowing that' construction that is an interesting problem. In what follows, I shall often disregard the elliptical uses of the direct object construction altogether.

There are other facets of the direct object construction that may be philosophically relevant. Certain philosophers, e.g., Bertrand Russell, have discussed what is often called *knowledge by acquaintance*.[10] Although this kind of knowledge cannot, without qualification, be identified with the kind of knowledge which is approximately expressed by means of the direct object construction, the two are obviously closely related, and a better understanding of the direct object construction can therefore be expected to throw some light on the idea of 'knowledge by acquaintance'.

In languages other than English, these different kinds of knowledge are sometimes expressed by different verbs. Here, one is reminded of the German distinction between *wissen* and *kennen* and the French distinction between *savoir* and *connaître*, although they do not completely coincide with ours. It is perhaps not irrelevant to point out that for the Greeks the idea of 'knowledge by acquaintance' was much more important than it usually is for modern thinkers.[11]

The connection between the direct object construction with 'knows' and the notion of acquaintance will be seen to point to the general direction in which a reduction of the direct object construction to the 'knowing that' construction is to be found.[12] I shall return to the relation of the direct object construction to the propositional constructions later in this chapter in discussing perception.

Emphasizing the difference between the direct object construction and the 'propositional' constructions may meanwhile help us to get rid of a misunderstanding. Whatever the direct object construction serves to express in the last analysis, it is somehow closely connected with such ideas as acquaintance and familiarity. Emphasizing the distinction therefore helps to keep in mind the fact that there are kinds (senses) of knowledge which are unlike the direct object construction and in which familiarity does not breed knowledge.

Another case of a construction which can be understood in different ways is the popular locution 'knowing how' which was exploited by Ryle in his criticism of what he calls the intellectualistic misinterpretation of intelligence, presented in the famous second chapter of *The Concept of Mind*.[13] Ryle contrasts 'knowing that' with 'knowing how' and claims that the latter is more fundamental than the former for the purpose of understanding our concept of intelligence and related concepts.

It is not my purpose here to criticize Ryle's criticism of what he calls 'the intellectualistic legend', although his criticism seems to me to rest on far too narrow a view of what it means to 'know that'. In any case, there is some truth in what Ryle says. However, it seems to me most unfortunate that the way in which he explains his point leans rather heavily on the ambiguous and frequently misapplied locution 'knows how'. Ryle's emphasis on the contrast between 'knowing that' and 'knowing how' would be justified if the similarity of these two constructions had been operative in misleading philosophers. Ryle does not claim this, however, and such a claim would be very unlikely to be true. For one thing, the skill sense of 'knowing how' is expressed in many other languages without using any counterpart to the verb 'know' at all. For instance, in German 'know how' would be *können* (*imstande sein*), whereas 'knowing that' would be *wissen*. No real danger of confusion can be said to obtain here.

What is confusing about the locution 'knowing how' is that it has several different uses. On one hand,

(11) a knows how to do x

may mean (and perhaps most often means) that a has the skills and capacities required to do x, i.e., that he can do x. However, it may also mean (and occasionally does mean) that a knows the answer to the question: How should one go about it in order to do x? In this sense, knowing how to do x does not entail being capable of doing it or even ever having been capable of doing it.

We might dub these two different senses of (11) the skill sense and the 'knowing the way' sense. Of these, the skill sense seems to be largely parasitic on the other one. Its presence in ordinary discourse can be partly explained in terms of pragmatic (conversational) forces. In fact, the other wh-constructions with 'knows' often have a similar 'skill sense' associated with them, albeit in a somewhat less marked form than with 'knows how'. For instance, in (9) the 'knows who' clearly suggests a definite skill on the part of the good doctor. However, this is easily explainable on the pragmatic level. For how else could Dr. Welby possibly know (even just in the minimal sense of being right *de facto*) who has pneumonia in each case among an unrestricted multitude of patents than by means of the appropriate skill? Thus it is the universal-quantifier reading of wh-constructions with 'knows' that gives rise (jointly with certain fairly obvious pragmatic assumptions) to the 'skill sense' of these constructions.

What happens with 'knows how' is basically only a more pronounced form of the same effect. If someone 'knows the way' to accomplish something in each of a wide range of problematic situations, it is a reasonable presupposition indeed that he 'knows how' to accomplish it also in the skill sense, which therefore appears little more than an unavoidable shadow of the 'knowing the way' sense. The latter use is thus the primary one logically.

It seems to me that we are sometimes uncomfortably aware of this secondary and derived character of the skill sense and that there are contexts in which this sense of 'knowing how' hence smacks of a vulgarism. Suppose, for example, someone asks me: "Do you know how to play the piano?" I would be tempted to reply: "Surely everyone *knows how* a piano is played; but nevertheless not everyone *can* play the piano, myself included." The same point can be illustrated by reference to the difference in logical force between such questions as "Do you know how to play the piano?" and "Do you know how to make a call from this extension phone?" Almost anyone *knows how* a piano is played, but not everyone *can* do it. Almost anyone *can* make a phone call, provided that he *knows how* to do it. It may also be suggested that knowing how in the 'knowing the way' sense is not always as much as a prerequisite for being able to do it. I *can* touch-type, but I do not *know how* I do it in the sense that I could recall the positions of the different keys (although my fingers find them 'on their own'), and thus, for instance, could not teach anyone to type without access to a typewriter.

It is typical that the situations in which we can thus neatly separate the skill sense of 'knows how' from the 'knowing the way' sense (and to dismiss the former as a solecism) are the ones in which the skill force does not come about by way of the pragmatic implications just adumbrated. We cannot likewise separate the two readings of 'Dr. Welby knows how to diagnose pneumonia', assuming of course the univeral-quantifier interpretation of the 'knowing the way' sense.

In general, it seems to me that it would have been much more useful for Ryle's own purposes to argue that there are elements of knowing how imbedded in the concept of 'knowing that' instead of taking the *knowing that/knowing how* contrast for granted and using it to criticize 'the intellectualistic legend'. For one thing, I believe that 'knowing that', in the last analysis, involves 'know-how' at the very least in the 'knowing the way' sense, and hence (via conversational implications) presumably also in the skill sense. Conversely, we have seen that the skill sense of 'knowing how' is largely parasitic upon the much more 'intellectualistic' sense ('knowing the way') sense of this expression. But, if so, then the 'intellectualistic legend' cannot be satisfactorily criticized in terms of an alleged contrast between 'knowing how' and 'knowing that' in the way that Ryle does.

It seems to me that, however refreshing Ryle's criticism of narrow interpretations of intelligence may be, in his own interpretation of the meaning of 'knowing that' Ryle himself succumbs to what I cannot help calling a narrowly intellectualistic view. Very briefly expressed, Ryle's mistake seems to be that he associates 'knowing that' for too closely with being able to tell, i.e., being able to produce the right information on request. Of course, Ryle would be the first to admit that what counts here cannot be the mere capacity to produce the right noises on appropriate stimuli. Neither a parrot nor a well-trained idiot *knows* what he is saying. What more has to be required is not easy to express briefly, but, in general, some reasonably good understanding of what one's words stand for is obviously required. And this understanding itself can scarcely be a purely verbal matter. It presupposes some idea of how one's words are related to the reality they are about. Now I have argued elsewhere that in the case of certain very simple logical words, namely, the quantifiers, it is useful to compare the mastery of the con-concepts they express with the mastery of certain games (in the precise sense of mathematical game theory).[14] Knowing the truth of a statement is, on this simple model, comparable to knowing certain things about what may happen in one's 'games of investigating the world', to use a phrase Ryle himself employs elsewhere. But if this model is at all representative, if it is at all like what is essentially involved in 'knowing that', then the contrast between 'knowing that' and 'knowing how' is useless as the kind of simple dichotomy which Ryle seems to assume it to be, for 'knowing that' will involve a great deal of 'know-how'.

In any case, we do distinguish between, for instance, 'knowing how the piano is played' and 'knowing how to play the piano', when the latter is taken in the skill sense. This already serves to show that the construction 'knowing how' is not always taken to indicate a skill but is sometimes naturally taken in the other ('knowing the way') sense.

The skill sense of 'knowing how' cannot be analyzed in terms of 'knowing that'. However, it can be largely dismissed from an analysis of the basic logical force of the different constructions with the verb 'know'. When it is not parasitic on the 'knowing the way' sense, it seems to be an illicit extension of this parasitic usage. Hence we shall not discuss the 'skill' sense further in what follows.

The other sense of 'knowing how' is comparable to the meaning of such locutions as 'knowing who', 'knowing when', etc., and can be reduced to the 'knowing that' construction in a parallel way. For instance, knowing how a call is made from a given extension phone is knowing of a certain sequence of manipulations (pushing a button, dealing certain numbers first, etc.) that a call can be made by their means.

Again, it may be useful to be shaken from our parochial ways of thinking and speaking by the realization that the Greeks viewed matters in a light different from ours. For them, there is scarcely any difference that corresponds to our distinction between *knowing that* and *knowing how*. As readers of the *Apology* will recall, in Socrates' view the skills of a craftsman constituted real knowledge or *episteme*. The difference between a real *episteme* and a mere blind *empeiria* is not one between factual knowledge and skill, but, roughly, between on the one hand knowledge or skill which is accompanied by conscious insight into its own aims and principles and on the other hand mere blind capacity.[15]

As far as the other terms which are important in epistemology are concerned, they give rise to the same or closely related problems. Among these terms there are the different words connected with belief ('belief', 'opinion', 'guess', etc.), perception ('perceiving', 'seeing', 'hearing', etc.), memory, awareness, and so on. All of these terms occur in some constructions analogous to those listed in connection with knowing, and most of them occur in almost all of these constructions. (It is interesting to see that the skill sense of 'knowing how' does not have any counterpart in the case of most of these other terms, however.) In addition, new constructions can make their appearance when we examine these other epistemic terms. The construction 'believe in' is an obvious case in point. My thesis concerning these terms is, by and large, the same as that concerning knowledge: the logical primacy of the that-construction. In other words, I think that all of these terms express *propositional attitudes* in a rather strong sense. Insofar as these terms are thought of as expressing relations, they hold between the person having this attitude and certain states of affairs or courses of events (propositions, if you want, conceived of as sets of 'possible worlds'). If we are discussing what a knows or does not know, the second term of the relation is (as I suggested above) the set of all possible worlds compatible with a's knowing whatever he does know. In the same way, when we are attributing any (typical) propositional attitude to a, we are implicitly considering the set of all states of affairs or courses of events (as the case may be) which are compatible with a's holding the attitude in question.

If propositional attitudes are conceived of as relations, they do not hold between a person and ordinary objects (individuals). In fact, the major implication of the reduction of the direct object construction to the propositional constructions is that these seemingly 'direct objects' can, in the last analysis, enter into a context governed by one of our terms only as members of a 'possible world' (or several such worlds).

This claim is especially interesting in the case of perception. The direct object constructions with perceptual terms appear independent of others, and perhaps even fundamental and irreducible. (Is not perception a physical and physiological relation between the perceiver and the perceived object or objects)? For this reason, the question of the reducibility of the direct object perceptual constructions to propositional constructions has to be argued much more carefully and at much greater length than I can do here.

There are of course differences between different uses (senses) of the direct object constructions. Some such uses admit of easy paraphrasing in terms of the propositional constructions. Cases in point seem to be 'believing what (i.e., that which) someone says' and 'seeing an accident', which presumably can be paraphrased in terms of believing that things are as the person in question says they are or in terms of seeing that the accident happened (or perhaps seeing how it happened). More generally, we have the locution 'believing someone' in the sense 'believing what he says'.

These uses will be called *elliptical* ones. However, the choice of this term is not calculated to suggest that they cannot given a semantical and grammatical analysis in their own right. On the contrary, such an enterprise would be highly interesting.

It is nevertheless obvious, especially in the case of perception, that there are other uses which do not reduce in these simple ways to propositional constructions and which clearly have a great deal of intrinsic interest. The most important case in point is undoubtedly a locution such as

> *a* perceives *b*

or

> *a* sees *b*

where '*b*' is a singular term (i.e., a term referring to a person or to some other individual object). I shall call these 'non-elliptical' senses of the direct object construction and shall largely restrict my attention to them.

The whole group of questions connected with the behavior of the direct object constructions (in their non-elliptical senses) is extremely interesting, for it is connected with a number of problems involving the nature of the objects of such propositional attitudes as knowledge, belief, memory, perception, and the like. These problems include the questions concerning the so-called intentionality of these attitudes. In this area we have queries such as the following: What precisely is meant by the intentionality of a concept? How does it manifest itself in the behavior of this concept? Are the basic epistemological notions intentional, and are they intentional to the same extent?

The connection I have sought to establish between such notions as knowledge, belief, perception etc., and the idea of possible world opens a line of attack on these problems of intentionality. Whatever is or may be meant by this term, it seems clear to me that normally the more the possible worlds admitted by a modal concept differ from the actual one, the more intentional the concept is. The more an attitude turns on one's own mental universe, the more the worlds compatible with this attitude are likely to differ from the objectively determined real world. Thus belief is more intentional than knowledge, for whatever is known by a (i.e., whatever is true in all of the possible worlds compatible with a's knowing what he knows) must also be true in the actual world, whereas this kind of similarity between the admissible possible worlds and the actual one does not have to obtain in the case of belief.

More important than such similarities or differences are those comparisons that pertain to the individuals that exist in the different possible worlds. For instance, is there a way of referring to each individual such that one can say that the same individual is picked out by this way of referring to it in every possible world compatible with the attitude in question? Under what conditions can an individual which exists in the 'merely possible world' compatible with a propositional attitude be said to be identical with an actual individual? These questions seem to me to distinguish rather sharply between the different degrees of intentionality of different concepts. By means of such questions, we can, among other things, approach R. M. Chisholm's semiformal criteria of intentionality with sharper tools than before.[16] Unfortunately, no details can be taken up here, apart from pointing out that since the admissible possible worlds can differ from the actual one in many different ways, there does not seem to be just one dimension of intentionality but a multiplicity of different ways in which a propositional attitude or other modal notion can be intentional.

Furthermore, there are questions concerning the way individuals enter into contexts governed by epistemic notions. What happens to the logical laws to which singular terms are normally subject? Difficulties arising here have fostered considerable discussion. As has already been hinted, these problems are especially closely related to the nature of the last two types of constructions we listed in connection with knowledge, and to the counterparts of these constructions for other terms.

The reduction of the direct object construction to the that-construction can be dealt with only briefly here. It is connected with the central problem which we confront almost at once when we try to analyze the interplay of propositional attitudes with quantification in terms of 'possible worlds' along the lines indicated above. This problem is posed by the question: When are individuals figuring in two different worlds identical with one another? By and large, it seems to me fair to say that 'cross-identifications' of this kind turn on criteria not entirely unlike those criteria of reidentification which have been studied by Strawson and others.[17] (Certain continuity properties will loom large in all such identification.) We might label these *physical or descriptive* methods of cross-identification. What makes the conceptual situation very complicated here is the fact that we may have a second set of criteria of cross-identification essentially different from the first set. The nature of this other set of methods is especially clear in the case of perception.[18] Here the different 'possible worlds' involved are really all of the different states of affairs compatible with everything a certain specified person perceives at a certain moment in time. When, then, are two individuals which occur in two respective states of affairs identical? Even if we disregard physical (descriptive) methods of cross-identification, we can still cross-identify individuals in terms of the situations in which they are perceived. These constitute frameworks, as it were, into which certain individuals fall and which serve to 'individuate' these individuals. The man I see in front of me (I am tempted to say) is one and the same definite individual even though I do not see who he is and even though in some of the different possible states of affairs compatible with what I see he will therefore be a different person (a different descriptively identified individual).

Since all use of quantifiers presupposes definite methods of cross-identification, the quantifiers relying on such *perceptual methods of cross-identification* will differ in meaning from those relying on physical methods of cross-identification. (In a sense they may nevertheless 'range over' the same individuals, which only goes to show that the 'ranging over' idiom is not a very useful one when used in connection with propositional attitudes.)

My suggestion is that direct object constructions like

(12)   *a* sees *b*

have to be explicated in terms of quantifiers that rely on perceptual cross-identification in a fashion similar to the explication of the interrogative construction

(13)   *a* sees who *b* is

in terms of quantifiers that turn on physical cross-identifications.

Roughly speaking, in (13) we typically start from a perceptually given individual and place it (as it were) among the physically cross-identified (individuated) ones, whereas in (12) we start from a physically given individual and find room for it (so to speak) among a's visually cross-identified individuals (among his *visual objects*, we are tempted to say, although there is no separate class of 'visual objects' or 'sense data' different from the ordinary kinds of object in any possible state of affairs).

The explicit (but not quite accurate) explications of (12) and (13), respectively, might thus be:

(12)*   there is a visually individuated individual (call it x) such that
         a sees that $(b = x)$

and

(13)*   there is a physically individuated individual (call it x) such
         that a sees that $(b = x)$.

The only construction in which the verb 'sees' occurs here is the 'sees that' construction. Of course it is also true that in (12)* we rely on the fact that we are dealing with visual perception in another, indirect way, in that we use visual methods of cross-identification. This does not diminish the interest of our reduction of the direct object construction to the that-construction in the case of 'sees'. It does not eliminate the fundamental fact that the only way in which individuals can be handled in a proper logical (semantical) analysis of the situation is as members of the different possible worlds we are considering.

It is less clear what the analogue to perceptual methods of cross-identification might be in the case of such notions as knowledge or memory. But then the truth conditions of the corresponding constructions

         a knows b

and

         a remembers b

in terms of knowledge and memory likewise seem to be less clear. The suggestion that ensues from the above remarks is that one can be said to remember someone (e.g., b) if and only if one can place him within the framework of one's personally remembered past, and that one knows b

if and only if one can place him within one's personal acquaintances.

Generally, this suggestion seems to square rather well with the logical behavior of the direct object constructions involving 'knows' and 'remembers', respectively, although the whole complex of problems that we encounter in this direction badly needs further study and discussion. In any case, we have already seen how questions that seem to pertain to general and abstract logical (and semantical) problems, such as that of cross-identification, naturally – not to say inevitably – lead to a satisfactory analysis of the problematic direct object constructions in terms of the that-construction (plus a suitable kind of quantification, of course).

What I have said may provide an interesting partial explanation for the preoccupation of the ancient Greeks with the direct object construction. (Such a preoccupation is easy to document.) Elsewhere, I have briefly noted some aspects of the tendency of the Greeks to think of logical, semantical, and epistemological matters from the point of view of some particular personal situation. If the suggestions made in the present paper are correct, then it is just this kind of personal situation that supplied the individuation methods (methods of cross-identification) which are relied upon in the direct object constructions. A preference for the direct object construction and the tendency to regard one's personal situation as a natural epistemological framework are thus two sides of the same coin. Incidentally, we seem to have found here a common denominator of the Greeks' inclination to think of semantical matters from the standpoints of particular speech situations (this tendency is demonstrated especially strikingly by the marked prevalence of temporally indefinite singular sentences in Greek philosophical literature) and their reliance on the model of perception as a paradigm for knowing (knowledge as 'a sort of mental seeing or touching'). [19] In both cases, an individual's immediate personal context is relied on as an epistemological framework.

Our parallel analyses of the different direct object constructions thus illustrate the fact that there often is a great deal of similarity among the different epistemologically important terms. There are also unmistakable differences, both of kind and of degree. Many of them have genuine philosophical and logical interest, but some of the differences seem to me to be largely accidental.

Among the differences that seem to be relevant, there is a difference between the questions one can ask in the cases of the different terms, as noted by Austin.[20] One can ask

> How do you know?

and

> Why do you believe?

but not the other way around. I shall not try to spell out this relevance here, however.

A difference which might *prima facie* seem accidental is the fact that the verb 'believe' lacks several of the constructions which were registered above for knowledge. For instance, we do not seem to have any locutions such as 'believes when', 'believes where', nor anything like a direct object construction with 'believes', except in its elliptical senses. Furthermore, although we can say

(14)   He knows whether p,

it would be taken to be a solecism to say

(15)   He believes whether p.

The absence of wh-constructions with 'believes' admits of an interesting explanation, however. A glimpse of (9)* is enough to show that on the universal-quantifier reading of subordinate wh-questions the main verb (e.g., 'knows' in (9)*) receives a kind of success force, independently of whether it has one in the that-construction. (For what the counterpart to (9)* for belief would say that Dr. Welby has the right opinion in each case of a pneumoniac patient. And saying this is of course little short of saying that he *knows* the right diagnosis in each case, in a weak but still natural sense of knowing.) Hence only verbs which can have a success force may enter into a wh-construction like (9). Since 'believes' clearly is not a case in point, we have an explanation for the absence of the missing wh-constructions with 'believes'. A generalization to other verbs without a success force (and without a logical connection with another verb with a success presupposition, such as the logical connection between 'forgets' and 'remembers') serves to supply further evidence for this explanation.

It is particularly instructive to see that some verbs, e.g., 'guess', which normally do not have a success presupposition acquire one when they occur in a wh-construction. For instance, the sentence

John guessed who would win the race

clearly has a success implication, meaning that John made a *correct* guess as to who would win.

The same explanation can be extended to account for the fact that 'believes' can enter into certain more complicated wh-constructions (they are the ones in which no success force is presupposed even on the universal-quantifier reading) and to cover the missing whether-constructions like (15).

In the absence of the universal-quantifier reading, my analysis of the logical structure of wh-constructions with epistemic main verbs would create an expectation that wh-constructions with such non-success verbs like 'believes' 'expects', etc., ought to be possible in English. For there is nothing wrong with the existential-quantifier readings of wh-clauses with these main verbs, e.g.,

(Ex) John believes that $---x---$

(Ex) Bill expects that $—x—$

Now we have nevertheless found – thanks to the universal-quantifier reading of subordinate wh-questions – an explanation why the corresponding constructions are missing from English. Thus even quite accidental-looking phenomena can have a natural explanations in my framework.

All this tends to confirm further my analysis of the logical form of the different constructions we have been studying and also tends to strengthen the logical parallelism between the different epistemic verbs.

Furthermore, it appears that the Greeks may have been more liberal with their constructions than we are. At least one of the missing constructions with words like 'believes' seems to have admitted a perfectly good (albeit rare) counterpart in the Greek. For there occurs in the ancient Greek texts a couple of times what amounts to a direct object construction with a verb which otherwise has the force of 'believing' or perhaps 'opining'. (Some features of the general background of the predilection for direct object constructions which this phenomenon illustrates were noted above.)

The general suggestion of (logical) similarity between the different propositional attitudes has to be qualified, however, by emphasizing a difference between two kinds of propositional attitudes, vague though this difference is. We have, on the one hand, more or less purely cognitive attitudes – attitudes which in some sense essentially turn on the informative (evidential) situation in which one finds oneself. Knowledge, memory, and perception are cases in point. On the other hand, we have attitudes which partly turn on one's non-cognitive decisions or states of mind, or on some similarly non-informational factor. The concepts of 'being sure' and 'faith' are likely to be as clear cases as one is apt to find.

Although this distinction is not easy to explain in general terms, it is important not to confuse the members of the two groups closely related though they may be. What makes things especially tricky is that there are concepts whose status vis-à-vis this distinction is not clear. The concepts of certainty and belief are cases of this sort. Thus it appears that in the map of our concepts belief lies somewhere between opinion (which is a predominantly 'informational' concept) and faith (which is not). This is also witnessed by the construction 'believe in', which has no analogue for knowledge or for opinion and which cannot be reduced (as far as I can see) to the 'believes that' construction.

Again, 'being certain' may occasionally have the force of '[really] knowing' but it may also be tantamount to *feeling* certain' or *feeling* sure'.

One further group of problems which can be mentioned but not discussed here concerns the relations of the different epistemologically important notions. Does knowledge imply belief, and perhaps even certainty? Can knowledge be defined as justified true belief? The philosophical interest of these questions is obvious, and they have in fact figured prominently in recent epistemological literature. They cannot be discussed here, however.

Instead, a general comment on what has been done may be in order. We have discussed the logical force of several different grammatical constructions as well as their logical relations. This sort of enterprise is an important prerequisite to any satisfactory account of the semantics of the grammatical constructions in question. In fact, it seems to me that the most promising source for applications of the ideas here adumbrated is in the direction of linguistic semantics. These applications will at the same time supply further evidence for the suggestions made in this chapter.

It is nevertheless important to-note what remains to be done to realize such applications. Even though I believe that the kind of rudimentary logical notation employed here can serve to codify semantical representations of the different constructions we have studied, it remains to see how these semantical representations are connected with the surface form of these constructions in natural languages. (That this remains to be done was noted above repeatedly in connection with certain particular constructions.) It already seems to be justified to think, however, that these further developments are going to be eminently successful, even if they may necessitate a further development of our framework of logical concepts, too.

NOTES

[1] Paul Ziff, *Semantic Analysis*, Cornell University Press, Ithaca, N.Y., 1960, especially the last chapter; Jerrold J. Katz, *Philosophy of Language*, Harper & Row, New York, 1966, pp. 287–317.

[2] This contrast has often been commented on by epistemologists. See, e.g., Roderick M. Chisholm, *Perceiving*, Cornell University Press, Ithaca, N.Y., 1957, p. 142; David Armstrong, *A Materialist Theory of Mind*, Routledge & Kegan Paul, London, 1967, p. 227.

[3] See especially my paper, 'Semantics for Propositional Attitudes', in *Philosophical Logic*, J. W. Davis *et al.* (eds.) (Synthese Library), D. Reidel Publishing Co., Dordrecht, 1968; reprinted in Jaakko Hintikka, *Models for Modalities: Selected Essays* (Synthese Library), D. Reidel Publishing Co., Dordrecht, 1969, pp. 87–111. Note that propositions can be re-introduced in this approach as sets of possible worlds (or as characteristic functions of such sets)

[4] Cf. my *Knowledge and Belief*, Cornell University Press, Ithaca, N.Y., 1962, p. 12.

[5] Cf. ibid., pp. 131–32.

[6] See W. V. Quine, *From a Logical Point of View*, Harvard University Press, Cambridge, Mass., 1953, especially essays 7 and 8; Quine, *The Ways of Paradox*, Random House, New York, 1966, especially essays 13–15. An excellent discussion of Quine's views is presented by Dagfinn Føllesdal in 'Quine on Modality', *Synthese* 19 (1968) 147–157. A detailed evualuation of Quine's views and of their consequences is presented in Chapter 6 below. In addition to that chapter and to the works already mentioned, see my essays 'Knowing Oneself and Other Problems in Epistemic Logic', *Theoria* 32 (1966) 1–13; 'Individuals, Possible Worlds, and Epistemic Logic', *Noûs* 1 (1968) 33–62; 'Existential Presuppositions and Uniqueness Presuppositions', in Hintikka, *Models for Modalities* (note 3 above).

[7] The two laws that typically fail are existential generalization and the substitutivity of identity. A somewhat different diagnosis is required in the case of the failure of these two.

[8] This distinction is extremely useful for many different purposes. Some of them are linguistic, as indicated briefly in Chapter 8 below.

[9] John L. Austin, 'Other Minds', originally published in the *Proceedings of the Aristotelian Society, Suppl. Vol.* 20 (1946) 148–87, and reprinted several times.

[10] See, e.g., Bertrand Russell, *The Problems of Philosophy*, Home University Library, London, 1912, Ch. 5; and my paper 'Knowledge by Acquaintance – Individuation by Acquaintance', in *Bertrand Russell: A Collection of Critical Essays*, David F. Pears (ed.) Doubleday, Garden City, N.Y., 1971, reprinted in my *Knowledge and the Known*, D. Reidel Publishing Co., Dordrecht and Boston, 1974.

[11] This point has been made repeatedly in the literature, most frequently in connection with some of the individual philosophers. See, e.g., W. G. Runciman, *Plato's Later Epistemology*, Cambridge University Press, Cambridge, 1962; R. M. Hare, 'Plato and the Mathematicians', in *New Essays on Plato and Aristotle*, R. Bambrough (ed.), Routledge & Kegan Paul, London, 1965, p. 23.

[12] Cf. my analysis of the direct object construction, briefly sketched toward the end of this chapter.

[13] Gilbert Ryle, *The Concept of Mind*, Hutchinson's, London, 1949; cf. also Gilbert Ryle, 'Knowing How and Knowing That', *Proceedings of the Aristotelian Society* 46 (1945–46) 1–16.

[14] See my paper, 'Language-Games for Quantifiers', *American Philosophical Quarterly*, Supplementary Monograph 2 (1968) 46–72, reprinted in my *Logic, Language-Games, and Information*, Clarendon Press, Oxford, 1973.

[15] See Ch. 2 of my *Knowledge and the Known*, D. Reidel Publishing Co., Dordrecht and Boston, 1974.

[16] See Roderick M. Chisholm, 'On Some Psychological Concepts and the "Logic" of Intentionality', in *Intentionality, Minds, and Perception*, Hector-Neri Castañeda (ed.), Wayne State University Press, Detroit, 1967; Chisholm, 'Notes on the Logic of Believing', *Philosophy and Phenomenological Research* 24 (1963–64), 195–201.

[17] See, e.g., Peter F. Strawson, *Individuals*, Methuen, London, 1959. Cf. also Chapters 2 and 6 below.

[18] Cf. my paper, 'On the Logic of Perception', in *Perception and Personal Identity*, Norman S. Care and Robert H. Grimm (eds.), The Press of Case Western Reserve University, Cleveland; 1969, pp. 140–75; reprinted in my *Models for Modalities*. See also Chapters 3 and 4 below.

[19] For the predominance of the temporally indefinite sentences in Greek thinking about semantical matters, see my paper, 'Time, Truth and Knowledge in Ancient Greek Thought', *American Philosophical Quarterly* 4 (1967) 1–14.

[20] Austin, 'Other Minds' (note 9 above).

CHAPTER 2

THE SEMANTICS OF MODAL NOTIONS
AND THE INDETERMINACY OF ONTOLOGY

I. QUINE AGAINST POSSIBLE INDIVIDUALS

Many philosophers dislike possible individuals. Professor W. V. Quine is a well-known case in point. According to him, possible individuals create an ontological slum, "a breeding ground for disorderly elements". At one point, he elaborated his apprehensions as follows: "Take, for instance, the possible fat man in that doorway; and, again, the possible bald man in that doorway. Are they the same possible man, or two possible men? How do we decide? How many possible men are there in that doorway? Are there more possible thin ones than fat ones? How many of them are alike? Or would their being alike make them one? ... Or ... is the concept of identity simply inapplicable to unactualized possibles? But what sense can be found in talking of entities which cannot meaningfully be said to be identical with themselves and distinct from another? These elements are well-nigh incorrigible."[1]

Another aspect of this incorrigibility has subsequently been expounded and argued for by Quine in *Word and Object*.[2] It is what Quine calls the indeterminacy of ontology. This means that all physically possible evidence would not enable us to decide how another man is splitting up his world into individuals, universals, and whatever other categories of entities he might countenance. By the same token, all I say and do is inevitably compatible with more than one way of structuring the world conceptually. The reason why this is but another aspect of the old problem of possible individuals is not hard to appreciate. If I could spell out, in the kind of behavioristic terms which Quine could accept, the principles on which his questions concerning thin and fat possible men could be answered, then these principles would describe the kind of linguistic behavior which goes together with one ontology rather than another.[3]

II. THE REVIVAL OF POSSIBLE INDIVIDUALS

Recently, something like a resuscitation of possible individuals has never-theless been taking place. For instance, in his 'Advice on Modal Logic' Dana Scott recommends to modal logicians a sandwich universe con-sisting of actual, potential, and virtual individuals.[4] The important domain *D* is the one which contains actual and potential but no virtual individuals. Of this class Scott writes: "I feel it is important to be thinking of *D* as *fixed in advance*" (his italics). According to Scott, we can quantify over *D*.

What is there to be said of this revival of possible individuals? It seems to me that it is not immune to challenges of the same type as Quine's and that it contains dangerous oversimplifications. There may be a sense in which the idea of possible individual can, and should, be restored to honor. Be this as it may, I am not convinced that the domain of possible individuals is anything we can start from in the sense of take for granted, at least not in some of the most important philosophical applications of modal logic. I am not sure, either, that all the possible individuals we in some sense have to deal with can eventually be pooled into one big happy domain. These are among the issues I shall try to discuss in this paper.

III. THE SEMANTICS OF MODALITY

The background of the recent renaissance of possible individuals is the development of a viable semantics for modal logics.[5] Many of the main ideas of this semantics can be discussed in terms of the vivid and precise idea of a 'possible world' which unfortunately has been partly pre-empted by logically minded metaphysicians from Leibniz to Heinrich Scholz.[6]

According to this semantics, understanding the attribution of necessity or possibility or a propositional attitude (to a person) in a given world turns on understanding which possible worlds are 'alternatives' to it. In the case of necessity and possibility, these alternatives to a given world *W* are those possible worlds that could have been realized instead of *W*. Possibility in *W* therefore amounts to truth in at least one of these alternatives to *W* and necessity to truth in all of them. For a propositional attitude *A*, attributed to *b*, these *A*-alternatives (with respect to *b*) to a given world *W* are all the possible worlds compatible with the presence of this attitude *A* in *b* (as a member of *W*). For instance, these might be all the worlds (epistemic alternatives) compatible with b's knowing what he knows in W, or the worlds (doxastic alternatives) compatible with what he believes in W.[7] Hence it is true in W that b knows that p if p is the case in all the possible worlds compatible with what b knows (and with his knowing it). Thus all attributions of propositional attitudes in W can be paraphrased in terms of the corresponding alternatives to W. In general, with a mild oversimplification one can say that all we want to say in the semantics of modal logics can be said in terms of the alternativeness relation.

IV. THE PROBLEM OF CROSS-IDENTIFICATION

This suggests at once an important reason why it is illicit to speak of well-defined individuals, whether possible or actual, in modal contexts without some further explanations. For the relatively unproblematic reality we face in the pragmatics of most modal notions, including especially prominently propositional attitudes, is a collection of possible worlds. We cannot, it is true, make actual observations of more than one possible world, to wit, of possible worlds other than the actual one. However, the other possible worlds can be described by conditional or counterfactual statements. What cannot be expressed by, or decided by means of, such statements about the observable or otherwise unproblematic features of possible worlds, is suspect or at least problematic in a much more radical way than possible worlds and their overt features.

This difficulty attaches, I claim, to the identity of 'possible individuals'. Each possible world contains a number of individuals (or, if you prefer the locution, manifestations of individuals) with certain properties and with certain relations to each other. We have to use these properties and relations to decide which member (if any) of a given possible world is identical with a given member of another possible world. Individuals do not carry their names in their foreheads; they do not identify themselves. We cannot – even counterfactually – observe bare particulars, only particulars clothed in their respective properties and interrelations. Ontological nudism may seem an attractive idea in the warm sunshine of a purely abstract semantics, but it is impossible to practice in the cold climate of a realistic pragmatics of modal logic.

The same point can be put as follows. Suppose, on the contrary, that one begins by postulating a fixed supply of prefabricated individuals. Then one obtains a semantics which could function as an actual means of communication, it seems to us, only if one could assume that there are no problems in principle about re-identifying one's individuals as they occur in the several possible worlds we are considering. Once this presupposition is made explicit, however, it is also seen at once how gratuitous it is for most philosophically interesting purposes.[8]

V. METHODS OF CROSS-IDENTIFICATION

Here the use of tense-logic as a conceptual paradigm, so fruitful in other walks of logic, is seriously liable to lead us astray. For in tense-logic the different 'possible worlds' are different contemporary slices of one and the same history of the world, and the identity of the members of the different slices is simply their ordinary identity as the same persons, physical bodies, or other equally familiar entities.

However, even here matters are in reality much more problematic than one first realizes. It is not clear to what degree it makes sense to speak of the continuing identity of an electron which after all can occasionally be thought of as a mere congestion of waves. Borderline cases of personal identity may be puzzling indeed, and the possible dependency of the criteria of continued personal identity on the criteria of bodily identity have caused much comment. In any case, it is clear that the identification (re-identification) of physical objects is as unproblematic (relatively speaking) as it apparently is only because our laws of nature serve to guarantee those continuity properties which in principle enable us to trace the continuous world line of an individual in space-time. Yet the applicability of these natural laws, or indeed any laws which can be used in the same way, has no logically (conceptually) necessary guarantee.

Of course similar continuity properties play a role in many other cross-identifications (identifications of individuals across the boundaries of possible worlds). However, they are not any longer capable of doing the whole job. The other considerations which here come into the play are somewhat less clear-cut and unproblematic. Instead of thinking of the model as following an individual along a continuous world line in space-time one might in many cases more profitably think of one's identificatory task as being comparable to identifying the originals of the characters of a *roman à clef*. Indeed, in many circumstances a course of events described by a sufficiently realistic *roman à clef* might in fact be one of the 'alternatives' relevant to the semantics of modal logic. It might be an account of what might actually have happened or what will happen, for all that I know. (Think, for instance, of the novel which Harold Nicolson wrote in the thirties and which obviously and intentionally sought to anticipate, however fancifully, the events of the next few years, with the well-known actors on the stage of history continuing the roles they had been playing so far.) Then it would be one of my epistemic alternatives to the actual world. It is clear that our actual criteria of identifying a character in a *roman à clef* are multiple and not without some vagueness. (Think of what arguments lawyers might present in a libel suit prompted by such a novel!) Here it is especially clear, it seems to me, that for any serious philosophical purpose our criteria of cross-identification have to be given a long hard look and cannot simply be taken for granted. It is nevertheless also clear what the main criteria of cross-identification are. They might be labelled 'continuity plus similarity', for the considerations that go beyond continuity seem to rely largely on the sharing of properties and relations – be it sharing some especially important properties and relations or a sufficiently large number of them – or both.[9]

VI. INDIVIDUALS AND INDIVIDUATING FUNCTIONS

Nothing in all this nevertheless contradicts yet the possibility of eventually forming a class of entities very much like Scott's domain of possible individuals. Elsewhere, I have tried to spell out a trifle more carefully what happens when a semantics is developed systematically.[10] What becomes of an individual is now an atemporal and non-spatial 'world line' through several possible worlds. In equivalent terms each individual in the full sense of the word is now essentially a function which picks out from several possible worlds a member of their domains as the 'embodiment' of that individual in this possible world or perhaps rather as the *role* which that individual plays under a given course of events. These functions I have called individuating functions. They may of course be only partial ones: a well-defined individual existing in one world may fail to exist in another.

This possible failure to exist – this gappiness of the world lines – is the only form of unorthodox behavior some modal logicians allow to their possible individuals. I find it arbitrary to impose so strict a regimentation on the behavior of world lines, and I seem to detect a trace of Quine's patrician distaste of ontological slums in this prohibition of disorderly world lines. Sometimes certain limitations seem in order, however, e.g., a prohibition against a world line's splitting when one moves from a possible world to its alternatives.[11]

Be this as it may, we can say that in any context of discussion – say, in considering a given statement p – we can make sense of an individual if and only if we can trace it through those possible worlds we are considering (however implicitly) in p. We may almost say that in such a context a well-defined individual *is* just a piece of world line. In any case, it goes together with one. Whenever it so happens that one of the individuating functions fails to have a value in the actual world, then it goes together with a merely possible individual, we might say.

VII. WELL-DEFINEDNESS OF INDIVIDUALS AND ITS LINGUISTIC EXPRESSIONS. THE OBJECTIVITY OF INDIVIDUATING FUNCTIONS

Not every free singular term (say, a) picks out from these possible worlds manifestations of one and the same individual. In fact, usually its references in different worlds are manifestations of different (well-defined) individuals. Such a term does not specify a well-defined individual in the context in question. For this reason we cannot instantiate or generalize with respect to such a singular term. The failure of the usual logical laws governing instantiation and generalization in such cases thus ceases to be a source of bewilderment and puzzle and becomes a matter of course.[12]

If we are speaking only of the alternatives to the actual world (plus, possibly, of this actual world itself), i.e., if there are no iterations of modal operations and if only one modal operator is present, then simple statements can be found to express explicitly that a term specifies a well-defined individual. These are statements of the type

(1) (Ex) b knows that $(a = x)$
         (Ex) b perceives that $(a = x)$
         (Ex) b remembers that $(a = x)$
         (Ex) b believes that $(a = x)$
         (Ex) necessarily $(a = x)$

When a success condition is not presupposed and when we are also talking about the actual world and not just its alternatives, we must make sure that the uniqueness of reference which (1) postulate extends to the actual world.

(2) (Ex) [(it appears to b that $(a=x)$) $\land$ $(a=x)$]
           (Ex) [(b believes that $(a=x)$) $\land$ $(a=x)$]
           ...

Several of these statement-forms have vernacular counterparts. For instance, the first four statements (1) can also be expressed as follows:

(1)* b knows who a is
           b perceives who a is
           b remembers who a is
           b has an opinion of who a is

That (1) serve the purpose I claimed for them follows from the interpretation of our variables of quantification. They are assumed to range over genuine well-defined individuals. Because of this, '(Ex) b knows that $(a=x)$' has the force of saying that 'a' always picks out, from the several epistemic alternatives to the actual world, manifestations of *one and the same* individual x.

Thus no unusual sense of quantification is being assumed here, certainly nothing remotely like that *bête noire* of Quine's, substitutional quantification.[13] Rather, what we face here are the consequences of an objectual interpretation of quantification in a situation where one is considering several possible worlds. In this situation, the objectual interpretation immediately leads one to ask how one and the same individual appears in the different possible worlds. If a substitutional interpretation of quantification is assumed, '(Ex) b knows that $(a=x)$' will only have the force of saying that for a suitable substitution-value inserted for 'x' in 'b knows that $(a=x)$' the result is true. Obviously, 'a' will serve this purpose, making all of (1) trivially true. Hence we have here a clear-cut formal difference between the substitutional and objectual quantification.

Moreover, the translations (1)* will obviously be spoiled if a substitutional interpretation is presupposed. Hence we are committed in more than one way to the normal objectual reading of quantifiers.

Another side of the same coin is that quantifiers are in modal contexts dependent on methods of cross-identification (i.e., on a supply of individuating functions), and their meaning will be relative to a given method of cross-identification. (To be precise, this refers to quantifying *into* a modal construction.)

In order for the truth-criteria of such statements as (1)–(2) to be objectively given, the supply of individuating functions (world lines) must also be objectively given, at least relative to a fixed class of possible worlds. I have argued that in a correct semantics for propositional attitudes this objectively given supply of world lines is the main range of entities over which we have to quantify.[14] They must therefore exist or at least subsist in some objective fashion. Among them, there are the individuating functions which give rise to (merely) possible individuals. They must thus also enjoy some sort of objective existence (or subsistence). Indeed, this seems to vindicate possible individuals completely. For surely they can be pooled together into one happy domain if we can even quantify over them. What more can we possibly ask of a vindication of possible individuals? No wonder that a reasonable semantics of modal logic seems to reinstate possible individuals if it leads to this result.

VIII. THE RELATIVITY OF INDIVIDUALS

This, in fact, is the sense in which – and the extent to which – possible individuals can be countenanced. We cannot go further, however. For instance, if we as much as say that individuals and individuating functions are just one and the same old things, we are already oversimplifying. There are facts about world lines that cannot naturally be spelled out in terms of prefabricated individuals. It seems to me that the situation can be described in functional terms. (Of course, these terms have to be taken to express logical rather than causal or temporal relationships.) The world lines cannot be drawn so as to connect blank worlds. They depend on the properties and relations that obtain in the several possible worlds we are considering. They come about, as it were, only through comparisons between these possible worlds. For this reason, we cannot start from individuals. We can only arrive at them as outcomes of trans-world comparisons.

All this is of course partly metaphorical. Since there is admittedly a one-to-one correlation of some rough sort between possible individuals (in any reasonable sense) and my individuating functions, all discussion of their relative priority may seem to resemble a dispute of the relative priority of hens vs. eggs.

There is a real issue here, however, or rather several issues. I shall by-pass the predominantly pragmatic point that the cross-identifications we in fact seem to be able to perform turn in reality on rather complicated processes. Instead, I want to argue that the primacy of individuating functions over possible individuals appears already on the level of semantics, provided we develop it with a view on certain applications of the greatest philosophical interest.

There are two main facts here, it seems to me, that are crucial for the applications I have in mind. The first is that the set of individuating functions is not given once and for all but is relative to a class of possible worlds.[15] It is objectively given, but only relative to this class. (This observation, if it can be sustained, is a partial semantical counterpart to the thesis – already aired in this paper – that individuating functions, i.e., world lines, depend functionally on those possible worlds they serve to tie together.) In other words, some world lines that run smoothly between a certain class of possible worlds may be impossible to continue to a wider class of possible worlds.[16] This fact (putative fact) I shall call the *relativity* of individuating functions or the relativity of world lines.[17]

This relativity, of course, is to be expected if the world lines are in the first place drawn (as it were) on the basis of similarities between the worlds and regularities holding in each of them. The members of the wider class of possible worlds may be dissimilar when compared with each other and irregular when examined alone.

It seems to me that when it is realized what the relativity of world lines means, it is immediately realized that this relativity obtains in our own conceptual system. In other (maybe somewhat more guarded) words, it has to be accepted if my general semantical framework is accepted. Otherwise one cannot have an opinion as to who a is unless one knows who that individual is in some guise or another or knows who a is unless everyone else also knows who a is under some suitable description or designation or other, and so on. I cannot help feeling that the main reason why the relativity of world lines has not been registered in the literature is a misplaced quest of mathematical elegance in one's logic.

IX. TECHNICAL CONSEQUENCES OF THE RELATIVITY

This point is worth elaborating, for the relativity of world lines has clear-cut consequences for our semantics.[18] The approach I have very briefly sketched may also be partly characterized by saying that in it we try to capture by means of explicit premises the precise conditions on which a singular term a will in a given context behave like a *bona fide* singular term of ordinary non-modal logic, i.e. obey the usual laws of instantiation and generalization.[12] It does so if and only if it picks out (apart from gaps) one and the same individual from all the possible worlds we are to consider. These possible worlds are determined by the context, and are relative to it. If we are merely considering what b believes or does not believe, we find the requisite condition in (1). If we are also considering the actual world, the condition is found in (2). If we are in addition considering what b believes (or fails to believe) that d knows or does not know, we are *ipso facto* considering epistemic d-alternatives to these doxastic b-alternatives, and the requisite condition has the form

$$(Ex) \ [(a=x) \ \& \ (b \text{ believes that } (a=x))$$
$$\& \ (b \text{ believes that } d \text{ knows that } (a=x))]$$

In general, the condition needed is a similar existentially quantified conjunction of modalized identities $(a=x)$. The modal prefixes of these identities indicate the classes of possible worlds as members of which a is being considered. These, in turn, are indicated by the several sequences of modal operators within the scope of which 'a' occurs in the sentence which constitutes the relevant context. (The prefixes are precisely these sequences except that the weaker operator in a pair of dual operators is always replaced by the stronger.)

All this is quite straightforward. However, it flies to the face of some of the most commonly used principles of modal logic. For instance, we cannot any more move from

$$(3) \qquad \vdash (p(a/x) \supset q(a/x))$$

to

$$(4) \qquad \vdash ((Ex) \ p \supset (Ex) \ q)$$

or to

$$(5) \qquad \vdash ((x) \ p \supset (x) \ q)$$

Since these are frequently used principles, some logicians have been reluctant to give them up. However, the need of doing so is a direct consequence of the relativity of world lines. Even if (3) is the case, (4) and (5) may fail to hold, for the simple reason that the uniqueness conditions presupposed in the antecedent of (4) for instantiation may be weaker than those required in its consequent. Hence the implication need not hold, although the corresponding implication holds for singular constants instead of variables. (In the case of constants, we need not worry about instantiation any more.) Similar (dual) remarks pertain to (5). Thus our approach forces us to give up some familiar and admittedly quite convenient and 'elegant' deductive principles.

X. THE FAILURE OF WORLD LINES FOR LOGICAL MODALITIES

What is remarkable about the relativity of world lines is nevertheless not its reality nor any of its technical by-products in our semantics, but rather its philosophical implications – or, more accurately, the philosophical suggestions it yields.

One of them I have already explained briefly elsewhere.[19] If world lines tend to break when extended further, there may eventually be no trans world heir lines left when all sorts of weird worlds are admitted into our class of possible worlds. In less metaphorical terms, if the world lines are to be drawn on the basis of similarities between worlds and of their intrinsic regularities, then this whole enterprise will break down when very dissimilar and irregular worlds have to be considered. And this is the case with logical modalities. Everyone will admit, I think, that logically possible worlds can be very, very irregular and entirely unlike each other. It is logically possible, for instance, that all the nice continuity properties which characterize the behavior of physical bodies vis-à-vis space and time should not obtain. This need not deter a logician from envisaging in purely abstract terms some unspecified system of world lines between them. However, every attempt to specify with any infinitesimal degree of realism how such world lines could conceivably be drawn in accordance with the criteria of individuation we normally use is doomed to fail. In connection with logical (analytical) modalities, individuating functions thus do not exist, if we presuppose a modicum of conformity with our actual ways with our concepts in other respects.

This implies that quantification makes no sense in a context of logical modalities, for quantification was seen to depend on a system of world lines. (To be precise, this affects only quantification *into* a context governed by operators for logical necessity and possibility.) Quine is thus seen to be right in his suspicion of quantified modal logic of *logical* modalities.[20] Quantifiers and *logical* modalities simply do not mix. In a context of logical modalities we cannot answer the questions that have to be answered in order for quantification to make sense, presupposing that the rest of our discourse is moderately realistic.

XI. RATIONALITY ASSUMPTIONS UNDERLYING PROPOSITIONAL ATTITUDES

This does not directly affect such other modalities, for instance propositional attitudes, as do not necessarily lead us into a comparable jungle of possible worlds. There may nevertheless be only a (vast) difference in degree rather than a difference in kind between logical modalities and (say) propositional attitudes. For one thing, logical modalities can occasionally be used in contexts (for instance, in a context where all talk is about numbers or other similar abstract entities) where the vagaries of cross-identification do not matter. For another, in discussing a man whose beliefs are few and irregular, we might fail to establish world lines and hence fail to make sense of quantification into *his* belief-contexts. We might perhaps say that some rudimentary rationality (in some rather weak sense) must be presupposed of someone's propositional attitudes in order for us to be able to use quantifiers and identity in discussing his attitudes. However, the fact that there is no a priori guarantee of such rationality does not make the general task of trying to make sense of quantification into contexts governed by operators expressing such attitudes any less interesting or important. However, other curious things happen in the case of propositional attitudes.

XII. THE INDETERMINACY OF ONTOLOGY

Consider, for the purpose of seeing what the situation is, people's systems of settled beliefs – their rational *Weltanschauungen*, one might say. When is an entity a member of the ontology of one such system of beliefs – say, of the beliefs *a* holds? This question is perhaps the main question one can ask concerning the individuals, possible and actual, that *a* countenances. In fact, one can almost paraphrase it by asking simply whether that entity *is* a member of *a*'s ontology.

Because of the relativity of world lines, the answer to this question is relative to the class of possible worlds we are considering. These are all the possible worlds compatible with *a*'s beliefs. Their totality determines precisely these beliefs, contentwise. Thus a man's ontology is relative to his beliefs in a radical sense. Not only does the selection of possible individuals that he believes to exist depend on his beliefs. Even the class of his *possible* (potential) individuals depends on his beliefs as to what predicates apply to what individuals. To determine my ontology, you would have to find out what my substantial beliefs are. In so far as these beliefs are behavioristically underdetermined, ontology is likewise indeterminate. Thus we have vindicated a thesis reminiscent of Quine's famous 'indeterminacy of ontology'. Our result is in fact very much like Quine's thesis in that in both cases the indeterminacy of ontology is essentially connected with the indeterminacy (if any) of beliefs. Our result is more limited than Quine's thesis, however, in that the relativity of a man's ontology to his beliefs matters only in so far as we are quantifying into a belief-context, i.e., explicitly or implicitly considering his beliefs. Even with this qualification, our result seems to amount to an important partial vindication of what Quine has been aiming at in speaking of the indeterminacy of ontology, for surely Quine's apprehensions about the inaccessibility of a jungle tribe's ontology are largely occasioned by the influence of the natives' beliefs on their linguistic behavior.[21] (Notice nevertheless that I have not discussed the question whether beliefs are really behavioristically underdetermined in the way Quine seems to think they are.)

XIII. REVIEW OF THE SITUATION

This result is also an additional reason for viewing with suspicion any facile postulation of a single unified domain of possible individuals, independent of people's beliefs and other propositional attitudes. Such a domain seems to me a completely unrealistic abstraction.

However, truth seems to lie between two extremes here. Although I agree with a version of Quine's relativity-of-ontology thesis, it seems to me that Quine's tendency to cast doubts on the use of quantifiers in each and every context in which the unreconstructed quantificational laws of instantiation and generalization do not hold (i.e. do not hold without supplementary premises) is not only exaggerated but misplaced. These laws fail as such as we are considering several possible worlds in their relation to each other and thus considering individuals as they appear in these different possible worlds. I have shown how these quantificational laws can be vindicated (formally *and* interpretationally) by means of supplementary premises. There is nothing in the failure of these laws to demonstrate the impossibility of quantified modal logic.

The possibility or impossibility of such logic hinges instead on the possibility of cross-identification, i.e. on the possibility of recognizing our individuals in their different roles in the different possible worlds our modal notions invite us to consider. It is here that Quine's critical arguments have their bite. A mere postulation of possible individuals does not help. Merely to assume a fixed set of individuals which are without any further ado presumed to crop up in the several worlds is to pretend that no problem is present, not to solve one. As was indicated above, this problem of cross-identification is unsolvable in the case of logical modalities, and Quine is therefore right in this favorite case of his. In the case of propositional attitudes, however, no insurmountable problems arise, provided that we recognize the important relativity of our methods of cross-identification (individuation) explained earlier. If we do so, we can even answer the pointed questions of Quine's which served to open this paper. For the purpose, we nevertheless need one more large-scale theoretical insight. Its scale is unfortunately too large for us to discuss it here, and forces us to leave it to another paper.[22]

REFERENCES

[1] W. V. Quine, *From a Logical Point of View*, Harvard University Press, Cambridge, Mass., 1953 (2nd ed., revised, 1961), p. 4.

[2] W. V. Quine, *Word and Object*, M.I.T. Press, Cambridge, Mass., 1960. For further elucidation of the precise nature of the indeterminacy of ontology and of radical translation, see also Quine's reply to Chomsky in *Words and Objections: Essays on the Work of W. V. Quine*, Donald Davidson and Jaakko Hintikka (eds.), D. Reidel Publishing Company, Dordrecht, 1969.

[3] Notice, however, that there may in principle be non-behavioristic ways of answering Quine's questions which therefore leave the behavioristic indeterminacy intact.

[4] Dana Scott, 'Advice on Modal Logic', in *Philosophical Problems in Logic: Some*

Recent Developments, Karel Lambert (ed.), D. Reidel Publishing Company, Dordrecht, 1970. Richard Montague's highly important work in this area also uses the idea of 'prefabricated' domain of individuals which just show up in the different possible worlds one is considering; see e.g. Richard Montague, 'Pragmatics' in *Contemporary Philosophy – La philosophie contemporaine* Vol. 1 (ed. by R. Klibansky), La Nuova Italia Editrice, Florence, 1968, pp. 102–122 and Richard Montague, 'On the Nature of Some Philosophical Entities', *The Monist* **53** (1969) 159–194.

5 The first big wave of work in this area was largely due to Stig Kanger and Saul Kripke; see Stig Kanger, *Provability in Logic* (Stockholm Studies in Philosophy, Vol. 1), Stockholm, 1957; Stig Kanger, 'The Morning Star Paradox', *Theoria* **23** (1957) 1–11; Stig Kanger, 'A Note on Quantification and Modalities', ibid. 133–134; Stig Kanger, 'On the Characterization of Modalities', ibid. 152–155; Saul Kripke, 'A Completeness Theorem in Modal Logic', *The Journal of Symbolic Logic* **24** (1959) 1–14; Saul Kripke, 'Semantical Considerations on Modal Logic' (*Proceedings of a Colloquium on Modal and Many-Valued Logics, Helsinki, 23–26 August, 1962*), *Acta Philosophica Fennica* **16** (1963) 83–94; Saul Kripke, 'Semantical Analysis of Modal Logic: I. Normal Modal Propositional Calculi', *Zeitschrift für mathematische Logik und Grundlagen der Mathematik* **9** (1963) 67–96; Saul Kripke, 'Semantical Analysis of Modal Logic: II, Non-Normal Modal Propositional Calculi' in *The Theory of Models* (Proceedings of the 1963 International Symposium at Berkeley), J. W. Addison, L. Henkin, and A. Tarski (eds.), Amsterdam 1965, pp. 206–220; Saul Kripke, 'The Undecidability of Monadic Modal Quantification Theory', *Zeitschrift für mathematische Logik und Grundlagen der Mathematik* **8** (1962) 113–116. See also Montague's work, partly mentioned above and partly referred to in these writings of his, and the work of E. J. Lemmon and Dagfinn Føllesdal. Most of my own early work here is collected in *Models for Modalities: Selected Essays*, D. Reidel Publishing Company, Dordrecht, 1969.

6 One danger here is to think of 'possible worlds' as being something weird and consequently philosophically suspect. Yet nothing is more commonplace in human life and in the life of science than to find someone considering several possibilities as to how some sequence of events might turn out (e.g. considering several possible outcomes of an experiment). Whoever does so, is dealing with as many 'possible worlds' in the general sense presupposed here.

It is instructive to see how pervasive and how unavoidable precisely analogous considerations are in the foundations of statistics, and how commonplace and innocent some of the intended applications of these concepts are. (Cf. e.g. L. J. Savage, *The Foundations of Statistics*, John Wiley, New York, 1954, especially Savage's discussion of 'states of the world' on pp. 8–10 and of 'small worlds' on pp. 82–86.) An ontological standard which (in the name of science?) tries to exorcise possible worlds from our conceptual system is likely to make shambles of statistics and applied probability theory.

7 There seems to be a bad ambiguity here between compatibility with *what* someone believes (knows, remembers, etc.) and compatibility (also) with his believing (knowing, remembering, etc.) it. For many purposes, including those of the present paper, we can simply leave the ambiguity there. It only matters when further questions (concerning the details of the behavior of the alternativeness relation, especially its possible transitivity) are asked. Contrary to what has been claimed, I have never traded on the ambiguity myself. Here we can simply leave it alone. (Cf. Jaakko Hintikka, '"Knowing that One Knows" Reviewed', *Synthese* **21** (1970) 141–162.)

8 There are nevertheless explicit doctrines to the contrary. Sometimes it is thought

that our primary vehicle in referring to individuals are names (individual constants), and that they are mere labels without descriptive content. Then clearly we can refer to individuals only in so far as we have succeeded in pasting these labels on them. As far as our ways with singular terms go, we then have to think ourselves as being rather in the position of an Adam who has associated names with the various beasts because they had come to him to be identified. I have called this view of the functioning of our language 'logical Adamism'. (Cf. *Genesis* 2:19.) It is clear that if it were acceptable, all those individuals we can meaningfully talk about can be recognized everywhere by means of their identificatory labels which we (so to speak) have to think of as already being strung to them. It is equally clear, it seems to me, that this is an unrealistic way of thinking about the use of our language. The values of quantifiers will on any reasonable interpretation leave behind all the individuals we have already witnessed and labelled.

9 Suppose that we are given two characters in two different *romans à clef*, both compatible with all my beliefs and asked whether they are the same person (individual) or not. One thing we can try to do is to follow each of them back and forward in his respective *roman*. The possibility of doing so of course depends heavily on spatial and temporal continuity of individuals within each possible world. If we are lucky, we can trace the two characters to the common part of the two novels, i.e. the part which represents my positive beliefs about the world. If they coincide there, they are identical; if they are separate there, they are different.

This strategy may of course fail. Then we fall back on some suitable requirements of similarity between the two individuals. Such criteria of cross-identification do not seem very sharp nor very conclusive. However, this probably is as it should be. We are in this case dealing with two 'possible individuals' about whom I have no beliefs. No wonder there is little one can say of the identification of such underdetermined individuals between my belief-worlds (worlds compatible with what I believe).

10 See the essays included in *Models for Modalities* (reference 5 above), especially 'Semantics for Propositional Attitudes' and 'Existential Presuppositions and Uniqueness Presuppositions'.

11 For the pros and cons here, see my 'Existential Presuppositions and Uniqueness Presuppositions' (reference 10 above). There it is also shown how this particular mode of good behavior on the part of individuals is connected with the problem of the substitutivity of individuals.

Gail Stine has claimed in effect that we cannot rule out splitting in the case of belief. (See 'Hintikka on Quantification and Belief', *Nous* 3 (1969) 349–408.) I am prepared to reserve judgement here, pending further discussion. This problem, vital to the evaluation of the Quine-Føllesdal position (as I am interpreting it), does not affect my constructive suggestions in this paper or elsewhere.

12 The precise conditions on which the usual quantificational laws apply in different circumstances are studied in 'Existential Presuppositions and Uniqueness Presuppositions' (reference 10 above). The next few paragraphs present only an intuitive summary of an analysis that can be made much tighter.

13 For Quine's distinction between objectual and substitutional quantification, see his new book, *Ontological Relativity*, Columbia University Press, New York, 1969, especially pp. 63–67, 104–108. See also W. V. Quine, *The Ways of Paradox and Other Essays*, Random House, New York, 1966, Ch. 14, and Ruth Barcan Marcus, 'Interpreting Quantification', *Inquiry* 5 (1962) 252–259, 'Modalities and Intensional Languages', *Synthese* 13 (1961) 303–322. I want to be especially emphatic here because

a substitutional interpretation of quantifiers has mistakenly been attributed to me.

[14] In 'Semantics for Propositional Attitudes' (reference 10 above).

[15] Of course, formally one might very well try to handle the situation in terms of one big unified class of individuating functions. Then each of them would have to be thought of as being defined only for some subclass of the class of all possible worlds we are considering.

[16] Technically, this means – in rough-and-ready terms – that the kinds of auxiliary premises contemplated in Section VII above do not coincide but have to be distinguished from each other in almost all interesting cases.

[17] We might perhaps express the relativity involved here by saying that what counts as an individual depends on the context of discussion. (The Prime Minister of Norway is a well-defined individual as far as Prof. Føllesdal's knowledge is concerned, for he knows who that high official of his country is, whereas the same Prime Minister unfortunately is not a well-defined individual as far as my knowledge and ignorance are concerned.)

This relativity of individuals has a terminological consequence which tends to create unnecessary confusion and perhaps even disagreement in this area. The inhabitants of each possible world, *when this world is considered alone*, are as good individuals as one can possibly hope. However, when our attention switches and we consider the same world (say) just as one particular alternative to another given world, these inhabitants suddenly become only so many 'embodiments' or 'manifestations' of the 'real' individuals who can also make their entrances and exits in other worlds, or perhaps rather so many different roles these individuals play. Hence referring to the good old inhabitants of one particular possible world as individuals may be perfectly appropriate in one context and yet quite misleading in another.

The same goes for the intuitive meaning one associates with the truth of an identity $a = b$ in some particular possible world. In one context, what is involved is a perfectly good identity between genuine individuals, while in another context only an identity between the ephemeral 'stages' or 'manifestations' of genuine individuals is what we ought to be thinking in terms of.

The main moral of this terminological and interpretational relativity is, it seems to me, that we need not be confused or misled by it.

[18] With the following (and with the preceding section) compare the related discussion in 'Existential Presuppositions and Uniqueness Presuppositions', Sections XVI–XVII.

[19] In 'Existential Presuppositions and Uniqueness Presuppositions', Section XIX.

[20] See e.g. W. V. Quine, *From a Logical Point of View* (reference 1 above), Ch. 8; *Word and Object* (reference 2 above), Ch. 6; *The Ways of Paradox and Other Essays*, Random House, New York, 1966, Chapters 13–15. Cf. also Dagfinn Føllesdal, 'Quine on Modality' in *Words and Objections* (reference 2 above), with further references.

[21] This is especially clearly in evidence in *Ontological Relativity* (reference 12 above).

[22] See 'The Objects of Knowledge and Belief: Acquaintances and Public Figures', Chapter 3 above.

CHAPTER 3

OBJECTS OF KNOWLEDGE AND BELIEF:
ACQUAINTANCES AND PUBLIC FIGURES

Recent work on the semantics of propositional attitudes[1] throws a great deal of interesting new light on the problem of the objects of these attitudes, it seems to me. These philosophical insights are rather precarious, however, for they can easily be spoiled by a wrong treatment of individuals in one's semantics. Some of the relevant differences among different kinds of treatments were discussed in my earlier paper 'The Semantics of Modal Notions and the Indeterminacy of Ontology'.[2] My own attitude indicated there can be summed up as a deep suspicion of those prefabricated 'possible individuals' which have recently become so popular.

Before we can understand the situation, a couple of features of the semantics of propositional attitudes have to be registered.[3] In the logical semantics of modal notions (in the wide sense of the word which includes propositional attitudes), the crucial idea may be said to be the alternativeness relation. Given a propositional attitude and a person, this relation associates with each possible world a number of others as its *alternatives*. When attributing the attitude to this person, we are in effect speaking of these worlds, which may be thought of as possible worlds compatible with his having that particular attitude in the original world. Thus we have (approximate) paraphrases of the following sort:

> a knows (believes, remembers, perceives) that p (in a possible world M) $\equiv$ In all the possible worlds compatible with what a knows (believes, remembers, perceives) in M it is the case that $p \equiv$ In all the epistemic (doxastic, mnemic, perceptual) a-alternatives to M, it is the case that p.

Here 'possible world' may have to be interpreted, depending on the concepts involved, either as a possible *course of events* (as the case normally is with, say, knowledge) or as a temporary *state of affairs* (as the case typically is with, say, perception).

The most intriguing feature of the resulting semantics is that in a context involving modal notions individuals have to be considered as members of several different possible worlds. An individual virtually becomes, for logical purposes, tantamount to the 'world line' (David Kaplan has called it a 'trans world heir line') connecting its manifestations in these possible worlds.[4] A singular term specifies a unique individual only if its several references in the relevant possible worlds are connected by one and the same world line. If these worlds are the epistemic (doxastic, mnemic, perceptual) alternatives to the actual world, 'b' succeeds in doing that if and only if the following statement (we shall call it identification statement) is true:[5]

(1) $(Ex) [a$ knows (believes, remembers, perceives) that $b = x)]$

These expressions have a neat idiomatic translation:

(2) a knows (has an opinion as to, remembers, perceives) who b is.

For clearly, knowing who b is means knowing of some definite individual x that *he* is b. (For certain qualifications, see Chapter 7 below, pp. 137–158.) Here we can see that in (1) a normal 'objectual' interpretation of quantifiers (as ranging over genuine, definite *individuals*) is presupposed.[6] For otherwise the 'x' in (1) would not range over such definite individuals as would make (1) synonymous (or nearly synonymous) with (2). It follows that (normally interpreted) quantification into a modal context makes sense only insofar as our individuals are defined for all the relevant possible worlds, i.e., insofar as a objectively given supply of 'world lines' can be presupposed.

A parenthetical remark may help to clarify the situation. Philosophers have occasionally yielded to the temptation of assimilating the class of singular terms 'b' for which (1) (or some analogue to it) is true with *proper names* in some 'logical' sense of the world. In other words, they have sometimes thought that since a proper name is a 'mere label' it cannot but apply to one and the same individual no matter in what possible world it is employed. There is indeed some connection between this kind of merely referential behavior and the notion of proper name, but the situation is much more complicated than philosophers usually realize. Notice, for instance, that even for (grammatical) proper names (1) is frequently false, for one can perfectly well fail to know or remember who the bearer of a proper name is. Hence in the context of propositional attitudes even grammatical proper names do not behave like 'logically proper names'.

One important point I argued at some length in Chapter 2 above is that the world lines are not absolute but depend on the internal structure of the possible worlds in question and on their similarities. One cannot draw world lines between bare particulars in blank worlds. Our supply of 'possible individuals' may be objectively given, but it depends on the set of possible worlds we are dealing with and on their structure. One can cross-identify, i.e., recognize an inhabitant of one world as a member of another, only if one can answer questions concerning these two worlds. These questions have to be more substantial than the Quinean questions I quoted with partial approval: "Take, for instance, the possible fat man in that doorway; and, again, the possible bald man in that doorway. Are they the same possible man, or two possible men? How do we decide? How many possible men are there in that doorway? Are there more possible thin ones than fat ones? How many of them are alike? Or would their being alike make them one?... Or... is the concept of identity simply inapplicable to unactualized possibles? But what sense can be found in talking of entities which cannot meaningfully be said to be identical with themselves and distinct from another? These elements are well-nigh incorrigible."[7] My questions are more substantial because they go beyond questions of identity and number envisaged by Quine.

Our observations open an even more radical line of criticism of 'possible individuals' than those put forward in the earlier paper. I said there that what counts as an individual, in a context that involves a class of possible worlds, is determined by comparisons between these possible worlds. If so, then it may in principle happen that the comparison can be carried out in more than one way, yielding two different domains of 'genuine', well-defined individuals although the possible worlds and all that can be said of each of them and its inhabitants (qua its inhabitants only) remain precisely the same. Then the situation will be as if we had a library full of *romans à clef* and found out that there was not one but two perfectly illuminating and irreducible *clefs* connecting the novels with one another (and, possibly, with the actual world).

Now a situation of this kind is not only a remote speculative possibility. It is realized, I claim, on a large scale right in the middle of our own conceptual scheme, and in fact in a context of lively philosophical discussion. Over and above the method of cross-identification (or, as we may also call it in *one* possible sense of the expression, method of individuation) which turns on continuity plus similarity, there is – in the case of many propositional attitudes – another type of method. This turns on the perspective, as it were, from which the person whose attitudes we are considering looks upon the world. I am not sure what would be a good terminology for the distinction. The former method I have tried to call physical or public, but I am not happy with either adjective. The latter may perhaps be called (in general terms) demonstrative, perspectival, or contextual, although these terms are not perfectly happy ones, either. Perhaps the best we can do is to call the former *cross-identification by description*, the latter *cross-identification by acquaintance*. At the very least this terminology indicates one interesting connection with earlier philosophical discussion.

Elsewhere,[8] I have tried to explain what individuation by acquaintance means in the case of perception, which offers us the clearest case of such an individuation method. Even if someone (say, *a*) does not see who the people around him are or what particular physical objects he is laying his eyes on, he can still consider these people or physical bodies as individuals in a perfectly good sense of the word. He can make statements about them as individuals, and for the purpose of specifying how the world appears to him he frequently has to do so.

Let us take one of these individuals, suitably described, for instance, the man in front of *a*. Let us use the abbreviating shorthand '*b*' for 'the man in front of *a*'. Then in discussing what *a* sees, *b* cannot be a well-defined individual because it was assumed that

$$a \text{ does not see who } b \text{ is.}$$

Since we can nevertheless, when discussing *a*'s visual perception, legitimate invest *b* with all the logical powers (and 'logical duties') of an individual, we must be relying on some method of cross-identification different from the physical (descriptive) one. What is this method? In the case of perception, the 'possible worlds' to be considered are all the different momentary states of affairs compatible with what *a* sees. Since *a* does not see who *b* is, different men have to be said to stand in these possible states of affairs in front of him, if one relies on the physical methods of cross-identification. These states of affairs must nevertheless be alike in that there is a man in front of a – a man in a certain visual relation to a. This similarity enables us to draw (as it were) that world line through all these men which justifies us in handling b as a well-defined individual.

This can immediately be generalized. The position different objects occupy in the framework of a's visual geometry creates a similarity among the possible states of affairs compatible with what he sees, a similarity which can be used to individuate them irrespective of whether they can be individuated by description. These are the individuals to whom a can point and say, "*That* is the individual I am talking about!" In brief, in the case of perception the second method of individuation which I have called *perspectival* or *demonstrative* is just that.

In an earlier paper[8] I have suggested that these perceptually individuated entities are essentially what the famous sense-data of earlier philosophers of perception were supposed to be, to wit, 'objects of immediate perception' (loc. cit., secs. *vi*, *x*, *xi*). The similarity becomes even more pronounced when sense-data are described as the subjects (individuals) that judgments of immediate perception are about. In fact, the main mistake of the sense-datum theorists is an illicit reification, an attempt to roll each world line into a ball that somehow can be located somewhere in the actual world.[9]

Since quantifiers range over well-defined individuals, i.e., over world lines spanning all the possible worlds we are considering (apart from admissible gaps, of course), our two different warps of world lines will be matched by two pairs of quantifiers.[10] Let us use (Ex), (y), etc. for quantifiers relying on descriptive methods of cross-identification and $(\exists x)$, $(\forall y)$, etc. for quantifiers relying on perceptual (demonstrative) methods. Both (Ex) and $(\exists x)$ can be used in individuating premises of form (1):

(3) $(Ex) \, [a \text{ sees that} \, (d \doteq x)]$

(4) $(\exists x) \, [a \text{ sees that} \, (b = x)]$

According to what has been said earlier, the former may be 'Englished' as

(3)* a sees who d is.

I have argued – if an argument is needed – that an approximate vernacular rendering of (4) is

(4)*   *a* sees *b*.

One way of explaining why (4) and (4)* have the same force is as follows. Although we do not have two different classes of objects here, only two methods of cross-identification, it is tempting to call the values of *x* in the old quantifiers (*Ex*) and (*x*) *physical objects* and its values in (∃*x*) and (∀*x*) *visual (perceptual) objects*. Now one can obviously say that one sees *b* if and only if one can locate *b* among one's visual objects; i.e., if and only if, for some visual object *x* that one has, one can visually identify *b* with *x*. This is just what (4) says.

This explanation is somewhat precarious, however, for the talk of 'values' of bound variables and their 'ranging over' certain individuals is often quite misleading in contexts where several possible worlds are being considered. Hence explanations of this sort have to be employed with caution.

Thus we have found a counterpart to the colloquial direct-object construction (with perceptual verbs) in an explicit, semantically interpreted symbolic language.[11] This counterpart relies essentially on perceptual (demonstrative) methods of individuation. The presence of the same direct-object construction with such verbs as 'remembers' and 'knows' suggests that something similar could be done with the latter, too. (Of course we have to disregard here those cases in which a grammatical direct-object construction is used to do duty for some other kind of construction.[12] Cases in point include the use of 'knowing the answer' for 'knowing what the answer is', of 'believing him' for 'believing what he says' or 'believing that the facts are as he says they are', etc.)

This expectation turns out to be justified. First, what are the contual or perspectival methods of cross-identification that can be used in connection with such notions as memory or knowledge? In the case of memory, the relevant possible worlds are in the simplest case all the courses of events ('stories') compatible with everything someone – call him *a* – remembers. Here *a* is not in the literal sense of the word looking at the world from a given perspective that would enable him to individuate people and objects demonstratively. However, *a*'s own role in his personally remembered past normally imposes a particular point of view on all the stories compatible with his memories. Even when *a* does not remember who someone (say *b*) is, he may be able to locate *b* uniquely in all these stories by reference to his own role in them. ("She is the blond girl I met at the New Year's party two years ago.") This enables us to draw, so to speak, a world line connecting all the persons who in the several stories play the same role vis-à-vis *a*, no matter whether they are descriptively the same individual or not.

In a somewhat similar way, one's personal cognitive relations to people and things create a perspective for cross-identifying them between worlds compatible with what one knows.

But how are these methods of cross-identification related to direct-object construction? What precisely is the meaning of these constructions in ordinary discourse, anyway? Let us take, for instance, the notion of remembering. What is expressed by an expression of the form (5)?

(5)   *a* remembers *b*,

for instance,

(6)   I remember the sergeant in my platoon.

In order for (6) to be true it is neither necessary nor sufficient that I remember who the sergeant was. For instance, I may perfectly well remember him vividly but fail to remember his name, address, age, civilian profession, or any other items that would give me a foothold for maintaining that I remember who he was. Conversely, I may remember who my divisional commander was but fail to remember *him*. There does not seem to be any fixed, closed list of factual items, either, that *a* would have to remember *about b* in order for (5) to be true. Independently of the rest of my line of thought in the present paper, the best account I could offer of the truth conditions of (6) is that it is true if and only if I can place the sergeant in question within my personally remembered past. The recollections I have of my own past create a framework into which I can fit some individuals but not others. The former are the ones I remember, the latter the ones I don't remember.

This is the kind of answer to the question concerning the truth conditions of (6), I think, that we have to give in any case, independent of any considerations of systematic logical semantics. It is immediately generalized to (5), and it is obviously precisely equivalent to the answer prescribed by my earlier remarks on individuation by acquaintance (contextual or perspectival individuation) for the truth conditions of

(7) $(\exists x)\,[a$ remembers that $(x=b)]$

with a quantifier relying on contextual methods of cross-identification. If these contextual methods do not yield as clear-cut truth conditions as in the case of perception, this vagueness is matched by the greater vagueness of the meaning of (5) in ordinary discourse as compared with that of (4)*.[13]

A similar analysis can be offered to show that the truth conditions of

(8) $(\exists x)\,[a$ knows that $(x=b)]$

with a contextual quantifier are the same as the truth conditions of

(9) a knows b

in ordinary language. The fact that both of these are again less clear-cut than in earlier cases is again predictable. The framework we have to rely on here is that created by one's first-hand knowledge of people and things, and this is much less clearly defined than the framework created by one's perceptual viewpoint or by one's personal memories.

Another way of describing the force of (8) and (9) is of course to say that they are equivalent to

(9)* a is acquainted with b

when the term 'acquaintance' is dissociated from its social overtones.[14] (If arguments are needed to support this connection between the notion of acquaintance and the direct-object construction with 'knows', Bertrand Russell has already supplied a few of them in 'Knowledge by Acquaintance and Knowledge by Description'.)

Thus we have found contextual methods of cross-identification (individuation by acquaintance) right in the middle of our own conceptual system, in the case of several important propositional attitudes. It is especially illuminating to see, I think, how an analysis of the meaning of direct-object constructions in ordinary discourse leads us precisely to the truth conditions predicted by my abstract semantical theory. This important insight calls for additional comments.

First, a well-worn word of warning. One cannot expect hard-and-fast rules to apply to ordinary usage. Thus, the vernacular distinction between the who- or what-construction and the direct-object construction does not invariably go together with the logical distinction between the two kinds of quantifiers and between the corresponding two kinds of cross-identification. Partly because the two constructions have a similar logic, they may be expected to be occasionally expressed in the same way in our everyday jargon. Examples are not hard to come by. For instance, a who-construction often serves to express acquaintance with the person in question rather than such descriptive knowledge of his attributes as would enable one to locate him in an impersonal history or in a parish registry. When asked, "Do you know who that man is?," I can idiomatically answer, "Yes, he is my next-door neighbor," even if I do not know his last name, occupation, age, or any of the other items that are usually relevant to my knowing or not knowing who some public figure is.

A highly interesting philosophical example of an idiomatic who-construction doing duty for the direct-object construction occurs in the beginning of Russell's essay 'Knowledge by Acquaintance and Knowledge by Description'.[15] I shall argue in another paper that an actual confusion is operative in Russell's thinking. However, merely using one locution in the role of the other is of course insufficient evidence for attributing any confusion to Russell.

Conversely, Russell's younger friend the Old Possum does not even have to claim poetic liberty in order to use the direct-object construction to express knowing who (individuation by descriptive criteria) when he writes of McCavity the Mystery Cat

> You would know him if you saw him
> For his eyes are very sunken in.

An ingenious example by Hector-Neri Castañeda concerning one's knowledge of one's own identity[16] serves as an additional warning against assimilating the two kinds of quantifiers to each other. In his example, the assimilation is encouraged by perfectly idiomatic uses of 'knowing who' where individuation by acquaintance is being presupposed. An additional interest of Castañeda's example is that it brings out some further colloquial clues as to the cross-identification principles a speaker or writer of ordinary language is presupposing.

By way of self-criticism I must also acknowledge that a failure to appreciate the distinction between the two kinds of individuation led me to offer some highly misleading explanations in my book *Knowledge and Belief* (note 1 above, pp. 155–156, 164). There it was in effect said that in expressions like '(Ex) [a knows that $(b=x)$]' (i.e., in expressions in which one quantifies into a knowledge-context) the bound variable in a sense ranges over individuals known to a. What was intended was not the set of a's acquaintances, but something that can be expressed more appropriately by speaking of individuals of whom a knows who they are. Thus ordinary usage is a highly unreliable guide to meaning here.

An entirely different kind of remark might also be in order. The inevitability of our contrast between contextual individuation and individuation by description in ordinary human life is amusingly shown by what has happened when students of 'artificial intelligence' have tried to make machines to behave like humans. In doing so, they have run into the very same contrast. In a computer representation of simply described scenes "one method is a space-oriented representation where information about a region of space is accessed by its coordinates. Another approach is to access the information by object, where, by giving the object name, its description and position are returned." This is to all practical purposes just the contrast we have been discussing. (Remember that perceptual individuation uses the coordinates of objects in one's perceptual space, whereas descriptive individuation operates much more like giving objects names which they have independently of their location and independently of at least some of their descriptive characteristics.)[17]

We can now see a partial reason why there is no direct-object construction in terms of 'believes' whose meaning would be analogous to that of the direct-object constructions already encountered. What is needed for the analogy is a contextual or perspectival method of cross-identification. But, unlike perception, memory, and knowledge, belief is not perspectival – or in any case is not perspectival to a sufficiently high degree. The other notions presuppose more of an actual connection between whoever has the propositional attitude in question and the objects of his attitudes than belief. (This is illustrated by the familiar contrast between the questions, '*How* do you know?' and '*Why* do you believe?') This connection can serve to establish the perspective needed for the use of individuation by acquaintance. It seems to me that this is essentially only a matter of degree, however, and that there is no difficulty in principle to applying to the objects of belief most of what has been said here about the objects of other propositional attitudes. (One's own role in one's belief-worlds can again serve as an individuating frame of reference.) The need of doing so for those mundane purposes catered to by ordinary language apparently was not strong enough to have prompted the Anglo-Saxons to introduce a construction in terms of 'believes' that would be parallel (logically parallel) to the direct-object construction in terms of 'knows'. This need not deter a philosopher from noticing the fundamental similarities between the different cases, however.[18]

The clarification obtained by realizing the prevalence – and the importance – of contextual methods of individuation is also measured by the fact that we can now answer Quine's pointed questions quoted earlier. The crucial point is that our answers will depend on whether a contextual or a descriptive method of individuation is used, i.e., whether the 'possible individuals' in question are acquaintances or public figures. In Quine's formulation the locution "*that* doorway" strongly suggests the former, and in fact suggests that perceptual individuation is used. If so, some answers to Quine are easily forthcoming. If it mistakenly appears to me that there is a man there in that doorway, this merely possible perceptual object can be bald or not bald, fat or not fat, in the several possible worlds that match my hallucinations, provided that my visual impressions do not determine his hirsuteness or his bulk. If the doorway is too narrow for me to fit more than one man there perceptually, the possible bald man there will have to be identical with the possible fat man there. In other words, if the doorway allows no room in my visual space for more than one man, all possible men there, visually individuated, will have to be one, whether they are descriptively alike or not. By the same token, there may be room there for more thin than fat (possible) men, again demonstratively individuated. However, since descriptive cross-identification turns on the characteristics of the members of the different states of affairs compatible with what I perceive, a possible fat man will seldom be identical with a nonfat one, and two descriptively individuated possible men who are alike are likely to be forced to coincide.

Pace Quine, questions of identity and number thus apply to possible individuals (well-defined world lines) at least in a rough-and-ready way. They may be incorrigible, but not necessarily with respect to their behavior vis-à-vis identity and number. It may be that we can successfully answer some of these questions partly because we have tacitly presupposed that our world lines run smoothly enough, e.g., that they do not split when going from a world to its alternatives or from one alternative to another. However, it seems to me that such smoothness can frequently be presupposed, and that most of Quine's questions can in any case be answered independently of it.

If the account I have given of the direct-object construction is mainly correct, some interesting consequences follow as to how we should think of the so-called objects of knowledge, perception, and memory. In the vernacular direct-object construction, we seem to be dealing with a more or less ordinary two-place relation between a knower and an object of his knowledge, a perceiver and an object of perception, and so on. Here the objects of knowledge seem to enter into the logical situation in an entirely different way than they do in the knowing that-construction, for there they figure merely as members of the different states of affairs we are considering.

In the analysis (8) of (9) the direct-object construction is reduced to the that-construction. (The fact that a special sort of quantifier has to be used does not vitiate the fact that the concept of knowledge is used in (8) only in the 'propositional' that-construction.) Hence it is deeply misleading to conceive of perception as a normal two-place relation between the knower and the object of his knowledge. The *only* role individuals can play in one's knowledge is as inhabitants of the worlds that are compatible with what one knows. They are 'objects' of knowledge in a sense different from the 'objects' of activities expressed by normal transitive verbs. Perhaps they can be called *objects* of knowledge only by courtesy.

These observations, straightforward though they are, are incompatible with many well-known philosophical doctrines. To mention only one, if my analysis (8) of the direct-object construction with 'knows' is essentially correct, I have in a sense disproved Russell's claim [19] that "our knowledge of *things*, which we may call *acquaintance*" is "logically independent of knowledge of truth". For in (8) the only construction in which 'knows' occurs is (a shorthand for) 'knows that', which surely expresses "knowledge of truths." Elsewhere,[20] I have argued in some detail that Russell's 'knowledge by acquaintance' can be roughly identified with the type of knowledge expressed by the direct-object construction.

Several other philosophical problems are illuminated by our insights into the description-acquaintance contrast – more problems indeed than can be taken up here.

NOTES

[1] The literature is already becoming too extensive – and too varied – to be summed up in a note. My own work in this area is represented by the two volumes, *Models for Modalities: Selected Essays*, D. Reidel Publishing Co., Dordrecht, 1969, and *Knowledge and Belief: An Introduction to the Logic of the Two Notions*, Cornell University Press, Ithaca, N.Y., 1962. Of the work of others in this general direction, I would especially like to mention Richard Montague's papers collected in *Formal Philosophy: Selected Papers by Richard Montague*, R. Thomason (ed.), Yale University Press, New Haven and London, 1974.

[2] *Synthese* **21** (1970) 408–424. Reprinted above as Chapter 2 of the present volume.

[3] For an elaboration of these points, see my *Models for Modalities: Selected Essays*, D. Reidel Publishing Co., Dordrecht, 1969, especially the chapters 'Semantics for Propositional Attitudes' and 'Existential Presuppositions and Uniqueness Presuppositions'.

[4] This reflects the fact that one can scarcely be said to have a conceptual grasp of an individual unless one can in principle recognize this individual under a variety of circumstances.

An important qualification is needed here, however. As I have emphasized in 'The Semantics of Modal Notions and the Indeterminacy of Ontology', op. cit., what counts as a well-defined individual depends on the context. Hence it is a relative matter how long or short world lines can be identified with a 'genuine' individual.

[5] When other possible worlds are being considered, other conditions are needed to guarantee uniqueness. For instance, if, in addition to alternatives to the actual world, we are also considering our actual world itself and if no success grammar is presupposed, we need instead of (1) conditions of the following form:

(1)* $(Ex)\,[a$ believes that $b = x \wedge (b = x)]$.

A somewhat more systematic discussion of the uniqueness conditions that are needed in different contexts is given in 'Existential Presuppositions and Uniqueness Presuppositions' in *Models for Modalities* (note 1 above).

[6] Quine's distinction between objectual and substitutional quantification is explained e.g. in his book *Ontological Relativity*, Columbia University Press, New York, 1969, especially pp. 63–67, 104–108. See also W. V. Quine, *The Ways of Paradox and Other Essays*, Random House, New York, 1966, Ch. 14. I have discussed the dependence of my approach on an objectual interpretation briefly in 'The Semantics of Modal Notions and the Indeterminacy of Ontology', Chapter 2 above.

[7] *From a Logical Point of View*, Harvard University Press, Cambridge, Mass., 1953 (2nd ed., rev. 1961), p. 4.

[8] 'On the Logic of Perception', in *Models for Modalities*, op. cit., pp. 151–183. This paper appeared first in *Perception and Personal Identity*, Norman S. Care and Robert H. Grimm (eds.), The Press of Case Western Reserve University, Cleveland, 1969, pp. 140–173. See also my reply to Romane Clark in the same volume, pp. 188–196.

[9] It is not the whole story, however. Many further peculiarities of sense-datum theories – especially in their less sophisticated variants – depend also heavily on certain phenomenological and psychological presuppositions about what can and cannot be immediately (noninferentially) perceived. According to these presuppositions, what we primarily and immediately perceive are colors and shades (cf. Quine's "two-dimensional continuum of colors and shades"). Because of this, sense-data – characterized as the objects of immediate perception – are turned into something much less substantial and less commonplace than my perceptually individuated individuals, which are nothing but ordinary persons, chairs, tables, rivers, mountains, etc., contextually or perspectively viewed.

I believe that these presuppositions are prejudices, but I cannot argue the point here. For further remarks on this subject, see Chapters 4 and 10 below.

[10] Once again, ontology is recapitulating etymology. In English, *some* is a cognate of *same*, just as the dependence of quantifiers on criteria of sameness in different possible worlds would suggest.

[11] A qualification is needed here. Like so many other ordinary-language expressions, (4)* is ambiguous in that it can be interpreted either as being *de dicto* or *de re*. In other words, it can be about b, 'whoever he is or may be', or about the individual who in fact is b. Since individuals are what bindable variables range over, we accordingly have two different translations of (4)* into our symbolic language:

(4) $(\exists x) [a \text{ sees that } (b = x)]$

and something like

(4)** $(\exists x) [(b = x) \wedge a \text{ sees that } (Ey) (y = x)]$

Whenever by 'seeing b' we merely mean 'laying one's eyes on an individual who in fact is b', the latter translation (4)** is what is needed.

[12] A couple of remarks on this subject are made in Chapter 1 above.

[13] Some philosophers have suggested that the meaning of 'remembering someone' involves, in at least one sense of this direct-object construction, having mental images of the object remembered. Norman Malcolm (see his *Knowledge and Certainty*, Prentice-Hall, Englewood Cliffs, N.J., 1962, pp. 205–209) is a case in point. He writes: "Apparently there is a real distinction to be got at here. Often we want to contrast remembering something with remembering that the something occurred or existed. ... On the other hand, we sometimes say 'Not only do I remember that there was a lad named Robin in my class but I remember *him*.' When we say those things, what point are we making, what information are we giving? – The point is not always the same. But sometimes it is to announce that we cannot *see in our minds*... the face of the classmate. This meaning comes out very strongly when we say 'I remember a great deal *about* him but I don't remember *him*.'"

It seems to me that this is not the primary or the most common sense of the direct-object construction with 'remembers'. I doubt very much whether I can be said to be able to picture all my high school classmates 'in my mind' in any clear-cut sense of the word. (I could not draw them or even offer a good verbal description of their respective appearances.) Yet I feel very strongly I remember each of them, and I am prepared to meet a challenge to the contrary by retailing all sorts of first-hand stories of their doings and sayings, our common experiences, etc. If somebody applied the direct-object construction with 'remembers' to Hellen Keller, we would not have any difficulty in understanding what is meant, and scarcely any feeling of logical oddity, in spite of the fact that in her case there could not have been any question of her being able to call up mental images of the same sort the rest of us have.

However, my argument does not depend on this point at all. If images or mental pictures are needed in 'remembering someone', this simply brings remembering closer to perception than I have so far indicated. And this should make it ever so easier to appreciate individuation by acquaintance in the case of memory, for it is just perception that offers the clearest example of such individuation.

This point is nevertheless easily overlooked. It is perhaps thought that merely having suitably vivid images of past scenes is not enough to create a context or a framework by means of which remembered individuals can be cross-identified. This worry is based on nothing more than an ambiguity, however. We have to make a distinction in any case between remembering (say) *a* (remembering him *as a*, we might perhaps say) and remembering a person who *in fact* is *a*. The former case is unproblematic, for what one there remembers is an encounter with *a*, i.e., an occasion or a situation in which *a* has a place or a role. This clearly suffices (in principle) for cross-identification.

It is the latter case that might look problematic, for no remembered occasion of this sort is presupposed there. However, if imagery is required for remembering *a*, this imagery must in this latter case be based on some previous perception or experience of *a* that actually did take place, for otherwise we could not speak of *remembering* at all. (Otherwise we could not distinguish between remembering and, e.g., imagining.) The context of that perception or experience constitutes the framework requisite for cross-identification.

Although further discussion is undoubtedly needed here, no objections to my account seem to be forthcoming.

A verb which is in some ways (but not in all) a mirror image of 'remembers' is 'expects'. This verb, too, admits both of the that-construction ('I expect that he will come') and of the direct-object construction ('I expect him'). Although there are certain further complications here, an analysis along roughly the same lines we have been following above can be given of its direct-object construction.

[14] The same warning as was issued in note 11 above for perception applies also to (8) as a rendering of (9) or (9)*. These can often be understood *de re*, and then their force will not be captured by (8), but rather by something like

$$(8)^* \qquad (\exists x)\,[(x=b) \wedge a \text{ knows that } (Ey)\,(y=x)].$$

[15] *Proceedings of the Aristotelian Society* 11 (1910–11) 108–128; republished in *Mysticism and Logic and Other Essays*, Longmans, Green and Co., London, 1918; Anchor Books, Doubleday, New York, 1957.

[16] 'On the Logic of Attributions of Self-Knowledge to Others', *Journal of Philosophy* 65 (1968) 439–456, and my reply, 'On Attributions of "Self-Knowledge"', ibid. 67 (1970) 73–87.

[17] See R. Paul, G. Falk, and J. A. Feldman, 'The Computer Representations of Simply Described Scenes', *Reports of the Stanford Artificial Intelligence Project* AIM-101, Computer Science Department, Stanford University, October, 1969, 66 pp.

[18] This is illustrated almost too neatly by the fact that the closest counterpart to our verb 'to believe' in ancient Greek, viz. *doxazein*, occasionally admitted of a direct-object construction semantically parallel to the direct-object constructions with 'to know'. The neatness lies in the observations that there seems to have been a matching tendency among the Greeks to look upon belief, too, from the vantage point of some given cognitive situation. Cf. my paper, 'Time, Truth, and Knowledge in Ancient Greek Thought', *American Philosophical Quarterly* 4 (1967) 1–14, reprinted in my *Knowledge and the Known*, D. Reidel Publishing Co., Dordrecht and Boston, 1974.

[19] *The Problems of Philosophy*, The Home University Library, Oxford University Press,

London and New York, 1912 (1946 edition, p. 46) (Russell's italics).
[20] 'Knowledge by Acquaintance – Individuation by Acquaintance' in *Bertrand Russell: A Collection of Critical Essays*, David F. Pears (ed.), Anchor Books, Doubleday, Garden City, N.Y., 1972, pp. 52–79, reprinted in Jaakko Hintikka, *Knowledge and the Known: Historical Perspectives in Epistemology*, D. Reidel Publishing Co., Dordrecht and Boston, 1974, pp. 212–233.

CHAPTER 4

INFORMATION, CAUSALITY, AND THE LOGIC
OF PERCEPTION

It is sometimes thought that there is a contrast between such approaches to perception as rely on causal notions ('causal theories of perception'), those discussions that emphasize the informational ('representative') nature of perception, and sense-datum theories of perception. This double contrast is largely spurious, however. In this chapter, I shall argue that an appropriate semantical analysis of the informational role of perception naturally, almost inevitably, leads us to assign an important role to causal relationships in the logic of perception. It is also suggested that this observation can be partially generalized to other notions which allow for individuation by acquaintance and that it puts into a new perspective several conceptual puzzles in this area.

The basis of my discussion is the semantical analysis of perceptual concepts outlined in my earlier paper, 'On the Logic of Perception'.[1] It is perhaps worth recapitulating the main features of this analysis so as to emphasize certain leading ideas behind it, especially the notion of information. One relevant observation is that my analysis squares rather well with the general ideas put forward recently by certain leading psychologists of perception. Here I shall use one particularly interesting writer as a representative (*mutatis mutandis*) for many. In his important book, *The Senses Considered as Perceptual Systems*[2], James J. Gibson pleads for a view of perception as pickup of information, not as registration of sensations. What a person perceives in the sense of detecting or becoming aware of is not a complex of sensations but certain information about his environment. "There can be sensationless perception, but not informationless perception" (p. 2). One can very well ask *how* certain objectual information is extracted by an organism from the stimulus flux but not *whether* this happens. "The individual does not have to construct an awareness of the world from bare intensities and frequencies of energy" (p. 319).

Gibson himself has suggested that his viewpoint yields 'New Reasons for Realism'.[3] This may perhaps be so, but it seems to me that it is not the most general nor the most important element in Gibson's salient insights. It may even betray a certain uncertainty in Gibson's own thinking as to what is at issue here philosophically. Gibson's viewpoint is admittedly realistic in the sense that he argues that people's conscious perceptions are geared to the information they yield about the environment, and that senses are 'perceptual systems' which serve this informational function so as to be "the instruments of our contact with the world".

However, this is a *de facto* thesis, and Gibson emphazises himself the problem of explaining precisely *how* it is that human 'perceptual systems' extract the information they in fact yield from the flux of stimulus energy. This *de facto* realism seems to me a rather far cry from the kind of philosophical realism which focuses on *de jure* questions, such as the certainty of perceptual knowledge. A realist of such a variety is confronted according to Gibson by new problems rather than conceptual reasons for realism, in that Gibson emphasizes the tremendous complexity of the process of extracting the actual information which can surface in consciousness from the stimulatory input. Gibson provides factual reasons for thinking that our perceptions reflect our environment usefully if not always faithfully, but a philosophical realist is surely uncomfortable when he is made to understand that they do so only in virtue of subtle, unconscious neural processes.

Although Gibson does not put his point quite in the same way, it seems to me that the upshot of the revolution he wants to carry out in the study of perception lies elsewhere. Gibson does not give conceptual reasons for thinking that our actual perceptions are necessarily close to their objects in our environment. Rather, the conceptual moral is that the *perceptions* that can surface in our consciousness *must be dealt with in terms of the same concepts as what we perceive*. The appropriate way of speaking of our spontaneous perceptions is to use the same vocabulary and the same syntax as we apply to the objects of perception. Otherwise, I do not see that it makes much sense to speak of perception as information pickup or to apply other informational ideas to perception. If there is a general conceptual or philosophical point to Gibson's book, it is surely this rather than anything connected with naive realism. Whatever else Gibson may be claiming, this much he will have to assume.

This point is furthermore independent of the question of certainty or reliability of perception. The information our senses or, rather, our 'perceptual systems' give us may be false or misleading, but these are themselves informational terms rather than terms referring to uninterpreted sensations.

I shall call the thesis we have found implicit in Gibson the thesis of *the informational character of spontaneous perception*. It might be called *conceptual realism* as distinguished from naive realism and from the epistemic realism which puts a premium on the certainty of perception.

The analysis of the logical status of perceptual terms I have offered earlier may be thought of as a corollary to this thesis. For if to specify one's perceptions is to specify the information they yield (or seem to yield), what follows concerning the logical status of perceptual concepts? What follows is that to specify what someone, say a, perceives is to describe what the world is like according to his perceptions (whether they be veridical or not). Since these perceptions do not fix the world uniquely, this description is logically speaking not unlike a disjunction of several different alternatives concerning the world. The most systematic way of spelling out these several alternatives is to make each one of them as full a description of the world as we can give by means of the resources we are using. Switching to an obvious semantical (model-theoretical) jargon, it is clear that what such maximal (consistent) descriptions describe is (in a slightly technical sense of the expression) *a possible world* (a possible state of affairs or a possible course of events). In this way we are led to say that to specify what a perceives is to specify the set of all possible worlds compatible with his perceptions. This is precisely the analysis of perceptual concepts I have explored earlier.[4] It is to be noted that the notion 'compatible with what a perceives' is to be taken as unanalyzable. To know what someone, say a, perceives in a world W *is* to know what-is-compatible-with-what-he-perceives among other possible worlds W', and the latter notion — it is a relation between the possible worlds W' and W — turns out to be a most powerful one for the purpose of semantical analysis. Attempts to analyse it have turned up nothing useful. If one could list all the facts that a perceives in W one can of course define the perceptual alternatives to W as those worlds which are logically compatible with that list in the sense that in which all the members of the list are true in the world in question. But this does not accomplish anything new, and it rules out those perceptual situations in which we cannot specify in some particular language all the facts *a* perceives. In short, it does not allow for unverbalized perceptions.

Thus the analysis I have offered of perceptual concepts may be thought of as a kind of corollary to the thesis of the informational character of spontaneous perception: to describe these perceptions is to describe the information (putative information) they convey.

One may put this point as follows: In spite of his frequent use of the term 'information' and its cognates, Gibson does not connect his approach with any precise explication of informational concepts. The line of thought just adumbrated provides such a connection, for the notion of (semantical) information is closely tied to that of a possible world: to specify an information-content *is* to specify a set of possible worlds.[5] The interpretation I have given to Gibson's ideas – or, rather, the viewpoint from which I am looking at them – is therefore as much a vindication as a criticism of them.

It is worth emphasizing, incidentally, that the thesis of the informational character of perception does not as such commit one to any particular view concerning the actual relation of one's sense-impressions to physical objects, nor to any view concerning the epistemological relation of the two. What it amounts to is the logical primacy of the language we use of physical objects and suchlike over the language we use to describe our unedited sense-impressions: the latter constitutes a special use of the former.

It seems to me that the thesis in question is of a considerable methodological significance to virtually all discussions of the logic of perception. It amounts to saying that in normal situations perception is an *informational* process. Hence *all* there is (in principle) to perception (at this level of analysis) is a specification of the information in question, and this amounts to a specification of the set of worlds compatible with what is being perceived.

In this form the thesis is in contradiction with an otherwise highly appealing discussion of the logic of perception. In his interesting paper, 'Perception and Individuation', Richmond H. Thomason has sketched a logic of perception which is a case in point.[6] In it, stepping from the plain extensional description of the actual world W to a discussion of what someone perceives is not only to specify the informative content of his perceptions by specifying the set of possible worlds compatible with them (and, possibly, to locate W with respect to this set), but also to import a whole new set of entities (individuals) into the actual world, viz. his perceptual individuals. I consider this an undesirable violation of the thesis of the informational character of spontaneous perception.

Another corollary to the informational character of perceptual concepts is an important difference between my analysis and the traditional sense-datum theories. My earlier remarks on the relation of the two approaches have perhaps been unduly casual, and given the appearance of representing the difference as a merely psychological or phenomenological one. This is misleading, because there is a clear-out logical difference between the two approaches as to how sense-experience should be conceptualized. Here, as in so many other cases, there is more logic than phenomena to phenomenology.

Sense-datum theories have typically been based on the assumption, which has often remained tacit, that the appropriate way of speaking of one's spontaneous uninterpreted visual impressions is to speak of a two-dimensional distribution of colors and shades, not of objects with more or less definite locations in a three-dimensional visual space, and analogously for other sense-modalities. The true phenomenology of perception is nevertheless quite unlike this view. However complicated the processes may be which lead from the physical input picked up by sense-organs to such sense-impressions as can be consciously beheld, and however dependent this process perhaps is on earlier experience, no traces are normally found either of this editorial process or of the formative learning processes in the actual perceptual experience. Our sense-impressions do not yield information of one's physical environment by a conscious process of inference. They are spontaneously organized so as to embody such information before they reach the purview of conscious experience. All this is entirely foreign to typical sense-datum theories, and contrary to much of what their adherents have actually said.

How far a cry the idea of our sensing 'colors and shades' is from the phenomenological realities of perception can perhaps be appreciated by recalling the conclusion of one of the foremost psychological analysts of color-perception that most of us virtually never see colors as colors only (called film colors), as colors should according to sense-datum theoreticians be *always* seen.[7] Instead, in usual situations colors are spontaneously seen as colors *of* certain objects (surface colors) or *of* a certain medium (space colors) or are otherwise spontaneously associated with the organization of our visual space into objects, their properties, their interrelations, etc.

In view of these deep differences it is quite remarkable how much of the central ideas of sense-datum theoreticians can nevertheless be recaptured within the framework I have outlined.[8] Moreover, many of those aspects which cannot incorporate into our own theory become understandable as results of tempting but illegitimate reification. Sense-data are primarily supposed to be the subjects of our perceptual judgements, the individuals (in the logical sense of the term) our perceptual statements are about – perceptual statements here being those in which the actual physical situation is abstracted from. I have argued that the proper subjects of perceptual judgements are *individuals perceptually individuated* (cross-identified). This idea is based on an insight which comes naturally after the informational character of perception has been recognized, viz. on the insight that cross-identification between the several possible worlds we have to consider when discussing what *a* perceives can take place in two essentially different ways (or types of ways). They are cross-identification by *descriptive* means and by *perceptual* means (more generally, by means of *acquaintance*). By cross-identification we of course mean here telling which individual in one possible world is identical with which individual in another. (Identification across the boundaries of possible worlds.) The possible worlds involved are of course those compatible with what the person in question – call him *a* – perceives. Earlier, I have considered them as possible states of affairs at the time of perception. It is both more realistic psychologically and more illuminating conceptually to consider them as courses of events compatible with whatever events *a* perceives (or spontaneously believes he perceives) during the specious present to which we are referring his perceptions.[9]

How we cross-identify between these worlds by those usual public or descriptive methods which we are apt to think of first in this sort of context is both so obvious in its general features and so problematic in its details that there is little point in discussing it here at great length. Suffice it to say that continuity with respect to space and time seems to be one of the most important considerations here.[10] Similarity is another important ingredient here, although it seems to be resorted to only when the normal spatio-temporal framework fails us. (Normally descriptive cross-identification is not only or even primarily a matter of similarity.)

These explanations may sound somewhat hazy. They can be made easier to grasp, if not much more definite, by pointing out the obvious fact that a singular term, say '*b*', picks out a definite individual by descriptive criteria, i.e., picks out the same individual descriptively cross-identified between *a*'s perceptual worlds, if and only if it is true to say

(1)   *a* perceives who or what *b* is

whose formal counterpart clearly is

(2) (Ex) *a* perceives that $(b = x)$

where the quantifier relies on descriptive cross-identification. Now precisely when can we say to perceive *who* someone is? There is clearly a great deal of borderline fuzziness present here, and frequently also discrepancies between criteria applied on different occasions. However, descriptive cross-identification is as objective as are the truth-conditions of 'perceiving who (or what)' locutions.

Although the other kind of cross-identification (perceptual cross-identification or, more generally, cross-identification by acquaintance) perhaps does not occur to a philosopher quite as readily as its descriptive counterpart, the main ideas on which it is based are easily explained and easily understood. Consider visual perception, say what *a* sees at a certain moment of time. It was argued already that the proper way of specifying what *a* sees is to speak of the world as it would be if his visual perceptions were veridical, that is, to speak of the individuals there would be in his environment, their properties, their relations, etc. Now often *a* does not recognize these individuals; he does not see what or whom they are. In spite of this, he sees definite individuals. There may, for instance, be a man in front of *a* of whom *a* does not see who he is. Then descriptively speaking the man in front of *a* is a different (descriptively individuated) person in some of the different possible worlds compatible with everything *a* sees. But in each such world there will have to be a man in front of *a*, more specifically in the precise spot of *a*'s visual space in which he sees this man. Obviously we *can* in principle use this fact for the purpose of cross-identification and as it were draw a 'trans world heir line' through all these men in their respective worlds. That we not only *can* do this but in fact *do* so can be shown by arguing that perceptual cross-identification is presupposed in the truth-conditions of such direct-object constructions as '*a* secs *b*'. The point is perhaps explained most quickly by pointing out that for *a* to see *b* (direct object construction!) is for *b* to find a place among *a*'s visual objects, that is to say, among the individuals – obviously perceptually individuated individuals – which *a* can locate in his visual space. A simple argument shows that this is the case when we have

(3) $(\exists x)$ *a* sees that $(b = x)$

with a quantifier '$\exists$' relying on perceptual cross-identification. The question whether one can appropriately be said to *see* on object or person without recognizing him[11] becomes simply the question whether the intended force of a direct-object construction of ordinary language is that of the *de dicto* sentence (3) or of the corresponding *de re* construction[12]

(4) $(\exists x)(b = x \wedge$ *a* sees that $(\exists y)(x = y))$.

As usual, a choice between a *de dicto* reading and a *de re* one cannot be made on *a priori* grounds. Both readings are legitimate in principle. Hence the philosophical part of our question is solved simply by observing that the distinction (3)–(4) is an excellent reconstruction of the traditional contrast between statements *de dicto* and *de re*.

The analogy between (2) and (3) is worth emphasizing. We might say that the direct-object construction is related to perceptual quantifiers $\exists$, $\forall$ (and hence to perceptual cross-identification) precisely in the same way as perceiving who (or what) locations are related to the descriptive quantifiers E and A (and to descriptive cross-identification).

It is interesting to see that perceptual cross-identification is closely tied – both conceptually and psychologically – to the notion of *perceptual space*. For instance, cross-identification by visual means is not unlike fixing the co-ordinates of the individual in question in the perceiver's visual space.[13] As a first approximation, we can say that for *a* to see *b* (in the *de dicto* sense) is for him to see where *b* is – as is intuitive enough. Equally intuitive is that 'where' has to be understood here as referring to locations in *a*'s visual space, not in physical space. (One can see *b* without seeing where it is physically speaking, viz. if one fails to see where oneself is.) This connection is important, for it shows the close connection there is between individuation and geometry – connection which is (among other things) highly pertinent to the evaluation and criticism of Kant's philosophy.[14]

This connection with seeing an object and seeing where it is may seem to be severed in more complicated cases. Suppose that I see John in a glass, but that I cannot tell perceptually whether it is a looking-glass or a transparent glass panel. Don't I then see John without seeing where he is even in my own visual space? Even if one answers this question in the affirmative, I do not see that such puzzle cases tell against my approach. Mirrors complicate one's visual geometry in any case, but they do not lead us away from questions of perceptual space to essentially different kinds of considerations, such as causal relationships. In the example mentioned (it was suggested to me by David Lewis) my visual perception fixes John's putative location down to two alternatives (either behind the transparent panel or else where the reflection originates). Without such relatively strict narrowing down of John's location in my visual space I could not truly say that I (knowingly) see him. It is even somewhat unclear whether it is correct to say *simpliciter* that I see someone when I see him (as we say) in a mirror. Thus I do not see that puzzle cases affect what was said earlier in this paper.

Individuals perceptually individuated constitute the partial reconstruction of the sense-data of sense-datum theorists which was mentioned above. They are in a fairly literal sense the subjects we judge about in unedited perceptual judgements. They therefore serve the very function for which sense-data were initially introduced.[15] Of course, they do not constitute a special class of members of the actual world. The contrast between sense-data and physical objects is on this view not one between two kinds of entities whose interrelations can be inquired into. The contrast pertains solely to comparisons between several different worlds, not to any particular world. Yet the reification of the perceptual trans world heir lines is the kind of tempting fallacy to which epistemologists are naturally and as it were professionally prone. Thus the only entities needed in the actual world are ordinary material objects and other familiar entities. No shadowy entities like sense-data are to be admitted as inhabitants of any world. They are literally 'neither here nor there'.

What has not been pointed out earlier is that there is a special case of perceptual cross-identification which is not covered by the explanations just given. Perceptual cross-identification was said to be based on the fact that all worlds compatible with what a sees must have a great deal similarity in that a's visual objects inhabit by and large the same (visual) locations in each of them. But of course the actual world does not have to be like the world as it appears to a. Hence something more has to be said of cross-identification between the actual world and its alternatives.

There is no way out of this fact by imposing a success condition on perceptual statements (such as 'a sees that p'). There undoubtedly is a success presupposition of some sort present in the perceptual statements of ordinary discourse. However, if it is made part of the force of such propositions as

(5) a perceives that p,

as ordinary usage certainly suggests, then (5) is no longer a disinterested statement of how the world appears to a, but contains also an evaluation of the veracity of these appearances. More importantly, (5) is then no longer a description of the putative information which the senses ('considered as perceptual systems') furnish to a. Hence the imposition of the success condition is (in a sense) in a conflict with the principle of the informational character of spontaneous perception. It seems much more appropriate to separate the specification of the possible misleading 'messages of our senses' from their evaluation and represent the perceptual claims which contain a success presupposition as explicit conjunctions of the following kind

(6)   (a perceives that p) $\wedge$ p.

Here the force of 'perceives that' is only that of 'it appears to a that'. (If a special *terminus technicus* is desirable for the notion of perception minus success condition, perhaps 'perhaption' might do.)

In any case, for the purpose of discussing the semantics of our concepts of perceptual appearance, we cannot assume a success condition, that is, assume that the actual world is among its own alternatives or, more generally, assume that the alternativeness relation used in the logic of perception is reflexive. If we assume the condition, we cannot discuss such epistemologically interesting problems as illusions, hallucinations, perceptual mistakes, impossible objects, etc. Hence we cannot use the similarities which obtain between the alternatives to a given world W and

which are used to cross-identify between them also to cross-identify between them and the world W – for W does not have to share these
similarities.

How, then, do we cross-identify between W and its alternatives?
This question is crucial for the truth-conditions of such propositions as

(7) $(\exists x)\,[(x=d) \wedge a$ sees (seems to see) that $(x=c)]$.

The trans world heir lines which are (go together with) the values of 'x'
here must be extended to the actual world in order for us to be able to
say, as we are attempting to do in (7), that in the actual world one of them
is (picks out) d.

From this we can see what the problem is intuitively. The question
concerns the principles according to which we say that one of a's
perceptual objects is or is not identical with an object in the actual world.
In what way do our perceptual objects reflect the real ones? It can undoubtedly be maintained that in some sufficiently abstract sense this
question could be answered in more than one way. One is reminded of
the fact that the descriptive trans world heir lines are sometimes extended
from world to world by means of resemblances between the respective
individual members of the two worlds. David Lewis has gone so far as to
suggest that this is the way in which 'counterpart relations', as he calls
them, are set up, thus overlooking the role of spatio-temporal frameworks
and of continuity.[16] In principle, one could thus use whatever similarity
there is between the members of a's perceptual worlds and the inhabitants of the actual world and the similarities between the two kinds
of worlds in drawing the world lines. This would imply, among other
things, that if a seems to see a definite visual object b (seen as b) at a given
location, and if b in fact is there, then the visual object in question is in
fact b. Although there do not seem to be binding a priori reasons for
ruling this out, it does not seem to be the way in which we in fact cross-
identify individuals in our own conceptual system. Correctness just is
not what decides here. Paul Grice has made essentially the same point
forcefully[17] by reminding us that it is logically conceivable that there
should be some method by which an expert could make someone, say a,
to have the right sense-experiences although the imaginary method in
question is totally independent of the actual objects apparently perceived.
(This method might be thought of as some kind of for instance stimula-

tion of the cortex or post-hypnotic suggestion.) If one of the objects apparently seen by a is b, then we are not inclined to say that any one of a's visual objects actually is identical with b. We do want to say this only when there is some sort of appropriate *causal* connection between the actual object b and the visual object a beholds.

Examples more realistic than Grice's are not easy to come by. This is neither surprising nor worrisome, however. We do not even need an Austin to realize that perceptual mistakes, let alone hallucinations, are relatively rare, philosophers' examples notwithstanding. Situations in which one has right perceptions for wrong reasons are apt to be even more recondite. It is nevertheless remarkable how well the artificial examples one can devise here enable us to make up our mind of the conceptual situation. I have myself used in teaching an imaginary situation in which it appears to a that a certain picture, say the first Hals portrait of Descartes, is on the wall in front of him, as it in fact is. However, it is further assumed in this example that what a 'really sees', as we say, is a reflection of a copy of the famous painting in a mirror which has been cleverly hidden between a and the wall. Here, as in Grice's examples, we undoubtedly would not say that the painting a thinks he sees is identical with the original, but rather say it is identical with the copy.

Grice also registers some of the difficulties in spelling out precisely what the causal connection is which has to obtain between one of a's perceptual objects and an actual object in his environment before we can tie them together with the same world line. It seems to me that the problem of giving a precise characterization of this connection is due more to general difficulties in analysing causal notions than to the special features of the causal connections relied on in perception.

Certain necessary conditions are nevertheless easy to formulate. If John hits you on the head and you therefore see stars, these stars are not to be identified with John although there is a causal chain connecting John with your having these visual objects. Clearly, the causal chain must pass through one's sense-organs in order for these chains to establish lines of perceptual cross-identification. This requirement is not yet strong enough to characterize fully the cross-identificatory link. However, I shall not inquire here what more is needed.

Thus we have reached the conclusion indicated in the beginning. It has been found that causal notions are deeply involved in the semantics of our perceptual concepts: they constitute an essential element in the truth-conditions of certain kinds of perceptual statements, viz. those which involve cross-identification between a world and its perceptual alternatives. Syntactically speaking, they are statements in which one and the same bound variable (bound to a *perceptual* quantifier) occurs both outside perceptual operators ('perceives that', 'sees that', etc.) and within the scope of one of them, as e.g. in (7). It seems to me highly interesting that an approach which initially emphasized the informational character of perception should turn out to accommodate not only a reconstructed version of sense-data but a version of what is sometimes known as the causal theory as well.

One aspect of our observations is especially important to the general conceptual aspects of the situation. If I am right, cross-identification between the actual world and its perceptual alternatives takes place in a way different from cross-identification between these alternatives themselves. The 'trans world heir lines' connecting these several worlds are as it were drawn differently when it comes to connect the actual world with its perceptual alternatives and when it is required to weave together these alternatives among themselves. Since such world lines are involved essentially with the truth-conditions of quantified statements, it is thus seen that the truth-conditions of statements in which one quantifies *both* into a perceptual context *and* outside it (thus requiring the alternatives to be compared with the actual world) involve considerations essentially disparate from those involved in the truth-conditions for statements in which one merely quantifies in. The former turn partly on causal considerations; the latter on the articulation of the perceiver's perceptual space only. This duality of considerations involved in the truth-conditions of perceptual statements is worth keeping in mind. It illustrates vividly the dependence of the truth-conditions of perceptual (and other modal) statements on the way bound variables enter into them. One's ontology as it were depends on the class of possible worlds as members of which one's individuals are being considered, and this depends on the way bound variables enter into the statement.[18] The contrast between geometrical and causal methods of cross-identification illustrates the futility of operating with just one big context-independent pool of individuals.

I have argued earlier that individuation by acquaintance (not unlike perceptual individuation) and the direct-object construction which goes with it are not restricted to perception but are found also with concepts like memory and knowledge.[19] If so, it is not surprising that similar but somewhat less clear-cut observations can be made concerning notions like memory which exhibit a similar direct-object construction. Although there is no direct-object construction with 'believes' whose meaning would be parallel with that of the construction *perceives* + *direct object*, similar but still vaguer points can be made concerning it. In all these cases, the vehicle for shuttling between a world and its alternatives for the purposes of identification by acquaintance is causation. Knowledge is unlike these notions only because it involves a success condition which makes the alternativeness relation reflexive and thus partly eliminates the special problems of cross-identifying between the actual world and its alternatives. In the case of a's memory, I have argued that the individuals which count as values of quantifiers relying on cross-identification by acquaintance are those for whom a can find a niche in his personally remembered past – which need not be *correctly* remembered. Such a 'remembered individual' is to be identified, if I am right, with that in-habitant of the actual world who caused (in some appropriate sense of the word) the recollections pertaining to this 'remembered individual'. This view certainly squares well with our conceptual practices, it seems to me. I may vividly remember, say, the actor who played a certain role at a definite time, without remembering who he was. Of course this 're-membered individual' is to be identified with the actor who by playing the role in question caused the relevant memories of mine.

Many questions can be asked concerning the relation of these seman-tical and pragmatic observations to other philosophical views con-cerning the role of causality in perception – and in the semantics of other propositional attitudes. Perhaps the most pressing question is whether the role I have assigned to causality has anything at all to do with what has in fact been called causal theories of perception.

Here a rather clear-cut answer is possible. One of the most authori-tative recent definitions of the causal theory has been offered by H. H. Price.[20] According to him, "the only sort of Causal Theory which is of philosophical importance is one which discusses *this* question", viz. the question what observation is. Price goes on to define a version of Causal Theory which does consider it. This theory "maintains (1) that... 'M is present to my senses' will be equivalent to 'M causes a sense-datum with which I am acquainted'; (2) that perceptual consciousness is fundamentally an *inference* from effect to cause."

Here we are not concerned with the second part of the definition, only with the first. Recalling the connection mentioned above, we can see that it comes as close to the role we have assigned to causality in the semantics of perception as one can possibly come within a nontechnical jargon. "A sense-datum with which I am acquainted" is, according to the reconstruction, one of my perceptually individuated individuals. According to my lights, it equals an actual-world object M if and only if it is caused by M, precisely as Price's definition requires.

Less striking but still relevant similarities are found with the views of even more venerable thinkers than Price. St. Thomas Aquinas already held that "to perceive X is to have a sense experience representative of X and caused by X, when X is something external to the body".[21]

Rather more recently than Aquinas, David Kaplan has offered a highly interesting analysis of 'Quantifying In'.[22] He operates there with the notion of belief rather than perception, but *mutatis mutandis* we can apply his discussion to perception, too. Kaplan discusses two different ways of judging names (singular terms): with respect to what Kaplan calls their *vividness* and with respect of whether they are *of* some particular entity or not. The vividness of (say) 'b' is in so many worlds equated by Kaplan with the truth of

(8) $(\exists x)\, a$ believes that $(b = x)$

in my approach. Over and above giving vivid examples, Kaplan explains the nature of this vividness in terms of a's having enough beliefs about the putative bearer of 'b' for him to fix this bearer. As Kaplan puts the point, a vivid name refers to a character filling a major role in the believer's 'inner story' which consists of all the sentences he believes. The role of vividness in Kaplan is thus to fix the reference of a name in this 'inner story', and the objective counterpart of this fixed reference can scarcely be but the identity of the individuals 'b' picks out in the different worlds compatible with what is believed by a. This, of course, is precisely what (8) says. Vividness is thus a matter of cross-identification between belief worlds (doxastic alternatives).

The other basic relation in Kaplan, a name's being *of* someone or something, is causal in nature. There has to be a suitable causal chain between the name and the person or object it refers to in order for it to be *of* this person or object. This relation is in so many words identified by Kaplan with the relation there is "between a perception and the perceived object". It thus is tantamount to the relation which according to the view defended here enables one to cross-identify between the actual world and its perceptual alternatives, generalized to doxastic alternatives. It is in effect used by Kaplan for the same purpose we needed this cross-identificatory step for, viz. to make sense of the truth-conditions of sentences in which bound variables occur both inside and outside operators. (A more accurate name for Kaplan's paper would thus be 'Quantifying In and Out'.)

Thus the approach represented here enables us to assign an appropriate place to both the main ingredients of Kaplan's discussion: vividness concerns cross-identification between alternatives while a name's being *of* someone or something is a matter of cross-identification between alternatives and the actual world. This also shows the underlying unity of the two elements in Kaplan's conceptual scheme: both are methods of cross-identification. Kaplan's lively examples and happy formulations are in fact highly useful in elucidating further the nature of these two kinds of cross-identifications.

What is missing from Kaplan's account is the insight that cross-identification can take place in two different ways. (This is clearer in the case of perception but holds also in some rather vague sense also for belief.) Although this conceptual feature is often overlooked, and although it has not been discussed very much by philosophers, it seems to me the most important fact about the logic (semantics) of perception and of several other propositional attitudes. Both my vindication of the role of causality in the logic of perception and my partial reconstruction of sense-data are made possible by this insight.

NOTES

[1] First published in *Perception and Personal Identity*, Norman S. Care and Robert H. Grimm (eds.), The Press of Case Western Reserve University, Cleveland, 1969, pp. 140–173, and reprinted in my *Models for Modalities*, D. Reidel, Dordrecht, 1969, pp. 151–183. See also Chapter 3 above.
[2] Houghton Mifflin, Boston, 1966.
[3] Cf. his paper with this title in *Synthese* 17 (1967) 162–172.

[4] See 'On the Logic of Perception' (note 1 above).

[5] Notice how this idea is closely related to probabilistic analyses of information. For the obvious interpretation of a sample-space point is just my 'possible world', and what measures of information measure are sets of such sample-space points.

[6] In *Logic and Ontology* (Studies in Contemporary Philosophy), Milton K. Munitz (ed.), New York University Press, New York, 1973.

[7] David Katz, *The World of Color*, Kegan Paul, London 1935. Cf. also Jacob Beck, *Surface Color Perception*, Cornell University Press, Ithaca, N.Y., 1972, Ch. 2.

[8] Cf. 'On the Logic of Perception' (note 1 above).

[9] What is of particular interest here, background knowledge (and background beliefs) is used to weed out many of the possible courses of events apparently compatible with one's perceptions within a given specious present *before* we cross-identify between the states of affairs compatible with one's perceptions. Thus there probably is no such thing in the last analysis as cross-identification by purely perceptual means, but only by means of perceptual information *cum* collateral non-perceptual information.

[10] Cf. my paper, 'The Semantics of Modal Notions and the Indeterminacy of Ontology', in *Semantics of Natural Language*, D. Davidson and G. Harman (eds.), D. Reidel Publishing Company, Dordrecht, 1972, pp. 348–414, reprinted as Chapter 2 of the present volume.

[11] This spurious problem is discussed at length e.g. in G. J. Warnock, 'Seeing', *Proceedings of the Aristotelian Society* **55** (1954–55).

[12] For the distinction between *de re* and *de dicto* readings of an ordinary-language expression, see my *Models for Modalities* (note 1 above), pp. 120–121, 141.

[13] In his paper, 'Analysis of Perceiving in Terms of the Causation of Beliefs' (in *Perception: A Philosophical Symposium*, F. N. Sibley (ed.), Methuen, London, 1971, pp. 23–64), J. W. Roxbee Cox in fact claims that "for a man to perceive a thing, a *y*, is for him to perceive that some thing, a *z*, which in fact is the *y*, is *at a certain place...*" (my italics).

[14] See my papers on Kant reprinted in *Knowledge and the Known*, D. Reidel, Dordrecht, 1974, especially '"Dinge an sich" Revisited'. Cf. also Robert Howell 'Intuitition, Synthesis, and Individuation in the *Critique of Pure Reason*', *Noûs* **7** (1973) 207–232.

[15] Cf. the recurring characterizations of sense-data as the objects of our judgements of immediate perception, as discussed, e.g., in K. Marc-Wogau, *Die Theorie der Sinnesdaten*, Uppsala Universitets Årsskrift 1945, no. 2, Uppsala, 1945.

[16] David Lewis, 'Counterpart Theory and Quantified Modal Logic', *Journal of Philosophy* **65** (1968) 113–126.

[17] 'The Causal Theory of Perception', *Proceedings of the Aristotelian Society*, Supplementary Vol. **35** (1961) 121–152.

[18] Cf. my 'The Semantics of Modal Notions and the Indeterminacy of Ontology' (Chapter 2 above).

[19] See my paper, 'Objects of Knowledge and Belief: Acquaintances and Public Figures', *Journal of Philosophy* **67** (1970) 869–883, and 'Knowledge by Acquaintance – Individuation by Acquaintance', in *Bertrand Russell: A Collection of Critical Essays*, D. F. Pears (ed.), Doubleday & Co., Garden City, N.Y., 1972, pp. 52–79. The former appears also as Chapter 3 of this volume (pp. 43–58 above), and the latter has been reprinted as the last chapter of *Knowledge and the Known*, D. Reidel, Dordrecht, 1974.

[20] *Perception*, Methuen, London, 1952, p. 66.

[21] William Kneale's summary of Aquinas' views in Sibley (*op. cit.*, note 13 above), p. 73.

[22] In *Words and Objections*, Donald Davidson and Jaakko Hintikka (eds.), D. Reidel Publishing Company, Dordrecht, 1969, pp. 206–242.

CHAPTER 5

CARNAP'S HERITAGE IN LOGICAL SEMANTICS

One of the most genuine tributes one can pay to any thinker who has already passed away is to be able to say that his work does not have to be given a special consideration as a kind of venerable museum specimen but can be discussed on its own merits as if its author were still among us. This tribute we can pay in full measure to Rudolf Carnap's work in logical semantics as in other areas, and I am sure that it is the way in which Carnap himself would have preferred to have his work remembered.

In this chapter, I shall therefore not shy away from those aspects of recent discussions of semantics which might at first appear to by-pass Carnap's work or even to stand in an opposition to it. An important additional reason for doing so lies in the fact (which I shall try to argue for) that much of this recent work in semantics is, appearances notwithstanding, an outgrowth of Carnap's ideas or consists of attempts to solve the important problems Carnap raised in semantics. Much of the credit of his successors' work is thus due to Carnap.

What, then, is crucial in Carnapian ideas? It was once said by David Kaplan that Carnap's *Meaning and Necessity* – the book I will mostly concentrate on – represents the culmination of the golden age of (logical) semantics.[1] This age, if I have understood Kaplan correctly, is supposed to extend from Frege to Carnap, and to be characterized by that familiar contrast which in its several variants has been known by such labels as *Bedeutungen* vs. *Sinne*, references (or nominata) vs. senses, or extensions vs. intensions. In *Meaning and Necessity* Carnap uses the last pair of terms.[2]

Carnap's work in *MN* and elsewhere may very well seem to be the end product of this tradition. The importance of the extension-intension dichotomy to him is amply shown by the table of contents of *MN*. It reads, in part:

And even in sections whose titles do not sport the terms 'extension' and 'intension' these two concepts loom large. For instance, the fourth of Carnap's five chapters is devoted almost exclusively to the question of how the distinction is to be accommodated in one's metalanguage.

MN represents the Fregean tradition also in that Carnap emphasizes the primacy of intensions over extensions, to the point of speaking of a reduction of extensions to intensions (*MN*, Section 23). In his own abstract of Section 27 we likewise read: "... a semantical rule for a sign determines primarily its intension; only secondarily, with the help of relevant facts, its extension." This goes back in some form or other to Frege who said in so many words that "in the conflict between extensional and intensional logicians I am taking the side of the latter. In fact I do hold", Frege continues, "that the concept is logically prior to its extension." [3]

The intensions we need in a Carnapian semantics include such old friends of philosophers as propositions, properties (as distinguished from the classes they determine), and individual concepts. Needless to say, their *prima facie* philosophical importance could not be greater. The postulation of such intensional entities has been claimed by Carnap's critics to violate the standards of enlightened scientific empiricism. The most important of these critics is W. V. Quine.[4] It has been made beautifully clear by Quine himself how much of his philosophy of language can be understood as a reaction to Carnap's semantics.[5]

This is not a place to try to adjudicate the whole of Carnap-Quine exchange. It seems to me fair to say, nevertheless, that Quine has spotted certain weak spots in Carnap's position, at least insofar as *MN* is concerned. This is not decisive, however, for I shall argue that Carnap's ideas allow for developments which serve to solve Carnap's difficulties to an incomparably greater extent than the critics, and the philosophical community at large, have so far acknowledged. At the same time, these developments show that the strict intension-extension contrast is far too narrow a framework for a realistic semantics, and that Carnap's own ideas can easily be extended so as to widen this framework essentially. These, at any rate, will be the main theses of the present chapter. If I am right, Carnap was not the last Mohican of Fregean semantics, based on the extension-intension contrast, but rather the first and foremost herald of a new epoch of possible-worlds semantics.

Usually, Carnap's critics have focused on what the critics claim amounts to the unobservability or perhaps rather inevitable empirical underdeterminacy of intensions. To put their point very briefly: We cannot ever hope to find out for sure what the intensions are that underlie a heathen tongue – or our own idiolect, for that matter. All the speech disposition of the speakers of any given language are compatible (according to Quine) with the postulation of more than one set of incompatible intensions.

These criticisms seem to me somewhat premature – as premature in fact as the views under criticism. We shall return to the problems of empiricism and observability later. Meanwhile, I want to emphasize that the true weakness of Carnap's position in *MN* is not the non-empirical character of his main semantical concepts. Especially in some of the papers appended to the second edition of *MN*, Carnap in fact presents plausible arguments to show that his concepts do carry an empirical import. The reason why these arguments have not swayed more philosophers than they have done is not so much due to the arguments themselves. It is due to the fact that the crucial intensional concepts themselves were not analyzed far enough by Carnap in *MN*. They were not developed in a way which would have created a viable framework for Carnap's own arguments and for the further development of his semantics, e.g., so as to allow a natural and convincing treatment of belief-sentences. What is missing in *MN* are not reasons for the empirical character of intensional concepts but rather all penetrating analyses of them in some more informative and more easily operationalizable terms.

Whoever deserves the credit for the analyses which we just found wanting in *MN*, they are found in a full-fledged form in what is often called possible-worlds semantics. Its main outlines will emerge from a comparison with Carnap's position in *MN*.

The historical fact which one cannot but find absolutely fascinating is that in *MN* Carnap came extremely close to the basic ideas of possible-worlds semantics, and yet apparently did not formulate them, not even to himself. The conceptual framework developed in the first chapter of *MN* is that of state-descriptions. It is in terms of state-descriptions that Carnap defines all his crucial concepts, such as those of range, L-truth, L-equivalence, identity of intensions, and so on.[6] Technically, this almost amounts to a possible-worlds semantics. All that Carnap had to do here was to take a good hard look at his state-descriptions and to ask: What are they supposed to be descriptions *of* in some realistic, down-to-earth sense? One natural answer is that they are descriptions of the different possible states of affairs or courses of events (in short, 'possible worlds') in which a speaker of the language in question could conceivably find himself and which he could in principle distinguish conceptually from each other. From this answer it is only a short step to the crucial idea that the rules for using the language will have to be shown – in principle – by the way a well-informed speaker would use it in these different circumstances according to the rules, i.e., by the extensions which the expressions of the language would have in those several 'possible worlds'. This is all we need to arrive at the basic ideas of possible-worlds semantics.

It is especially tantalizing to see that Carnap in fact says in so many words in *MN* that his state-descriptions "represent Leibniz' possible worlds" (p. 9). In his intellectual autobiography,[7] Carnap likewise mentions Leibniz' possible worlds as one of the original guiding ideas of his distinction between logical truth and factual truth (p. 63). What is missing is thus apparently only an insight into the possibility of using these possible worlds for the purpose of analysing the intensional objects Carnap in fact leaves unanalysed in *MN*.

The move from *MN* to possible-worlds semantics is closest at hand in the case of intensions of sentences, i.e., in the case of propositions. The class of those state-descriptions in which a sentence '*S*' is true is called the *range* $R(S)$ of '*S*' (*MN*, p. 9).[8] According to Carnap, this range determines the identity of the intension $I(S)$ of '*S*' in the sense that $I(S) = I(S')$ iff $R(S) = R(S')$ (*MN*, p. 23, Def. 5–2). In the same sense, $R(S)$ determines the proposition expressed by '*S*'. What, then, is more natural

than to *define* this proposition as $R(S)$ or as something closely related
to $R(S)$, such as the characteristic function of the set of worlds described
by the members of $R(S)$? In the latter case, propositions will be functions
from possible worlds to truth-values. This definition is most natural
because it is natural to say that to understand a proposition is to know
what restrictions its truth places on the world. Such restriction is precisely
what the membership in the set of worlds described by the members of
$R(S)$ amounts to. Here we have a good example of the kind of structural
analysis of fundamental semantical notions which possible-worlds
semantics enables us to carry out but which I found missing from MN.[9]

This kind of structural insight is not restricted to intensions of sentences. Historically, perhaps the most crucial question is what can be said
of the intension $I(i)$ of an individual expression 'i'.[8] In MN, Carnap never
formulates explicit criteria for the identity of the intensions $I(i)$ and $I(i')$
of two individual expressions 'i' and 'i'' comparable with his criteria for
the identity of the intensions of sentences. Implicit in his discussion (see
e.g. p. 40) is nevertheless a criterion according to which $I(i) = I(i')$ iff
'$i = i'$' is true in every state-description. By the same token as in the case
of the intensions of sentences, this naturally leads us to identify the intensions of individual expressions (dubbed by Carnap *individual concepts*)
with functions that for each possible world W pick out a member of some
domain of individuals (or with some essentially equivalent entity). (This
domain must obviously be thought of as depending on W, if we want to
have a flexible, presuppositionless treatment of the situation.[10]) Thus if
$I(i)$ is the intension of 'i', the function I must be thought of as having
a second argument, too, and thus as being of the form $I(i, W)$, where W
is the possible world in which we are considering the reference of 'i'.

In fact, one's interpretation of the intensions of sentences as sets of
possible worlds (or, essentially equivalently, functions from possible
worlds to truth-values) tends rather strongly to prejudice the case for
a similar treatment of individual expressions. As I have pointed out on
several occasions,[11] if one introduces the modal operators 'N' ('necessarily') and 'M' ('possibly') and formulates the truth-conditions in the most
natural manner imaginable, merely requiring the substitutivity of identity
for atomic expressions, then it can be shown that be criterion of substitutivity (say of 'a' and 'b' for the case of just one layer of modal operators)
is the truth of '$N(a = b)$'. According to the treatment of sentences, how-

ever, this is true iff '$a = b$' is true in all (relevant) possible worlds, i.e., iff 'a' and 'b' pick out the same individual from each of these possible worlds. This is the analogue to Carnap's explicit criterion for the identity of the intensions of two sentences, and in the same way suggests the identification of $I(i)$ with a function from possible worlds to their respective domains of individuals.

What is remarkable in this analysis of individual concepts is how very closely it comes to the intentions (with a 't'!) of modern semanticists from Frege on. Frege said that the intension (*Sinn*) of a name must include more than just its reference. It must also include *the way in which this reference is given* (*die Art des Gegebenseins*, 'Sinn und Bedeutung', p. 26 of the original edition[12]). Now the functional dependence which this phrase "way of being given" clearly means can – and must – be spelled out by specifying how the reference depends on everything it might depend on, which in the last analysis is the whole possible world we are dealing with.[13] (Of course this does not preclude that it depends only on certain particular aspects of that world!) But this is precisely what the function $I(i,W)$ gives us. Here, possible-worlds semantics therefore follows as closely as one can hope in Frege's and Carnap's footsteps. I cannot but find it very strange that it apparently never occurred to Frege that to speak of "die Art des Gegebenseins" is *implicite* to speak of a functional dependence of a certain sort. There does not seem to be an inkling of this idea in his writings.

Clearly predicators can be dealt with in the same way as individual expressions. Their intensions will be functions from possible worlds to sets of n-tuples of the members of their domains, or some similar entities.

This completes my sketch of the step from MN to possible-worlds semantics. The step is so short that it is not surprising to find a report according to which in his unpublished work Carnap did take something essentially tantamount to it. Richard Montague reports in his paper, 'Pragmatics and Intensional Logic',[14] last paragraph, that "Carnap had... proposed in conversation that intensional objects be identified with functions from possible worlds to extensions of appropriate sorts...". In fact, in addition to conversations, Carnap's 'Replies and Expositions' in the Schilpp volume contain a sketch of what he calls "translation of a modal language into an extensional language" (pp. 894–6). Apart from minor technical differences, this 'translation' is to all practical purposes an outline of a model-theoretical treatment of intensions, with what Carnap called models playing the role of possible worlds. In fact, propositions are in so many words 'represented' as classes of models, certain other intensions as functions from models to suitable specifications of the properties of their individuals, and the necessity of a proposition amounts to its truth in all possible worlds. In brief, we seem to have here a full-fledged possible-worlds semantics explicitly outlined by Carnap. Yet this impression is definitely misleading. Carnap has most of the basic technical ingredients of a possible-worlds semantics right there in his hands, but he does not know what to do with them philosophically and interpretationally. His notion of a model is not that of a possible world, for he is, e.g., allowing descriptive predicates to be arbitrarily re-interpreted in a model.[15] In a different possible world surely those and only those things are to be called red that *are* red there. Hence the interpretation of descriptive predicates must be assumed to be constant between different possible words. This is *not* required of Carnap's models, however.

Montague reports that, according to Carnap's verbal suggestions, too, "possible worlds [are] identified with models".[16] In other words, possible worlds were not thought of by Carnap as the real-life situations in which a speaker might possibly find himself, but as any old configurations – perhaps even linguistic – exemplifying the appropriate structures. As we shall see, it is this apparently small point that precludes Carnap from some of the most promising uses of possible-worlds semantics.

Although possible-worlds semantics thus may be said to be (in some respects) a natural and perhaps even fairly small further development beyond Carnap, it nevertheless puts the whole of the classical Frege-Carnap semantics into a radically new perspective. Here I shall only comment on three aspects of the new perspective. (1) First, the new semantics opens the door to the treatment of a large class of philosophically interesting notions, thus answering a number of Carnapian questions. (2) Second, I shall argue that possible-worlds semantics shows conclusively the insufficiency of a semantics which is primarily based on the intension-extension distinction. (3) Third, I shall suggest that possible-worlds semantics perhaps points to a way of removing the objections which Quine and others have raised against intensional concepts because of their alleged unobservability, empirical vacuousness, behavioral non-specificity or because of some similar defect.

1. Already in MN[17] Carnap put his semantics to work for the purpose of spelling out the logic of modalities ('necessarily' and 'possibly'). It is not always appreciated sufficiently that this made Carnap into the first modal logician to employ semantical methods.

The details of Carnap's modal logic are rather predictable, and need not detain us here. If Carnap had formulated his point in the suggestive terminology of 'possible worlds', all that is really involved in Carnap's modal logic (apart from the treatment of individuals, their existence, and their uniqueness) is the old idea that necessity means truth in every possible world and possibility truth in at least one possible world. Once again, the necessity of dragging along all intensions as unanalyzed entities leads Carnap to a lengthy discussion of how we ought to address them in our metalanguage.

Carnap's failure (in MN) to analyze his intensional concepts seems to be a partial reason for a much more serious oversight, however, than his worry about a bunch of somewhat scholastic problems concerning one's metalanguage. The point is perhaps made most forcefully in a somewhat technical-sounding jargon. When propositions become functions from possible worlds to truth-values and individual concepts functions from these worlds to members of their respective domains of individuals, all sorts or interesting conceptualizations can be reached by restricting the domains of these functions (in the relation-theoretical sense of domain) to subclasses of the class of all possible worlds.

The first major novelty in the subsequent technical development of the semantics of modal logics was in fact the idea that not all possible worlds are on a par. Given a world W, only some possible worlds are relevant alternatives to W. Then necessary truth of a sentence in W has to be characterized as its truth (truth *simpliciter*) in all the alternatives to W, and its possibility *a fortiori* as its truth in at least one alternative to W. The first heady discovery in this area was that by imposing simple restrictions on the alternativeness relation we obtain the semantical counterparts to all of the most important axiomatic systems of modal logic.[18] Their semantics is (with one exception) unobtainable in the simple-minded Leibniz-Carnap assumption of the parity of all possible worlds.

This does not seem to affect Carnap's immediate purpose, for he was trying to explicate the notions of *logical* necessity and *logical* possibility. For them, it is natural to argue, all worlds are equal: what is necessary or possible in one is likewise necessary or possible, respectively, in any other. Hence Carnap's modal logic seems to be unobjectionable as far it goes, and the advantages of the alternativeness relation appear primarily technical.

This is not the whole story, however. The most important philosophical uses of alternativeness relations are for the purpose of studying certain notions in which Carnap was interested, especially the notion of belief. The use of an alternativeness relation makes it possible to accommodate such notions within possible-worlds semantics.[19] In fact, the interpretation of the alternativeness relation itself is exceptionally clear in this case. (It turns out that it has to be relativized to a person.) Worlds alternative to W (with respect to a person a) are then worlds compatible with everything a believes in W. Understanding the concept of belief will then become tantamount to mastering this particular kind of alternativeness relation (relation of *doxastic* alternativeness). How close this comes to our actual ways with notions like belief can perhaps be seen by pointing out that to know what a believes (say, in the actual world) is clearly very close to knowing which possible states of affairs or courses of events are ruled out by his beliefs and which ones are compatible with it. This, of course, is just what the alternativeness relation specifies. Our analysis thus constitutes an important step beyond Carnap in the analysis of the concept of belief.

Carnap was apparently prevented from analyzing the concept of belief in this way by the very same peculiarity which made us say above that he never reached full-fledged possible-worlds semantics, viz. by his failure to interpret his models as genuine possible worlds, i.e., real-life alternatives to our actual world. This does not matter as long as one is merely studying the notions of logical necessity and logical possibility. It already begins to matter if we are interested in analytical necessity and analytical possibility, for here arbitrary reinterpretation will destroy those relations of synonymy (or whatnot) which do not reduce to the formal truths of logic. This may perhaps be handled by means of explicit meaning postulates, but no comparable trick has much appeal in the case of belief. Hence the step from Carnap's "translation of modal language into extensional language" to possible-worlds semantics, small though it might seem, makes all the difference in the world to our analysis of belief. By the same token, it enables us to undertake similar analyses of several of the most important philosophical concepts, including knowledge, memory, perception, obligation, etc.

One marriage of the problem of belief to possible-worlds semantics does not solve all the problems concerning belief-sentences Carnap discusses in *MN*. However, it opens the door to new developments in this direction. Carnap's own terminology enables us to describe the situation succinctly. Carnap called an expression *intensional* iff the identity of intensions (*L*-equivalence) is a necessary and sufficient criterion of substitutivity in that expression. (For a more accurate definition, see *MN*, p. 48.) Carnap pointed out that belief-expressions are not intensional in this sense. In fact, the failure of intensionality is here twofold. If '*i*' and '*i*'' are individual expressions, $I(i) = I(i')$ is neither a necessary nor a sufficient condition of substitutivity. Carnap's discussion in *MN* is addressed solely to the problem created by the latter fact. What is at issue here is of course the fact that even if '*i*' and '*i*'' are L-equivalent (logically equivalent), a rational believer may very well be unaware of their equivalence, and an interchange of '*i*' and '*i*'' may therefore make a difference to his beliefs. For this reason, we need for the purpose of analyzing the concept of belief a relation which is (at least sometimes) stronger than logical equivalence. In the Schilpp volume (pp. 897–900) Carnap in effect calls equivalence classes with respect to the former (stronger) relation senses, those with respect to the latter intensions. This does not alone help us very much, however. The main problem here is the characterization of the new, stronger relation.

This problem is not automatically solved by possible-world semantics but remains a problem there. However, gradually we seem to be getting even this problem under control.[20]

Carnap's own attempted solution to this problem was in terms of what he called intensional structure.[21] Roughly speaking, two expressions have the same intensional structure iff they are built up in the same way of logically equivalent unanalyzed parts. The intensional isomorphism of *S* and *S'* is proposed by Carnap as a sufficient criterion for the logical equivalence of '*a* believes that *S*' and '*a* believes that *S*''. This solution appears to me *ad hoc*, however, until some general theoretical reasons are given why it is just differences of intensional structure that essentially tend to obscure our insights into logical interrelations of sentences. For it was precisely this failure of us humans to be 'logically omniscient' that causes the failure of intensional isomorphism to be a sufficient condition of substitutivity. Hence the formal restrictions on substitutivity ought to reflect those structural factors that are principally responsible for the failure of 'logical omniscience'. However, if the question is put in this way, it seems to me clear that more interesting candidates for this role can be suggested.[22]

Let us leave this half of the problem and return to the failure of L-equivalence to constitute a *necessary* criterion of substitutivity. What the fault-finders uniformly overlook is that this part of the problem is beautifully solved by possible-worlds semantics. According to this semantics, 'i' and 'i''' are interchangeable in discussing a's beliefs iff they pick out the same individual in all the possible worlds we have to consider here. These worlds, in turn are all the worlds compatible with what a believes. Hence the identity of the references of 'i' and 'i''' in these worlds means that a believes that $i - i'$. But if so, quite obviously 'i' and 'i''' *are* interchangeable in discussing a's beliefs, provided they are consistent. Hence possible-worlds semantics at once leads to the right condition of substitutivity, thus carrying the analysis of an important problem of Carnap's essentially further.

The reason why the identity of intensions is not a necessary condition for substitutivity here is nicely brought out by the fact that $I(i) = I(i')$ means that the functions which pick out the references of 'i' and 'i''', respectively, coincide on the whole set of possible worlds, while the truth of

$$\text{`}a \text{ believes that } i = i''\text{'}$$

in a world W only requires that they coincide on the much smaller set of alternatives to W.

2. This brings us already toward my second main point. It is that possible-worlds semantics conclusively shows the insufficiency of a semantics based solely on the distinction extension-intension or *Bedeutung-Sinn*. This distinction is all right, but it just does not do the whole job nor even one of the most important parts of the job that a satisfactory semantical theory must do. Hence, the classical Frege-Carnap semantics is very seriously incomplete, notwithstanding its closeness in some respects to possible-worlds semantics.

In order to see what the problem is, it may be useful to try to have an overview of the aims of the Frege-Carnap semantics. For our present purposes, the relatively unproblematic part – the part to which Frege in fact paid less attention – is the semantics of purely first-order (quantificational) notions. Only a small selection of the problems concerning it were taken up by Carnap. (Some of them are in fact very naturally suggested by the basic ideas of possible-worlds semantics, but I shall not discuss them here.) The problems I want to focus on here are due to the failure of our expressions to behave in modal contexts (in the wide sense of the word in which 'propositional attitudes' like belief are also considered modal notions) in the same (relatively) unproblematic way as in first-order contexts. Now the *locus classicus* of the Frege-Carnap semantics is of course Frege's paper 'Sinn und Bedeutung'.[23] The very first question Frege asks in this paper concerns the behavior of identities like '$i = i'$' vis-à-vis the notion of knowledge. More generally, to explain the failure of the substitutivity of identity in modal contexts is obviously one of the basic tasks of any satisfactory semantics.

The basic answer Frege-Carnap semantics gives is that what matters in modal contexts are not the *extensions* of one's expressions but rather their *intensions*. At first blush, this seems quite wrong-headed, for the right criterion of substitutivity in, say, belief-contexts (doxastic contexts) is certainly not the identity of the intensions (*Sinne*) of the intersubstituted expressions. As was already noted, we do not need to have $I(i) = I(i')$ in order to have 'i' and 'i'' interchangeable in discussing a person's beliefs. Hence Frege's answer to his own first and foremost question seems to be seriously amiss. Likewise, it was already indicated that Carnap failed to say very much of interest about substitutivity in belief-contexts in terms of his theory of extensions and intensions.

However, here possible-worlds semantics rushes to the rescue of Frege and Carnap. When the intensions of (say) individual expressions are analyzed as functions from possible worlds to the members of their respective domains of individuals, it becomes clear that intensions are after all essentially involved in the substitutivity conditions. The only new thing that happens in belief-contexts is that it is not the identity of these unrestricted functions that matters, but rather the identity of their restrictions to a certain subset of the set of all possible worlds. (Typically, it is the set of worlds compatible with everything someone believes.) The same account is seen to work for many other propositional attitudes.

Hence the Frege-Carnap semantics does come close to giving the right answer to the question of substitutivity conditions in modal contexts, although their own formulations did not spell out the matter quite fully. It is instructive to notice how our treatment of the substitutivity problem was made possible by the insight into the relation of the possible worlds to the notion of belief via the doxastic alternativeness relation. Here the tremendous advantages that accrue from the insignificant-looking step from models to possible worlds are beginning to tell. Both our *prima facie* objection to the Frege-Carnap treatment of substitutivity and the simple answer to it would have been impossible to formulate without this step. Among other things, Frege's first and foremost problem would have remained unsolved as a consequence.

However, the substitutivity problem is not the only one here, and those logicians who have tried to make it into the only major problem in interpreting modal logic have only succeeded in clouding the issues. The substitutivity problem is a paradigm problem caused by the failure of the usual *identity laws* in modal contexts. Another set of problems is created by the failure of *quantificational laws* in these contexts. The paradigmatic problem here is to account for the failure of existential generalization, i.e., of many inferences of the form

(EG) $F(a)$, therefore $(Ex) F(x)$.

where '$F(x)$' contains modal operators.

Possible-worlds semantics at once yields a natural explanation. The individual expression 'a' may pick out different individuals in the different possible worlds we have to consider in '$F(a)$'. If so, the truth of '$F(a)$' does not give us any opening for maintaining that '$F(x)$' is true *of some particular individual x*, as '$(Ex)F(x)$' claims. Hence (EG) is not valid in general.

It is also seen at once (at least roughly) when (i.e., on what additional conditions) (EG) is valid. It is valid iff 'a' picks out one and the same individual from all the different possible worlds as a member of which we are tacitly considering a in '$F(a)$'. What these worlds are can be read from '$F(a)$', and it turns out that the requisite uniqueness condition can even be expressed by a suitable sentence of our modal language.[24]

Precisely how this happens is an interesting question, but it need not concern us here. Our main interest lies in the fact that in order to make sense of the reasons for the failure of existential generalization as well as of the conditions of its success we have to be able to *cross-identify*, that is, to say of a member of (the domain of individuals of) one possible world that is or is not identical with a member of another. (For we had to say that '*a*' picks or does not pick *the same individual in different possible worlds*.)

The interpretational aspects of cross-identification offer all sorts of problems. However, the overriding fact is clear enough, and sufficient for our purposes: cross-identification must make objective sense.

To see what this means, consider a 'world line' connecting the 'embodiments' or perhaps better the 'roles' of one and the same individual in all the different possible worlds. These members of the different possible worlds may be thought of as being picked out by a function. This function is of the nature of an intension in the sense that it is of the same logical type as those functions which serve as intensions of individual expressions. Let us call à la Carnap functions of this kind *individual concepts*. The objectivity of cross-identification then means that a subclass of the class of all such special individual concepts has to be objectively given, viz., the class of those special functions which define world lines of one and the same individual.

Clearly, it will be a *proper* subclass of the class of *all* individual concepts, for obviously not any old function which picks out an individual from a number of possible worlds picks out *the same* individual from all of them in any conceivable sense of identity. Let us call the narrower class of those functions that do so the class of *individuating functions*.

When an explicit semantics is developed,[25] it turns out that individuating functions, or, rather, their restrictions to certain sets of possible worlds, are the main ingredients of the truth-conditions for quantified sentences. They are the most important entities we have to quantify over in these truth-conditions.

Now it is obvious that the class of individuating functions cannot be defined in the sole terms of the class of individual concepts. As far as I can see, it cannot be reduced in any other sense, either, to the class of individual concepts.

What this means is that a semantics which only recognizes the whole unanalyzed set of individual concepts as a primitive idea will be incapable of formulating satisfactory truth-conditions for quantified sentences in modal contexts and also incapable of explaining the failure of existential generalization in modal contexts. The classical Frege-Carnap semantics is a case in point, give or take a few minor qualifications. Hence their type of semantics is insufficient for dealing with quantified modal logics. More specifically, it is incapable of dealing with the other paradigmatic puzzle case in this field, viz. the failure of existential generalization. No wonder Quine has been unhappy with Carnap's semantics, for unlike Frege he has explicitly considered the problem of existential generalization in modal contexts over and above the problem of substitutivity of identity. Small wonder, too, that Quine has directed his main attack against the idea of quantified modal logic.

From one important point of view, the classical Frege-Carnap semantics is thus seriously incomplete, requiring an essentially new conceptual element in order to be able to deal with the problem which more than perhaps anything else has been the bone of contention between Carnap and his critics, viz. the problem of combining quantification and modality. To put the main point in a nutshell, the Frege-Carnap semantics explains the behavior of identity in modal contexts (and propositional-attitude contexts), but not the behavior of quantifiers in such contexts. The difference between the two problems is almost like a quantifier-switch. In the case of identity, the problem is to tell when *two* singular terms pick out the same individual in *each* possible world (of a certain sort). In the case of quantification, we have to ask when *one and the same* singular term picks out the same individual in *all* possible worlds (of a certain kind). Only the second problem involves cross-identification between possible worlds. For this reason, it does not reduce to the first.

At the same time, possible-worlds semantics supports Carnap against his critics in the crucial matter of the possibility of using intensional concepts in a way which makes it possible, e.g., to construct a semantics for quantified modal logic. Admittedly there are further problems here which may bring out the bite of some of Quine's specific criticisms.[26] However, on the level at which most of the Carnap-Quine controversy has been carried out, possible-worlds semantics is not only an outgrowth of Carnap's ideas but also their partial vindication.

This conclusion is so important that it deserves a few further comments and a few supplementary arguments in its favor. It is not only the case that the dichotomy extension-intension requires some supplementation in order to be workable. What is even worse for those dichotomizers who still try to rely on the contrast, the introduction of individuating functions messes up thoroughly the neat intuitive contrast between references (extensions) and meaning entitites (intensions) which is one of the apparent attractions of the Frege-Carnap semantics. For the position of individuating functions in the alleged dichotomy of references and meanings is hopelessly ambivalent.

On the one hand, individuating functions constitute a subclass of the class of those paragons of intensionality, individual concepts. Moreover, they serve to solve one of the main problems for the treatment of which meaning entitites (intensions) have usually been introduced in the first place.

On the other hand, what individuating functions do is to give us the individuals which serve (albeit in some cases only potentially) as the references of our individual expressions. Almost the only reason, it may be suggested, why we have to deal with such functions here is that we have to keep an eye on more than one possible world and hence to keep track of our individuals – the very normal unexciting kinds of entities that inhabit our actual universe – in these different worlds. The technical counterpart to this (essentially correct) intuitive view is that the main role of individuating functions (or suitable restrictions of them) is to supply the entities one's quantified variables range over in modal contexts (more accurately, when we quantify into a modal context) precisely when we insist on quantifying over normal, down-to-earth sort of individuals in the normal 'objectual' sense of quantification (to use Quine's terminology).[27]

The details of the truth-conditions can easily be spelled out, but they are not our concern here. They have been spelled out – to some extent at least – elsewhere.[28]

The role of individuating functions and/or their similarity with intensions is sometimes overlooked in possible-worlds semantics. Sometimes this semantics is developed by postulating a class of individuals (possible individuals, if you prefer) which then simply show up or fail to show up in the several possible worlds. This procedure, though entirely justified for many purposes, is seriously oversimplified, however.[29] It hides the processes by means of which cross-identifications are actually carried out and which may rely on many things besides the individuals themselves, such as the structure of each of the two possible worlds in question and comparisons between them. However, the postulation of possible individuals is not only oversimplified pragmatically. It is also oversimplified semantically. The behavior of individuating functions can in principle be such that the 'manifestations' of individuals they connect cannot simply be appearances of one and the same individual.

For one thing, it has been argued that world lines can split when we move from a possible world to another.[30] Although this particular point is controversial, it seems very hard to rule out all splitting altogether.

What is more important, in some situations we have two different classes of individuating functions in operation at one and the same time.[31] Such a situation cannot be done justice to by simply speaking of a given class of (possible) individuals. The functional character of individuating functions, and hence their similarity with intensions, has to be recognized. We simply cannot save the traditional dichotomy by considering individuating functions as unproblematic dramatizations of the identity functions.

3.   While possible-worlds semantics thus demonstrates a major insufficiency in the traditional semantics which operates with the intension-extension contrast, it seems to me that in a deeper sense Carnap's work in semantics will perhaps be only enhanced by this insight. It seems to me that there are many suggestions and ideas in his writings which will be thrown into a sharper relief by the perspectives which possible-worlds semantics opens. This semantics may perhaps even be said to be closer to the spirit of Carnap's semantical ideas than the traditional intensions-extensions contrast.

The main new perspective that opens here consists of certain increased prospects of convincingly and systematically demonstrating the empirical and perhaps also behavioristic import of both intensional concepts and also of propositional attitudes such as belief, even when they are used non-extensionally. Quine is undoubtedly right in emphasizing that the two are apt to stand or fall together. Hence it suffices to discuss the notion of belief.

In MN (pp. 53–5), Carnap proposes as the first approximation toward interpreting belief-sentences the following paraphrase of 'John believes that D':

(B)   'John is disposed to an affirmative response to some sentence in some language which expresses the proposition that D'.

This analysis suffers from several difficulties.[32] Among them there are the following:

(i) There is no guarantee that under (B) belief is invariant with respect to intensional isomorphism (see above) as Carnap assumed. (John might respond differently to two intensionally isomorphic sentences.)

(ii) Interpretation (B) leads to problems whenever John understands a language incompletely or wrongly. (He might assent to a sentence expressing the proposition that D thinking that it expresses something else.)

(iii) An explication along the lines of (B) is inapplicable to unverbalized and perhaps unverbalizable beliefs (e.g., the beliefs of a dog).

(iv) In the form (B), Carnap's criterion is largely inapplicable, because it presupposes that the applier knows which sentences express which propositions in different languages – and also in one and the same language. Finding this out easily leads to considerations of the beliefs of the speakers of the languages in question. Hence (B) ought to be reformulated in terms of John's responses to 'D' itself, not to its synonyms or L-equivalents.

The source of all these difficulties (except the first one, which becomes spurious as soon as one gives up the belief in intensional isomorphism as the touchstone of substitutivity in belief-contexts) is Carnap's reliance in (B) on John's responses to certain *sentences*. In this respect, an entirely different procedure is suggested by the possible-worlds analysis of belief. Knowing what John believes means on this analysis knowing which possible worlds are compatible with his belief and (by implication) which ones are not. In order to explain what it means for John to believe something one thus has to explore what this dichotomy between two different kinds of possible worlds (in relation to John) amounts to. Now it clearly lies close at hand here to explain it in terms of John's different reactions to the two different kinds of worlds.

In brief, the idea is this: put John suddenly in a world incompatible with his (current) beliefs, and he will react in one way. Put him in a world compatible with his beliefs, and he will evince a different reaction. John will then believe that D if he exhibits the first reaction in no possible world in which it is the case that D.

This suggestion is of course oversimplified. However, it is neither trivially unrealistic nor subject to the difficulties which bothered Carnap's analysis. Nor does it necessarily violate reasonable standards of empiricism and observability. In short, it seems to open a much more promising line of thought than the analysis of belief in terms of responses to sentences.

For instance, the problem of attributing unverbalised beliefs to people and even animals (cf. (iii) above) reduces to the much more general problem of spelling out the responses which distinguish doxastic alternatives from other possible worlds. In fact, a dog's beliefs are likely to present a much simpler case vis-à-vis this general problem than the beliefs of us humans, for in the case of dogs it is clear that we do not attribute beliefs to them on the basis of what we think of as going on inside their minds but on the basis of their characteristic behavior when a belief turns or fails to turn out to be true.

Likewise, the problem of linguistic mistakes (cf. (ii) above) presents no difficulties in principle. A person believes that p quite apart from his responses to any particular sentence synonymous with 'p' if and only if his reactions to worlds in which 'p' is true and to those in which it is false exhibit the appropriate difference. Such a difference may even obtain between two complementary classes of possible worlds which are *not* the ranges of 'q' and 'not-q' for any 'q' in some given language L. Then a believes a proposition which is not expressible in L.

Moreover, insofar as the a's different responses to worlds compatible and incompatible with his beliefs can be spelled out, we have an explication of the notion of belief which even satisfies some of the stringent methodological canons apparently adhered to by Quine. For this belief will be more or less on a par with any old dispositional concept, and Quine explicitly admonishes us to "remain free to allow ourselves one by one any general terms we like, however subjunctive or dispositional their explanations".[33]

True, Quine seems to be completely happy with dispositional terms only when the dispositions in question are believed to be somehow tied to the physical structure of the objects they are dispositions of.[34] As long as we are not required to spell out this structure, however, I do not see that this desideratum is not satisfied in the case at hand, given some fairly reasonable view of the physiological basis of our beliefs. (Cf. here Carnap's remarks on the intensions of a robot in 'Meaning and Synonymy in Natural Languages'.)

Moreover, Quine's desideratum is hardly a reasonable one in the first place, if it is intended to imply that some unique structure is present in all cases of the dispositional concept. Surely computer scientists can legitimately speak of the software of computers without committing themselves to a particular way of realizing them in actual hardware. Statements like 'such-and-such an item of information is stored in the memory of a computer' may have a well-defined and unambiguous sense even if the kind of memory involved is left completely at large. Hence it appears that Quine's reservations about dispositional terms do not constitute valid reasons for denying the possibility of explicating the concept of belief along the lines suggested by possible-worlds semantics.

Similar remarks can be addressed to intensional concepts proper instead of the concept of belief. They, too, can perhaps be analyzed in terms of an informed language-user's behavior in different possible worlds. I find it rather strange that the promising new opportunities that are opened here by possible-worlds semantics for the philosophy of language have not been explored or commented on by philosophical semanticists.

In fact, virtually the only extant discussion that can (almost) be fitted into this framework is Carnap's own. In his highly interesting paper 'Meaning and Synonymy in Natural Languages' (*MN*, second ed., pp. 233–47),[35] Carnap envisages a procedure of empirically determining not only the extension but also the intension of a predicate. At first blush, it looks rather analogous to the explication of belief sketched earlier, and it seems to me that it is basically very much in the same spirit. The extension of a predicate to a speaker is the class of actual objects to which he would apply the predicate. In order to get from this to intensions, Carnap says, we only have to take into account also 'possible cases'.

It is here that differences come in. Carnap is thinking of people's reactions to possible *objects* or kinds of objects–these locutions are actually used by him – rather than possible *worlds*. Thus he relies on the dubious notion of a possible individual, which in any case greatly restricts the applicability of the procedure, for often the applicability of (say) a general term to an individual depends on other things besides this individual itself. (One and the same possible flea can be a big flea in one world and not a big flea in another, even if its size remains the same, depending on the size of the other fleas in the two worlds.)

This is connected with the fact that Carnap allows in his formulations the consideration of a respondent's reactions to *verbal descriptions* of non-actual but possible cases. On our explication, we are dealing with dispositions to respond in certain way to possible situations, perhaps ultimately including the whole 'possible world' in question. Only in this way will our intensions of predicates be of the right logical type. Once again, Carnap fails to interpret 'possible worlds' realistically and to use them systematically as a tool of his semantics and/or pragmatics. This failure has probably been especially unfortunate in the present context, for Carnap's overt reliance on language has apparently suggested to critics a covert reliance on mental entities of some sort or other. The possible-worlds reformulation makes it at once clear that, however much we have to rely on counterfactual considerations here, this does not necessarily imply reliance on mental entities or other non-behavioristic factors.

In spite of its shortcomings, I therefore find it exceedingly puzzling that Carnap's paper has not made a greater impact on the philosophical community. The probable reason for this seems to be that most philosophers have not realized how extremely demanding – not to say unrealistic – the standards of observability are that such critics of Carnap as Quine have been presupposing. In his recent formulations, Quine operates with the notion of "the totality of possible observations of nature, made and unmade" and "the totality of possible observations of verbal behavior, made and unmade".[36] He claims that those notions that cause the indeterminacy of intensions, prominently including the notion of belief, are underdetermined by these totalities of observations. On our explication, however idealized it may be, this simply is not the case. The extensions which a speaker would pick out from all the different possible worlds will determine (what he believes to be) the intension of the predicate, for this intension *is* the function that determines these extensions as a function of the possible world in question. This is a place in which the possible-worlds analysis of intensional notions (and of the notion of belief) turns out to have a powerful methodological thrust. Critics like Quine have probably felt that somehow the procedures envisaged by Carnap, even when amplified along the lines I have sketched, will be powerless to exhaust the content of such apparently mental entities as beliefs and intensions. On the possible-worlds analysis, the very idea of a possible world serves to guarantee this kind of exhaustiveness. There cannot be any conceivable import to a feature of someone's beliefs which does not show up in his attitudes to some conceivable world or other.

The true explanation of this discrepancy between Quine and our reconstructed Carnap is the wide gap between what Quine would count as "possible observations" and what most other philosophers, including Carnap, would presumably include under this heading. There is an ambiguity in Quine's notion of "the totality of possible observations". It would naturally be taken, it seems to me, to refer to observations one could have made had the course of events been different, i.e., observations made in certain different 'alternative' possible worlds. However, Quine's latest explanations [37] show that he means possible observations of the actually realized course of events, i.e., observations that could have been made in this actual world of ours. This is so restrictive an idea that it tends to cast doubts on the admissibility of any dispositional terms, including the ones Quine is himself using (e.g., 'stimulus meaning').

Furthermore, it is clear that Quine does not admit counterfactual concepts referring to the past, for otherwise there would not be any problem of separating the effect of past information from the influence of meanings in people's linguistic behavior. (Cf., e.g., *Word and Object*, pp. 62–3.) For in order to spell out this crucial difference we only have to specify what someone's behavior would have been if the information (stimulations) he received earlier had been different. All this helps to explain the contrast between Quine's views and our reconstructed Carnapianism, but it also shows how extremely rigid a standard of empirical significance has been presupposed by Carnap's critics and how little persuasion the criticisms therefore are apt to produce when their basis is fully understood.

Another possible reason for critics' dissatisfaction with Carnap's discussion in 'Meaning and Synonymy in Natural Languages' is that the pragmatical suggestions he makes there are not tied in any natural way to his semantics. For instance, Carnap does not in fact define the intension of a predicate as a class of possible objects (or perhaps of kinds of possible objects), as his discussion of how to find empirically the intension of predicate seems to presuppose.[38] This is one of the many places where Carnap's failure to analyze his intensional concepts can be used against him with a vengeance. When this failure is corrected, however, Carnap turns out to be on the side of the angels, it seems to me.

Needless to say, tremendous difficulties remain for a possible-worlds semanticist in his attempts to demonstrate the empirical and possibly even behavioral character of beliefs and intensions. For instance, I tend to think myself that the totality of possible worlds with which one has to operate here is a highly dubious notion, however legitimate it may be to consider particular possible worlds one by one or even certain restricted sets of possible worlds. For another thing, there clearly is no unique, easily characterizable response which would separate worlds compatible with someone's beliefs from those incompatible with it. Rather, belief must somehow be construed as a theoretical term. Furthermore, I have not said anything constructive in the present paper about the problems due to the failure of the identity of intensions to be a *sufficient* criterion of substitutivity in belief-contexts.

But even so, it seems to me that possible-worlds semantics overwhelmingly suggests that Carnap was on the right track. It makes the weight of his reply to Quine (that is what 'Meaning and Synonymy in Natural Languages' essentially is) felt in a new way, and it puts the onus of producing specific criticisms much more on Carnap's critics than has been recognized in recent discussion. What is even more important, it suggests new constructive, empirical approaches to the pragmatics of beliefs and intensions. As such, it amounts to an important partial vindication of Carnap vis-à-vis his critics, and shows the power of his ideas to inspire and to guide further development of the studies to which he himself already contributed so much.

NOTES

[1] Rudolf Carnap, *Meaning and Necessity*, University of Chicago Press, Chicago, 1947; second ed., with additions, 1956. In the sequel I shall refer to it as *MN*.

[2] A distinction is made by Carnap between intensions and senses in 'The Philosopher Replies' in *The Philosophy of Rudolf Carnap*, P. A. Schilpp (ed.), Open Court, La Salle, Illinois, 1963, especially pp. 897–900. The reasons for the distinction, which does not matter at this stage of our study, will be mentioned later.

[3] Gottlob Frege, 'Kritische Beleuchtung einiger Punkte in E. Schröders *Vorlesungen über die Algebra der Logik*', *Archiv für systematische Philosophie* 1 (1895) 433–56 esp. p. 455.

[4] See W. V. Quine, 'Carnap on Logical Truth' in the Schilpp volume (note 2 above),

pp. 385–406 and Quine's other writings on the philosophy of language and of logic since 1941.

⁵ See Quine's commemorative note on Carnap in *Boston Studies in the Philosophy of Science*, Vol. 8, Roger Buck and Robert S. Cohen (eds.), D. Reidel Publishing Company, Dordrecht, 1971.

⁶ *Meaning and Necessity*, first chapter.

⁷ Schilpp volume (note 1 above), pp. 3–84.

⁸ As usual, I am treating (for simplicity) such *placeholders* for sentences as '*S*' and such *placeholders* of individual expressions as '*i*' (see below) as if they were themselves sentences or individual expressions, respectively. I shall also let quotes be absorbed into such functions as *R* and *I* (for the latter, see below).

⁹ The role of possible-worlds semantics in providing structural analyses of various intensional concepts has been stressed especially forcefully by Richard Montague. See, for instance, 'Pragmatics' in *Contemporary Philosophy – La philosophie contemporaine*, Vol. 1, R. Klibansky (ed.), La Nuova Italia Editrice, Florence 1968, pp. 102–22; 'On the Nature of Certain Philosophical Entities', *The Monist* 53 (1969) 159–94; 'Pragmatics and Intensional Logic', *Synthese* 22 (1970–71) 68–94.

¹⁰ The first to carry out systematically this liberalization seems to have been Saul Kripke.

¹¹ See, for instance, 'Existential Presuppositions and Uniqueness Presuppositions' in Jaakko Hintikka, *Models for Modalities: Selected Essays*, D. Reidel Publishing Company, Dordrecht, 1969, pp. 112–47, and 'Individuals, Possible Worlds, and Epistemic Logic', *Nous* 1 (1967) 33–62.

¹² *Zeitschrift für Philosophie und philosophische Kritik*, Neue Folge, **100** (1892) 25–50.

¹³ In R. M. Martin, *Logic, Language and Metaphysics*, New York University Press, New York 1971, pp. 59–60, it is objected to this point that the difference in "the *expressions* that do the referring" suffices as the relevant difference between the ways in which different objects (or the same object) can be given. This objection is surely completely foreign to Frege's intentions, for senses were for him non-linguistic entities. In 'Sinn und Bedeutung', p. 27, he emphasizes that *Sinn* is independent of language and can be shared by different expressions in one and the same language. For another thing, Frege's very first puzzle about the epistemic difference between the identities '*a* = *a*' and '*a* = *b*' would have been vacuous on Martin's view.

Instead of 'the way of being given' we could also say '*how* the reference is given'. It turns out that the analysis of the relevant how-expression requires in general the consideration of several possible worlds, just as happens in the possible-worlds semantics. See, for instance, my survey 'Different Constructions in Terms of the Basic Epistemological Verbs' (reprinted as Chapter 1 of the present volume).

¹⁴ See note 9 above.

¹⁵ There are no restrictions to rule this out in Carnap's characterization of a model in the Schilpp volume, pp. 890–1.

¹⁶ 'Pragmatics and Intensional Logic' (note 9 above), p. 91. In general, Montague emphasized (before any one else I know of) clearly and appropriately the crucial difference between possible worlds and models.

¹⁷ *Meaning and Necessity*, Chapter 5.

¹⁸ The first to put forward this idea explicitly in print was Stig Kanger; see his dissertation *Provability in Logic* (Stockholm Studies in Philosophy, Vol. 1), Stockholm,

1957. The same discovery was made independently by others, especially by Saul Kripke.

[19] In his paper, 'The method of Extension and Intension' in *The Philosophy of Rudolf Carnap* (note 2 above), pp. 311–49, Donald Davidson already pleaded persuasively for a uniform treatment of intensional contexts and belief-contexts in logical semantics.

[20] See my paper, 'Knowledge, Belief, and Logical Consequence', *Ajatus* **32** (1970) 32–47, and the literature referred to there. (This paper is reprinted below as Chapter 9 of the present volume.)

[21] *Meaning and Necessity*, pp. 56–64.

[22] Cf. 'Knowledge, Belief, and Logical Consequence' (note 20 above).

[23] Note 12 above.

[24] I have tried to examine the conditions on which it is valid in several papers, most fully in 'Existential Presuppositions and Uniqueness Presuppositions' in Jaakko Hintikka, *Models for Modalities: Selected Essays*, D. Reidel Publishing Company, Dordrecht, 1969, pp. 112–47.

[25] A sketch is found in my paper, 'Semantics for Propositional Attitudes' in *Models for Modalities*, pp. 87–111.

[26] Some important further problems are discussed in Jaakko Hintikka, 'The Semantics of Modal Notions and the Indeterminacy of Ontology', *Synthese* **21** (1970) 408–24, reprinted as Chapter 2 of this volume.

[27] See W. V. Quine, *Ontological Relativity and Other Essays*, Columbia University Press, New York, 1969, pp. 63–67, 104–8.

[28] See, e.g., the papers referred to in notes 24 and 25 above.

[29] See 'The Semantics of Modal Notions and the Indeterminacy of Ontology' (note 26 above).

[30] For the systematic background of this problem, see my *Models for Modalities*, pp. 130–3, 140. For an argument for allowing splitting, see Gail Stine, 'Hintikka on Quantification and Belief', *Nous* **3** (1969) 349–408.

[31] See my papers, 'On the Logic of Perception' in *Perception and Personal Identity*, N. S. Care and R. H. Grimm (eds.), The Press of Case Western Reserve University, Cleveland, 1969, pp. 140–73, reprinted in *Models for Modalities*, pp. 151–83, and 'Objects of Knowledge and Belief: Acquaintances and Public Figures', *Journal of Philosophy* **67** (1970) 869–883 (reprinted above, Chapter 3 of this volume).

[32] They are discussed perceptively by Barbara Hall Partee in her contribution to *Approaches to Natural Language: Proceedings of the 1970 Stanford Workshop on Grammar and Semantics*, Jaakko Hintikka, Julius M. E. Moravcsik, and Patrick Suppes (eds.), D. Reidel Publishing Company, Dordrecht, 1973, pp. 309–336. I am greatly indebted to Mrs Partee's paper.

[33] *Word and Object*, The MIT Press, Cambridge, Mass., 1960, p. 225.

[34] Cf. op. cit., p. 223.

[35] First published in *Philosophical Studies* **7** (1955) 33–47.

[36] See W. V. Quine, 'Replies' in *Words and Objections: Essays on the Work of W. V. Quine*, Donald Davidson and Jaakko Hintikka (eds.), D. Reidel Publishing Company, Dordrecht, 1969. (See p. 302.)

[37] See 'On the Reasons for Indeterminacy of Translation', *Journal of Philosophy* **67** (1970) 178–83. In order to spell out fully the logic of the situation, we would have to use relative modalities in the sense of Hilpinen and distinguish observations that are possible for us humans to make (leaving the rest of the world intact) from observations

that are possible *simpliciter* (observations made in a possible world which differs from the actual one also in its non-human aspects). Cf. Risto Hilpinen, 'An Analysis of Relativised Modalities' in *Philosophical Logic*, J. W. Davis, D. J. Hockney, and W. K. Wilson (eds.), Synthese Library, D. Reidel Publishing Company, Dordrecht, 1969, pp. 181–93.

[38] *Meaning and Necessity*, pp. 236–40.

CHAPTER 6

QUINE ON QUANTIFYING IN: A DIALOGUE

This chapter is an attempt to bury a problem, not to praise it. The problem is, as the title indicates, the possibility of quantified modal logic and, more generally, the possibility of using such referential notions as quantifiers and identity meaningfully in combination with modal notions in the narrow sense (necessity and possibility) and with the concepts known as propositional attitudes (e.g., knowledge, belief, memory, wishing, striving, hoping, etc.). Why such usage presents us with a problem will be explained later in this chapter.

It would nevertheless be an eminent injustice toward our *quantifex maximus*, Van Quine, not to emphasize what a splendid achievement it has been of him to pose the problem of quantifying in as forcefully and lucidly as he has done. Attempts to deal with it have produced some of the most interesting conceptualizations in recent philosophical logic and epistemology, notably those embodied in what is sometimes known as possible-worlds semantics. It is a measure of Quine's influence that they have largely been developed under his influence or provocation, by his friendly opponents (Carnap), their students (Montague, David Kaplan), his students and associates (Føllesdal, Kripke, David Lewis), or by philosophers and logicians who have otherwise come under his spell (Hintikka). Beside the merit of having prompted this development, the question as to whether Quine or his critics are in the last analysis 'right' is of lesser importance.

The author's task was considerably facilitated by the discovery of certain tapes which apparently had been recorded when some former Junior Fellows and their friends were guests at a recent Monday night dinner at the Society of Fellows at Harvard. The speakers could not be positively identified, but with some difficulty a dialogue could be assembled from the garbled remarks. The suspicion is that besides Quine himself Dagfinn Føllesdal, David Kaplan, Burton Dreben, Charles Parsons, and Jaakko Hintikka may have contributed to the exchanges. Some of the rejoinders echo Quine's ideas, but the lack of his customary elegance rules out the attribution of some others to him. Apparently too much devil's and other adversaries' advocacy was practiced during the evening for us to attribute any single remark definitely to any particular person. The two sides of the dialogue are labelled Q. and C. (for critic) for convenience only. A number of footnotes were added in the process of editing, mainly spelling out references which the speakers did not provide. (References to works whose author is not specified are all to Quine's writings.) For what it is worth, here is the dialogue.

Q. Modern modal logic was conceived in sin, the sin of confusing use and mention.[1] It originated from C. I. Lewis' notion of strict implication, which was an unwitting and illegitimate attempt to say *in* a language something *about* that language. Hence one can never hope to make decent interpretational sense of modal logic, and the same goes *a fortiori* for quantified modal logic.

C. You may be right about the historical origins of contemporary modal logic. If so, your apparent conclusion from this original sin is merely an instance of the genetic fallacy.

Q. No conclusion was intended. Modal logic does not require confounding use and mention. Rather, it is the confusion that has engendered an irresistible case for modal logic.

C. If so, you have not given a single objective reason yet why concepts like 'necessarily', 'known', or 'provable' cannot be accommodated in our object language, no matter what else it contains. Your *ad hominem* reference to C. I. Lewis can be parried by an equally *ad hominem* reference to Kurt Gödel, who can scarcely be blamed for confusing use and mention. Although not everyone knows it, his 1933 note even contains the first formulation of that basic system of propositional modal logic which was subsequently rediscovered by Feys and by von Wright.[2]

Q. Your appeal to Gödel is indeed *ad hominem*, I must say. For recall that modal involvement comes in degrees, not all of them equally pernicious.[3] What happens in Gödel is that he uses necessity as a statement operator. Such operators can often be converted into predicates of statements, and their innocence thus established. (For instance, in this way the referential opacity of modal contexts becomes a mere corollary to the trivial opacity of quotation or quasi-quotation.)

What I find especially objectionable in modal logic is the use, or misuse, of modalities as sentential operators, applicable also to open sentences. It is only this practice that leads us to the temptation of quantifying in, in other words, of binding from the outside a variable occurring in a modal context. And this practice cannot be justified in the same way as the use of modalities as statement operators.

C. I am beginning to see why you insist on considering quotation the referentially opaque context *par excellence*.[4] But I must say that your whole outlook on the different degrees of modal involvement is gravely misleading. What you are willing to grant to modal logicians they cannot have in any case, and the real defence of their position remains unrecognized by you.

Q. That strikes me as a rather far-fetched charge.

C. It is not fetched any farther than from that note of Gödel's we have been discussing. The ideas foreshadowed there were taken up and generalized by Richard Montague in his important 1963 paper.[5] Montague showed there that you just cannot consistently interpret modalities as predicates (of any sort) of expressions (your 'sentences'), provided only that you also have a modicum of ordinary logic and elementary arithmetic in your language and that you uphold the usual laws of modal logic.

The details of Montague's arguments are many, but the main point is clear. It is but a kind of generalization of Gödel's second incompleteness theorem. If you interpret the necessity operator 'nec' as expressing provability, as you have yourself signalled some willingness to do,[6] then what is it that the following familiar law of modal logic says?

(1) $\text{nec}(\text{nec } p \supset p)$

The answer is obvious. Having

(2) $\text{nec } p \supset p$

as a law means that what can be proved is true, that is, our system is consistent. Having (1) as a law means that this consistency can be proved in the system itself. Of course this is just what is proved impossible in Gödel's second theorem, provided that enough elementary arithmetic is present.

Montague's main theorem is in effect a way of making this intuitive observation respectable.

Q. So much the worse for modal logic. What you are averring is simply that even the lower degrees of modal involvement cannot be defended in the teeth of unproblematic elementary arithmetic. What could vindicate more completely my criticism of modal logic?

C. That would not be the only possible conclusion nor the most plausible one from Montague's results. One way of looking at these results is to take them to show that the usual laws of modal logic are to be revised. This course was suggested already in Gödel's note, and it is an especially natural – and especially interesting – idea as applied to epistemic notions like 'knows' instead of logical modalities.

What is even more important, however, is that Montague's results do not in the least reflect on the possibility of giving a semantical (model-theoretical) justification for modal logic or for the logic of propositional attitudes. This possibility was never denied by Montague, not even when his somewhat unstable estimation of modal logic was at its lowest ebb.[7] His findings may belie the particular partial justification of modal logic you have contemplated, but they have no bite as a general criticism of modal logic.

Q. Your use of the term 'semantics' is itself in need of semantical scrutiny. (For one thing, what you call 'semantics' has presumably little to do with my use of the term 'semantical predicate' in connection with modalities.)[8] However, I grant you the usefulness of the general idea of semantics for our present argument. It leads us to ask how our language in fact operates, how its several sentences hang together with the world they can be used to convey information about.

Now the problem of quantified modal logic turns on the semantics of singular terms and other referring expressions. How are they related to their objectual targets? It ought to be a tautology to say that the task of such referring expressions as proper names is to refer to individuals, to pick out members of one's universe of discourse. But the striking thing about modal contexts is that this is not what our referring expressions do there, or is not all that they do. If it were, substitutivity of identity (SI) and existential generalization (EG) would apply in these contexts. Recall first SI. If 'a' and 'b' refer to the same individual, and if *all* that each of them does is to refer to (pick out) this individual, they ought to be inter-substitutible *salva veritate* everywhere. And similarly for EG.[9]

Thus the notorious failure of these laws in modal contexts shows that in these contexts our referring expressions do not just refer. Something else is involved here besides the references of our terms. The truth of modal statements does not depend only on the individuals referred to, but also on the referring expressions themselves. It is in this sense that the expressions used matter as soon as modal operators are being employed. Of course this does not mean that we mention them in the literal sense of the word, but we do something that almost amounts to the same.

That is only a symptom of the malady, however. What really counts here is the problem of interpretation. And here I assuredly have 'semantics' on my side. Indeed, if referentiality fails in a way that vitiates EG and SI, quantification makes little sense. For what sense would it make to ask whether there exists an individual satisfying an open sentence $F(x)$ if an individual's satisfying this open sentence does not depend on it alone but also on the way it is referred to?

C. Your remark makes it even more understandable why you have so strenuously endeavored to reduce other opaque constructions to quotation.[10] Your substantial point seems to me exaggerated, however, Do you really mean that there is something wrong with the use of quantifiers and identity in any and every referentially opaque context? Are SI and EG really touchstones of the correct usage of quantifiers? Does each and every failure of these laws show that we are as it were mentioning our expressions in a way that makes quantification into them impossible?

Q. It is not the quotation-like character of modal contexts as such that is crucial here, but their opacity, that is, the failure of SI and EG in these contexts. These principles are our bridge to the notions of individual and ontology.[11] If they are destroyed, we do not know where to turn for our individuals. It is for this reason that the failure of the SI and of EG is absolutely crucial interpretationally. It shows that in modal contexts it is not clear what the individuals are that we are really speaking of, for in such contexts we just are not any longer speaking of ordinary individuals alone in an ordinary way.

However, in principle there is one line of interpretation open to modal logicians here. If ordinary individuals are not what is being evoked in modal contexts, they can try to draft into their service extraordinary individuals, usually called intensional objects, to act as the values of their bound variables. Only this does not seem to work. One natural course to follow here would seem to be to use logical (analytical) equivalence as a criterion of individuation for intensional entities. However, I have shown that this expedient is not viable.[12] It does not reconcile modal logic with the unrestricted use of the crucial principles of the SI and EG.

C. But that doesn't exclude some other individuation principle.

Q. No, it does not. But what it shows is that the onus of proof is on modal logicians, not on their critics. In any case I am wary of all outlandish intensional entities. Their nature and behavior have never been explained satisfactorily.

My main point nevertheless is a simpler one. The failure of laws like SI and EG shows that something or else is wrong with quantified modal logic. Either modal logicians are using language in some incoherent nonreferential fashion or else they are tacitly presupposing unacceptable, empirically underdetermined intensional entities. In this sense, my answer to your question is yes. The failure of SI and EG does show that something is wrong with quantified modal logic, or at the very least that some further explanations have to be provided by modal logicians. We can understand how the essentially referential apparatus of identity and quantification operates in referentially transparent contexts. The onus is on you to provide an equally convincing account of what happens in modal contexts and in other, comparable referentially opaque contexts.

C. I am happy to accept the challenge. In fact, I believe that a satisfactory account of the meaning of your own referentially transparent expressions already provides us a clue to a satisfactory semantics of modal logic. However, before taking up the challenge, I must return the compliment and wonder how you are going to make sense of much humanly important discourse. What are you going to do with the ubiquitous uses of propositional attitudes *cum* quantifiers and identity? Surely we all speak all the time of somebody's loving you, my knowing something about the same individual as you, and so on. Furthermore, interrogative constructions with epistemic verbs involve quantification into a propositional-attitude context. For John to know who is coming is for John to know of some particular person that *he* is coming. The logical form involved here is clearly

(3) (Ex) John knows that x is coming.

Surely you are far too severe here in trying to exorcise all such constructions from our discourse.

Q. I doubt that for strictly scientific purposes intentional notions like
knowledge, belief, love, etc., are needed in the last analysis.[13] That thesis
is too broad to be argued here, however, and I recognize the need of
making interim sense of the kind of locutions you just mentioned.[14]
There are various ways of doing so. One thing is to acknowledge that
propositional-attitude verbs have a dual use, that they are in a sense ambiguous. They are sometimes used transparently, and it is this transparent
sense that is always involved when we quantify into a propositional-
attitude context. At other times they are used opaquely.

Another, better, possibility is to construe propositional attitudes in
their relevant usage as relations of an agent to a person and an attribute.
Then we can avoid quantification into an opaque context. For instance,
in your example knowledge can be construed as a relation between the
knower, the object of knowledge, and the attribute $\hat{x}$ (x is coming), for
instance thus

(4)   --- knows $\hat{x}(x$ is coming) of ---.

Then (3) becomes

(5)   John knows $\hat{x}(x$ is coming) of someone.

Although I do not altogether approve of the kind of reification of attributes involved in (4) and especially (5), at least quantifying in is being
dispensed with.

Moreover, we can also try to replace these intensional attributes here
by the very expressions expressing them, thereby gaining a useful ontological economy.

C. The intensional-attribute analysis of propositional attitudes which
you are half-heartedly suggesting does not cut much ice with me. In
order to see precisely what the problem is, let's take your old example
of Bernard J. Ortcutt and the man in a brown hat. Since the existence of
the colloquial 'who' and 'what' constructions with 'knows' provides us
with a few additional clues as compared with what we have in the case
of belief, I hope that you allow me to transpose your example from belief
to knowledge, however. The changed story will then run as follows.[15]
'There is a certain man in a brown hat whom Ralph has witnessed

several times under incriminating circumstances on which we need not enter here; suffice it to say that Ralph knows he is a spy. Also there is a gray-haired man, known to Ralph rather as a pillar of the community, whom Ralph is not aware having seen except once at the beach. Now Ralph does not know it, but the men are one and the same.'

Now by your admission the undeniable parallelism between knowledge and belief commits you to say among other things the following.[16]

(6)   Ralph knows $\hat{z}(z$ is a spy) of Ortcutt.

and

(7) (Ex) Ralph knows $\hat{z}(z$ is a spy) of x.

But (7) is the best candidate, and in fact the only serious candidate, that you can avail yourself of for the role of

(8)   Ralph knows who is a spy.

But in terms of the story, (8) simply is not true. Ralph does not know who the spy in a brown hat is, not being able even to connect him with good old Bernard J. Ortcutt.

To put the point in more general terms, your treatment either yields wrong results or else deprives you of any possibility of making sense of who-constructions with epistemic verbs. The joker here seems to be basically the dual requirement, implicit in your printed discussions of this problem, that a context like

(9)   Ralph knows $\hat{z}(z$ is a spy) of x.

is referentially transparent with respect to x and that this is the only kind of propositional-attitude context into which we can quantify. For what happens then is that when Ralph knows an attribute to apply to someone under any description of that someone, Ralph knows it to apply to him under every description. Moreover, Ralph must be said to know that this attribute applies to a certain individual, which is precisely to know to whom it applies.

As an especially striking special case, consider the following. If Ralph knows anything at all of the man in a brown hat, then surely

(10)   Ralph knows $\hat{x}$(the man in a brown hat $=x$) of the man in a brown hat.

But (10) implies, according to your lights,

(11) (Ez) Ralph knows $\hat{x}$ (the man in a brown hat $= x$) of z.

And it is especially hard for you of all people to deny that (11) could be paraphrased as

(12)   Ralph knows who the man in a brown hat is,

for you have always insisted especially forcefully that the values of our bound individual variables must be genuine, well-defined individuals. What more can possibly be meant by knowing who the man in a brown hat is than knowing of some such genuine objectual individual that *he* is the man in a brown hat?[17] Yet the implication from (10) to (12), to which you are thus committed, is absurd.

Q. Perhaps my example was formulated in an unfortunate fashion. You have exploited my admission of (6), in its doxastic version. But there is nothing intrinsic in my approach or in my example that should prejudge this matter. There are in fact many different things one can try to do here. One of them is the following.[18] I can perfectly well deny (6) and describe the same facts by the following statement.

(13)   Ralph knows that the man in a brown hat is a spy.

Of course I must then be able to assert (13) and yet deny

(14)   Ralph knows $\hat{z}(z$ is a spy) of the man in a brown hat,

(14) here being what basically led us to assent to (6). If we follow this course, we need not accept (7)–(8), and no difficulties ensue.

This strategy can be used generally. Whenever existential generalization on statements of the form

(15) a knows $\hat{z}(---z---)$ of b

threatens to force us to assent to the illegitimate 'knows who' or 'knows what' statement

(16) $(Ex)\, a$ knows $\hat{z}(---z---)$ of x,

we can say that the true facts of the case ought to be described, not by the relational statement (15) but rather by the corresponding propositional statement

(17) a knows that $(---b---)$

which need not imply (15) and which therefore leads to no mischief.

The precise conditions on which (17) does imply (15) I prefer to leave to the likes of yourself to formulate. They import into our treatment a distinction between those attributes $\hat{x}(---x---)$ for which (17) does imply (15) and those for which it does not. This move thus marks an unfortunate admission to essentialism, which is why I don't particularly like it.[19]

C. I admit that you do not then run the same risk of outright fallacies as before. But you must pay a price in the form of equally insurmountable interpretational difficulties. The modification you envisage means, first of all, a radical change in your original treatment. It is not just that your changes of carrying out the further reduction and of replacing intensional attributes by expressions for these attributes are shattered by the modification. What is more important is that in your earlier treatment you were willing to consider a move from (17) to (15) 'in general as implicative'.[20] In so far as the reservations you seem to be signalling by the caveat 'in general' pertain to possible failures of existence, we can forget about them. They do not touch on the real problems here, although they have been made much of by Sellars and Sleigh.[21] The extra requirements you are now introducing into the truth-conditions of (15), over and above what is included in the truth-conditions of (17), cannot be in terms of the existence of the individuals involved, for failures of existence played no part in our little story. (Ralph may be assumed to know the existence of all the characters involved there all right, irrespective of whether we want to pack such existential presuppositions into the truth-conditions of knowledge-statements in general.) So what are your extra requirements? It is readily seen what force they must have: they must be such as to rule out the truth of (15) unless *a knows who or what b is* under some description or other. For otherwise I can reduce your modified approach to absurdity along the same lines as in (6)–(8).

This is an important observation. For one thing, we seemed to agree that the natural way of spelling out the semantics of 'knowing who' and 'knowing what' is in terms of quantifiers and bound variables. Hence there is in effect a quantifier tacitly tucked into (15) as distinguished from (17). As long as the nature of this quantifier has not been explained, we have not really made any progress in our task of trying to understand the interplay of propositional attitudes with quantifiers. An attempt to drive a semantical wedge between (15) and (17) means moving in a circle, if you excuse the metaphor.

Q. We have avoided quantifying into an opaque context, which is the crucial point here.[22]

C. Even that remains to be seen until the precise truth-conditions of (15) on the new interpretation are spelled out. And let me emphasize that in discussing the explication of 'knowing who' and 'knowing what' we are not dealing with a marginal problem but with what probably is the most central one in epistemic logic. For instance, Hintikka has argued that it is extra premisses of the form

> a knows who b is

that serve to restore EG, that touchstone of referentiality, in simple (i.e., noniterated) epistemic contexts.[23]

But our insights into the nature of the proposed truth-conditions of (15) as distinguished from (17) yield further suggestions. They show that what is crucial here is not so much a difference between essential and accidental attributes as the truth-conditions of 'knowing who' and 'knowing what' statements. And I do not see any evidence that these truth-conditions have much to do with essentialism.

Q. Admittedly we face serious problems here. However, the repertoire of solutions available to me here has by no means been exhausted. And even if it had been, I would view the situation with tranquility. For I am not in the least reluctant to acknowledge difficulties in the semantics of propositional attitudes.

Incidentally, can we not also try to resort to the two-uses idea I mentioned earlier in order to deal with quantification into epistemic contexts?

C. That idea is subject to all of the same objections as I made against your other idea, and to some further ones besides. A sample of these new objections is that referential transparency or opacity is essentially an attribute to each occurrence of a singular term in a context, not of this context as such. If someone says,

> John believes that an immoral adventurer has seduced his sister,

why should we assume that the sentence is transparent with respect to *both* 'an immoral adventurer' and 'his sister' or *neither*? The most plausible reading seems to make the latter occurrence extensional, but not the former. For presumably John knows his sister otherwise than so described, while her seducer might turn out to be his trusted, otherwise respectable and unadventurous best friend. But this would be impossible if your two-uses idea were correct. For then we had only two alternatives: a context is either opaque or transparent. We must not ask the question again of each singular term occurring in the context. Yet this was just found to be necessary. The list of your difficulties can be continued.

Q. These are admittedly difficulties. However, I do not see that they are conclusive. In any case, our duel ought to be fought according to Duhemian rules. I doubt that we can make a real decision here before someone develops a general semantical theory of questions (including subordinate questions with an epistemic main verb) in natural languages. Only such overall theories can be profitably compared with each other.

C. Once again, this is a challenge I am happy to accept. I believe that the kind of theory which will satisfy you can be developed on the basis of ideas that soon will be available in print.[24] Unfortunately, the subject is too large to be covered here. I can nevertheless say for instance that the additional conditions which serve to restore EG turn out to have a crucial role in answering such central questions as the characterization of the notion of answerhood. Moreover, the possibility of reconstructing the old *de dicto* – *de re* distinction within epistemic logic already gives us something like a general analysis of the situation which you rightly want to see.[25]

Q. Pending your promised theory, the upshot of our discussion seems to be merely a further difficulty in making as much as interim sense of quantification into propositional-attitude contexts. That upshot tends to reinforce rather than to dispel my wariness of propositional attitudes *tout court*. But we still have an even bigger bone to pick here. Are you going to rise to my earlier challenge and provide a satisfactory semantics for modal notions and propositional attitudes?

C. That task has already been carried out in the possible-worlds semantics for those very notions, of which you are undoubtedly well aware. (I prefer to call it possible-worlds semantics rather than Kripke semantics, for it was discussed in print by several other logicians well before Kripke.[26])

Q. I do not see that the model theory of modal logic which you propose to call possible-worlds semantics is an answer to your prayers.[27]
Models are useful tools for consistency proofs and other technical
purposes. They also have heuristic value, but they do not constitute
explication. Models may still leave us at a loss for the primary, intended
interpretation.

C. You are looking at possible-worlds semantics as if it were the same
thing as Carnap's ancient use of models in explicating modal logic. But
that is simply to miss the point of what has happened since. What
Montague and others have done is to replace the abstract idea of a model,
in the sense of an arbitrary reinterpretation of a part of our vocabulary,
by the realistically conceived notion of a possible world – a world considered as a serious rival to the actual one. This step was repeatedly
emphasized by Montague,[28] and it has been discussed at some length
by Hintikka.[29] Whatever difficulties there may be connected with it, one
cannot begin to appreciate what is going on in possible-worlds semantics
without taking it into account. As Hintikka points out, it is a *conditio sine
qua non* of all the applications of possible-worlds semantics to the analysis
of propositional attitudes. Mind you, I am not saying that the step from
models to possible worlds is unproblematic or even clear. But that is
what we have to discuss here, not some clever logician's applications of
model theory to the technicalities of modal logic.

I do not want to repeat what has already been said in the literature on
the subject. Let me nevertheless try to show how it bears on your question
of the behavior of referential expressions. What we can obtain by means
of possible-worlds semantics here – and what would have been completely
impossible to achieve by means of the old idea of a model – is a kind of
general theory of meaning entities. Although the idea seems to have
been implicit in the earlier work by Kripke and Hintikka, the merit of
spelling it out and emphasizing its general significance belongs to
Montague.[30]

This general theory shows precisely why your model of how singular
terms operate is too narrow. You spoke of singular terms as referring to
or picking out individuals. All right, let's see what is involved in such
locutions. I shall argue that what is involved is not just the references our
singular terms actually have, but also as it were potential references in a
number of unrealized situations. The model you were relying on is

essentially a correlation between singular terms and the individuals they refer to. There obtains a rare unanimity, however, that this is not all that is involved in our understanding of a language.[31] There is no getting around the fact that there is more to meaning than reference. When one understands a singular term, one does not just know what it stands for. One also knows something about how its reference is picked out, what rule or function takes us from the term to its reference. Frege tried to express this by means of his notion of *Sinn* which according to him includes, over and above the reference of a term, also the way in which the reference is given (*die Art des Gegebenseins*).[32] Now the crucial insight here is that all such talk of rules or ways of being given is functional. To specify a rule (a 'how') is to specify the function which gives us the reference, depending on circumstances. And some of the arguments which such a function depends on are inevitably counterfactual, that is, unrealized states of affairs. You just do not find the relevant arguments within the actual state of affairs or course of events. Some of your remarks seem to suggest the use of the referring expressions themselves as such arguments.[33] Others seem to be best construed as being based on the idea that referring expressions, or some of them, are to be interpreted on the model of descriptions, specifying their references by specifying certain properties of these referred-to individuals (and thus easily creating conceptual asymmetries between different properties).[34] Both models are far too narrow, it seems to me, especially the first, which overlooks completely the functional character of the establishment of referential relalationships. An expression itself just is not viable candidate for the role of the way in which its reference is given. The second model is too narrow in that there are all sorts of other ways in which the reference of a singular term may be specified.[35]

Q. Your quandary suggests that it is hopeless to try to be specific about these 'arguments'.

C. Not really. Whatever these meaning functions may specifically depend or not depend on, they depend in any case on the whole world in which the reference is supposed to be located. And of course to say that is already to reach a Montague type meaning analysis: in understanding a singular term, say 'b', we grasp the function f_b which gives its reference in different possible worlds, and analogously for expressions of other logical types.

Such a function f_b is thus precisely a Fregean *Sinn*, for it comprises the way in which the reference is given, functionally interpreted. Modern modal logic hence is not based on the original sin you imputed to C. I. Lewis. Its semantics is based on an original *Sinn*, to wit, on Frege's notion of sense as distinguished from reference.[36]

Q. Assuredly that is not at all what Frege actually meant. There is not a hint of such an analysis in the actual historical Frege.[37] You are twisting what he says quite unjustifiably in order to press him to your service.

C. All right, I admit that I am twisting what Frege says, but not unjustifiably. Frege did not see in sufficiently abstract terms what he was saying. He did not see what the most general form of the argument of a function like f_b is. In general, it depends on some special features of the possible world in which we are considering the reference of 'b'. However, the only thing we can say on our present level of general semantical theorizing is that in any case it depends on the whole world in question, however we can narrow this dependence down in special cases by means of a more refined analysis. There just is nothing else the reference could conceivably depend on. Thus Frege's intuition ought to lead us straight to a Montague-type analysis of the meaning of a singular term as a function from possible worlds into individuals, in spite of the fact that Frege himself apparently got stuck to the dependencies of the reference on some particular aspects of the world in question.

Q. What you are saying is still seriously oversimplified. If you force Frege into your mold, you should at least recognize that Fregean *Sinne* are more like algorithms or recipes for computing your meaning functions than like those functions themselves.[38]

C. I agree, but these criticisms of yours are beside the main point. Your criticisms admittedly will have to be taken care of in future, more refined versions of Montague-type meaning analysis. However, we already have perfectly good indications – and in fact much more than mere indications – of what can be done to meet your points, for instance Dana Scott's neighborhood semantics[39] and Hintikka's surface semantics.[40] These details do not affect the paramount fact that in possible-worlds semantics we have a model of how language operates which shows that your model is far too narrow.

This point is worth emphasizing. You said that the failure of SI and EG shows that something else is involved besides the reference of the singular term in question. I already argued that we cannot identify this 'something else' with the expression as distinguished from its reference. Now we can in any case see that there is a superior candidate available to us for the role of this 'something else' in the meaning function or *Sinn* associated with the term in question. Notice, in particular, that once we see this, we can also see that the failure of SI and EG is the most natural thing in the world, and does not violate the referential character of our discourse in any deeper sense of referentiality. The very way you posed our problem was too restricted. You said that the failure of SI and EG in modal contexts shows either that modal discourse is nonreferential and therefore does not admit of the use of quantifiers or else that some outlandish entities must be tacitly involved as the values of our bound variables. Possible-worlds semantics shows conclusively that this dichotomy is misconceived. In this semantics, what we have are perfectly ordinary singular terms referring to perfectly ordinary entities in a perfectly ordinary way. The only novelty is that we have to consider those entities as members of several possible situations or courses of events. This is the basic reason for the failure of SI and EG, not any real failure of referentiality, any reliance on intensional entities or mental entities, nor any general incoherence. Possible-worlds semantics provides just the kind of clear semantic account of modal contexts you have always wanted.

Q. There is still an embarrassment of epistemological difficulties about possible worlds. They are unobservable, and hence problematic for an honest empiricist like myself. Do they enjoy a genuine existence apart from our beliefs and other alleged mental constructions? I am afraid that a great deal of unclarity is still lurking here.

C. I am prepared to argue at some length that something like possible worlds are inevitably involved in all our understanding of language. Perhaps we should leave this point alone for the time being, however. Let me note only that the main epistemological difficulty in my talk of possible worlds is not that they are mental constructions or intentional entities or even that they are unobservable. This talk is problematic only in so far as it is counterfactual.[41] And I just do not believe you can get rid of counterfactuals to such a degree that you are not tacitly relying on my possible worlds.

However, at this stage my main point is much simpler, and much more obvious. You cannot deny that possible-worlds semantics has cleared up the very difficulties you used to complain about, and hence taken the whole problem of quantified modal logic to a new level altogether. Take something very concrete as an example, for instance the breakdown of SI. Now you can see precisely how and why SI and EG fail. The substitutivity of identity fails – I am tempted to say, fails as a matter of course – because two singular terms 'a' and 'b' which refer to one and the same object in the actual world (and hence make the plain identity '$a = b$' true) may fail to do so in other worlds. Hence they need not be interchangeable *salva veritate* in a context where these other worlds are implicitly considered. The same goes for EG *mutatis mutandis*.

This diagnosis is at once confirmed by the fact that we can see from our possible-worlds semantics what additional premises are needed to restore the substitutivity of 'a' and 'b'.[42] What we need is not only that the identity '$a = b$' holds in the actual world, but that it holds in all the worlds we are considering in the sentence 'S' where the substitution takes place. They depend on 'S' and can be read off from it. For instance, if 'S' speaks only of what John knows, the worlds in question are all the worlds compatible with what John knows. The truth of '$a = b$' in all of them means of course that John knows that $a = b$. Hence for this particular 'S' substitutivity is restored by the collateral premise

John knows that $a = b$.

Notice also how this treatment in a sense vindicates Frege. Frege tried to explain the peculiarity of referentially opaque contexts by saying that in them the *Sinne* of our expressions are involved instead of the usual references of these expressions. What the additional premiss says that is needed to restore the SI is that the meaning functions or *Sinne* associated with 'a' and 'b' coincide on those possible worlds we are considering in 'S'. Hence it is the identity of the senses (*Sinne*) of 'a' and 'b' that counts in opaque contexts as Frege in effect suggested, though with the added clause that these *Sinne*, being functions, must be considered as restricted to the relevant set of arguments (possible worlds).

This observation has a general moral. Even if we could, Montague notwithstanding, use modalities as predicates of expressions (e.g. statements), we could thereby create a wrong impression, to the effect that the crucial things here are these expressions themselves. The important things are the meaning functions associated with these expressions, reflected in the diverse equivalence classes of expressions whose meaning functions match, either absolutely or restricted to some suitably narrow class of possible worlds.

In brief, the problems of identity are solved by possible-worlds semantics in one fell swoop.

Q. By no means. At the very least qualifications of the same sort are in order as you were yourself willing to make in connection with Frege.

C. Sure. But they do not affect the thrust of my remarks.

Q. Possibly not. But I have even more important *caveats*. It may be true that possible worlds semantics has lifted the discussion to a new level. But has it really solved my problems? Scarcely. So far you have not said anything of the problems of cross-identification, that is, of the problem of telling which members of one possible world are identical with which members of another world. This is an important aspect of that problem of individuation which has always been my principal concern in criticizing quantified modal logic. And you are yourself committed to considering it a serious problem. Elsewhere you have yourself argued against Dana Scott, Dagfinn Føllesdal, and Richard Montague that such cross-identification is not unproblematic, that we cannot just assume a set of individuals which – or some of which – then make an appearance in the different possible worlds.[43] You have yourself pointed out that such cross-identification can in principle be carried out in more than one way, and even gone on to argue that in perceptual contexts and more generally in contexts involving a sort of Russellian acquaintance we actually employ two different kinds of trans world heir lines (that is, lines connecting the 'embodiments' of same individual in different worlds).[44] You have thus recognized yourself that there are all sorts of problems about cross-identification. What I want to add is that all the difficulties in making sense of quantified modal logic that I have emphasized continue to haunt us precisely in the form of difficulties about cross-identification.[45]

C. That is at best a half-truth. It simply is not true that all your old problems reappear in a new guise in possible-worlds semantics. The problems connected with identity do not. They are disposed of for good. The reason should be obvious. No comparisons between different possible worlds are involved in the problems connected with the substitutivity of identity, and hence no cross-identification. An identity '$a=b$' fails to be true in a world if *in that world* 'a' and 'b' pick out different individuals. The identity '$a=b$' is known to John if in *each* world compatible with what John knows 'a' and 'b' refer to the same individual, and so on.

In no such case do we need any comparisons between different worlds. Hence what I said above of the reasons for the failure of SI remain untouched by the problem of cross-identification.

Q. What you say is correct, but inconclusive. For one thing, the EG half of my claim is still unanswered. Moreover, my share of truth is by any token more than fifty per cent, for you have not yet completely solved the problems of identity, either. The SI principle has two forms, the free singular term version and the bound variable version. Schematically, they may be represented as

(18) $(a=b) \supset (F(a) \supset F(b))$

and as

(19) $(x)(y)(x=y \supset (F(x) \supset F(y)))$.

respectively.

What you have done is to provide a diagnosis of the failure of the free term version (18). This is not what is at stake here, however. The principle (18) fails as a matter of course in your approach because you allow as substitution-instances of 'a' and 'b' singular terms which in different possible worlds pick out different individuals. This may or may not be a natural thing to do, but in any case it hides the real problem. This problem is the substitutivity or, rather, the parity of identical *individuals*. It is the question whether two terms either of which specifies a well-defined individual (the same in all relevant possible worlds) are intersubstitutable everywhere if they as a matter of fact refer to the same individual. This question is precisely that of the validity of (19), for we agree that the values of bound variables must be well-defined individuals. It is the validity of (19), not of (18), that is connected with the interpretability of quantified modal logic, and it is what our intuitions about the SI principle really pertain to.

C. Are you not sidestepping the main issue? Possible-worlds semantics shows that the validity of (19) is an interesting but marginal problem which has no bearing whatsoever on the interpretability of quantified modal logic.

Q. Why? Isn't the parity of identical individuals fairly obviously a *sine qua non* for making sense of quantifying in?

C. No, fairly obviously it is not. We can make sense of quantification in modal contexts as soon as we can cross-identify. Intuitively speaking, all that is needed are the trans world heir lines connecting the relevant possible worlds. We would presumably like to have these TWA's[46] running as smoothly as possible, but that is an additional desideratum, not an indispensable condition of the semantical interpretability of quantifiers.

As you can easily work out on the basis of any satisfactory treatment of possible-worlds semantics,[47] the question of the validity of (19) is essentially[48] the question whether trans world heir lines must not split when we step from a world to one of its alternatives. This is an interesting question when asked of different specific modal notions or propositional attitudes. However, as far as its general significance is concerned, I am tempted to say: Who cares? The question is how smoothly we can make our trans world heir lines run, but no questions of general significance hang on the answer.

It is also quite clear that for some propositional attitudes (19) fails. If you are willing to treat perception by means of possible-worlds semantics,[49] as I am convinced we must do, you are committed to allowing (19) to fail, for otherwise you cannot accommodate the perfectly possible phenomenon of seeing double. What more do you need to convince yourself that the failure of (19) has nothing to do with the deep questions of the possibility of quantified modal logic?

Q. One thing more that is in any case needed is an explanation of certain consequences of adopting the schema (19). These consequences include the validity of

(20) $(x) (y) (x = y \supset \text{necessarily } (x = y))$.

Indeed, (20) has much of the same power as (19).[50] But what (20) apparently says is that those traits that determine an object do so necessarily.[51] Doesn't this have plenty to do with the deep question of interpreting quantified modal logic? The upshot of adopting a principle like (20) seems to be Aristotelian essentialism.

C. By no means. Whether I accept (20) or not, the values of its variables are normally individuals – persons, physical objects, or something equally real. But when they are considered *qua* members of several possible worlds, it may be asked whether identities between such individuals are transferable from one possible world to another, that is, whether they hold in other worlds if they hold in one. Clearly, one's possible worlds will be somewhat messy if such transfers are not always possible, but this messiness is not interpretational and apparently cannot be completely avoided. Above all, no reference to essentialism or intensional entities is involved here.

Q. I suppose that if I grant your general framework of possible worlds, I am bound to accept your diagnosis of (20). But I do not see that it precludes further interpretational problems. Suppose that (19) is violated for some propositional attitude, that is, suppose that one object o in the actual world corresponds to two objects o' and o'' in one of its alternatives. Suppose that we make a statement about the presumably well-defined individual o. Now which individual are we talking about? The one which in the alternative world appears as o' or the one which appears as o''? I hope that I can convey to you my residual puzzlement.

C. You are puzzled merely because you have lapsed back into the kind of absolutism vis-à-vis our individuals which you yourself rejected earlier when you first raised the question of cross-identification. In asking 'which individual' you are envisaging a fixed domain of individuals that can make their appearance in different possible worlds. Undoubtedly we would like to have such a constant domain underlying our actual everyday semantics, but we cannot begin by assuming that we can have one. Such 'bare particulars' are not and cannot be the basic ingredients in our semantics. The network of trans world heir lines is much more basic, and we just cannot rule out sight unseen such complications as the splitting of world lines. Questions as to what the 'real' individuals are that we are quantifying over in epistemic contexts are presuppose the kind of 'metaphysics of individuals' that neither of us is likely to find acceptable.

An example will perhaps press my point home. The kind of situation you described in abstract terms actually arises when someone sees the object o as two objects, o' and o''. In all the states of affairs compatible with what one sees, there are then two objects corresponding to the one real-life object o. What on earth is supposed to be unclear here? Nothing is unclear here in spite of the fact that you can raise precisely the same abstract question as to which individual o' or o'' we are speaking of in mentioning o. In this concrete example the question suddenly becomes jejune.

Q. Now I am getting suspicious. In handling this problem your emphasis has tacitly shifted from logical modalities to epistemic notions like perception. For modalities proper, we presumably must require (19).

C. You want to improve on Bishop Butler and to say that whatever is, necessarily is what it is, and cannot be another thing. Even if that were right, it would not follow that whatever is, is known not to be another thing.

Q. How could it help following? If no world lines branch when we go from a world to another logically possible world, surely no world lines can branch when one steps from a given world to one of its epistemic alternatives, for those alternative possible worlds are *a fortiori* logically possible, Hence (19) for logical modalities entails (19) for other modalities.

C. There is no *fortior* here. The point you are making is merely a terminological one. I am not convinced that (19) is valid for logical (conceptual) modalities. Assuming that it is may be just a corollary to the bad 'metaphysics of the individual'. But even if we try to impose (19) on analytical (logical) modalities, we still are not yet committed to requiring (19) of epistemic modalities. Earlier, I have described my 'possible worlds' as counterfactual. You should be the last person to object if I say that by the same token we can afford to let them be in certain specifiable respects counter-analytical, for you have consistently denied all ultimate difference between factual and analytical truths.

What is involved here is in fact entirely straightforward. Take a 'rigid designator' like 'the first Earl of Avon'. Very likely this cannot help referring to whomever it refers to for conceptual ('logical') reasons. But if we say that David here does not know whom it refers to, we are in effect envisaging states of affairs – states of affairs compatible with everything he knows – in which the title 'the first Earl of Avon' belongs to someone to whom Queen Elizabeth did not in fact confer it. Nor are such states of affairs shadowy metaphysical entities.[52] They might be precisely what David must be prepared for should he want to interview this noble lord. Thus even the so-called rigid designators can be bent by epistemic considerations.

There is nothing awkward here. For the purpose of discussing one's knowledge of logical and mathematical truths we need alternative quasi-worlds which are even less like the actual one. But their theory can still be developed without any serious problems.[53] In the more modest cases we are here discussing, I can have (19) valid for logical modalities and yet invalid for epistemic modalities, simply by allowing the branching of worlds lines only when we step to one of those epistemic alternatives which are not analytically possible.

Q. Isn't it embarrassing to have epistemically possible worlds which are not logically possible?

C. Only terminologically embarrassing.

Q. Can't one nevertheless still ask whether you are in your semantics quantifying over the inhabitants of some one world or over the world lines connecting several such sets of as it were parochial individuals?

C. You can ask, but you are not entitled to receive an answer one way or another. For suppose that we start out by trying to quantify over actually existing individuals only. But in a suitable modal or epistemic context you are inevitably considering these concrete individuals also *qua* inhabitants of certain alternative worlds. The upshot is precisely the same thing as quantifying over those bits and pieces of world lines which span these alternatives plus the actual world. So what's the difference?

Conversely, suppose that we start out by quantifying over certain world lines. Suppose further that we happen to consider them in a context in which only their nodes in the actual world matters, that is, in a context in which the question of cross-identification does not arise. What happens? It turns out that the outcome is precisely the usual traditional quantification over actually existing individuals.

I might try to express my point by saying that an existential quantifier involves inextricably two apparently different ideas or dimensions: existence in some particularly world and identity in several different worlds. Which of these comes to the fore depends merely on the context. (In emphasizing the second component, I seem to have etymology on my side, for the English existential quantifier 'some' is a cognate of 'same one'.)

All sorts of small technical questions are being begged by these theses of mine, but they are not important. Even if we do not take them up, I think you can see why I said that your question does not matter.

Q. You have my abstract sympathy in your criticism of prefabricated individuals. However, all that you have said still leaves unanswered all the concrete questions of trans world identification. You need cross-identification with vengeance when dealing with quantification. For instance the reason why EG fails in that although a sentence like '$S(a)$' is true, there need not be any genuine individual x of which we could truly assert '$S(a)$', for 'a' may pick out different individuals in the different worlds as denizens of which we are considering 'a' in '$S(a)$'. Here comparisons between different worlds are vital. Now what do we have available to help us to make such comparisons? You said that possible-worlds semantics is based on a suitably generalized and modified notion of a Fregean *Sinn* – your 'original *Sinn*' of modern modal logic. However, in dealing with the problem we are now facing, this notion is utterly useless. It is one thing to ask which individual is picked up in different worlds by a free singular term. That is what told to us by the function according to your lights is the *Sinn* of that term. It is an entirely different thing to ask whether these individuals are the same or different. There is nothing in your notion of meaning function ('*Sinn*') which helps to answer these questions of cross-identity, and the same goes for instance for Montague's semantical theories. Your notion of *Sinn* may be useful in dealing with the problems of free singular terms, but they are helpless with respect to quantifiers and bound variables. And I expect you to agree that these latter problems are the fundamental ones here. One can even reduce the former to the latter by considering all free singular terms as hidden definite descriptions.[54] Because of this primacy of quantificational problems, the failure of your meaning functions to deal with them is a telling argument against possible-worlds semantics.

C. I have my doubts about your use of definite descriptions, but for other reasons I agree with your point about the primacy of the problems concerning quantification. What is more, I agree that meaning functions do not help us here, either. But that does not exhaust the resources of possible-worlds semantics, which is here gradually turning into possible-worlds pragmatics. It is precisely in dealing with quantification and cross-identification that possible-worlds semantics has taken the longest step beyond Frege and even Carnap.[55]

Q. But the whole idea of cross-identification is unrealistic, not to say absurd. More than anything else, it is arbitrary. For instance, I can envisage a series of possible worlds in which David Kaplan is transformed by infinitesimal steps into Rod Chisholm and another series in which he is likewise imperceptibly transmuted into Saul Kripke. This shows that we cannot go by continuity from one world into another, for then even the transitivity of identity fails. We cannot cross-identify by similarity, either, David Lewis notwithstanding, for again transitivity fails.[56] (I forego here the temptation of asking you to tell me precisely what kinds of similarity are supposed to be operative and precisely how they are to be weighted.) Hence the whole enterprise is doomed, and the prospect of quantified modal logic hopeless.

C. Not at all. You have yourself practiced a kind of cross-identification and consequently a kind quantified modal logic. Moreover, your own cross-identification methods can be generalized beyond the special application you have so far countenanced.

Q. That is an extraordinary allegation. I cannot even surmise what you might have in mind.

C. Among the applications of possible-worlds semantics is the one in which the different 'possible worlds' are simply states of affairs of the world at different moments of time. In brief, quantified tense logic may be considered a special kind of modal logic.

In that area you have yourself emphasized not only the possibility but the virtual necessity of quantifying over individuals persisting in space-time, i.e., individuals which can in principle be cross-identified between different temporal cross-sections of the world. You have gone as far as to doubt that a coherent application of quantification theory to temporal matters is possible on any other basis.[57]

Such an alternative basis might be to try to quantify always over the members of some fixed time-slice (temporal cross-section) of our world history. I do not see any incoherence in such an attempt, and I cannot help wondering how your doubts on this score mesh with your insistence elsewhere that we cannot in the last analysis tell whether the next man is quantifying over rabbits or over rabbit-stages.[58] If the second attempt is incoherent, this very incoherence should enable us to tell it from the other interpretation.

However, my point here is not the alleged necessity but only the obvious possibility of quantifying over persisting, re-identifiable individuals in temporal contexts. In admitting this possibility you are yourself practicing a kind of quantified modal logic.

Q. But the kind of cross-identification used in temporal contexts – I think that the term 'tense logic' is a misnomer – is a far cry from what is needed for quantifying in. In it, we just follow the object or the person in question back and forth in space-time. All we need for this purpose is spatiotemporal continuity of our individuals. But cross-identification is not like re-identification. Nothing like spatiotemporal continuity works in cross-identification, for no continuity considerations can enable us to follow an individual from one world to a different one.

C. You still don't appreciate my point. One of the main vehicles, perhaps the main vehicle, of cross-identification is just continuity in space and time.[59]

Q. Let's call space a space. Each world has its own space and time. Hence your method of cross-identification cannot possibly take us from one world to another by means of spatiotemporal continuity.

C. Not alone, you mean. Fortunately we have something else going for us here. Let's consider a typical situation we face in cross-identifying individuals, let's say a situation in which we are talking of what someone, say John, believes. The 'possible worlds' involved here are all the worlds compatible with everything John believes. We may think each of them represented by one of Richard Jeffrey's 'complete novels'.[60] They all usually have a recognizable part in common, viz. that specified by John's definite beliefs about the world. Usually that part is rather extensive. We may think of it as printed in a way different from the rest of the novel, say in red ink.

Cross-identification is now like taking a character mentioned in one novel and a character mentioned in another one and asking whether they are one and the same individual. One way of answering this question is implicit in what has already been said. We follow each individual back and forth in his respective world, trying in both instances to reach the red-letter part (common ground) of the two novels. This we can try to do as soon our individuals are continuous in space and time. When we come to the red-letter part, we can decide the cross-identification question simply by seeing whether the individuals coincide there.

If you pause and think for a moment how we actually cross-identify between (say) my knowledge-worlds, you will soon see that this is just what we in fact do. What does it mean for a person to be identical with my friend Bill in a possible further course of events compatible with everything I know? It means for him to be a spatiotemporal sequel in that world to the career I know Bill has so far enjoyed.

The most important feature of my cross-identification procedure is that no tricks are used in it that were not already employed in your own reidentification procedures. It was in this sense that I suggested that you have yourself been practicing quantified modal logic.

We might thus say that both kinds of extremists are mistaken here – both the philosophers who refuse to worry about cross-identification and those who rely completely on abstract comparisons of possible worlds. What is needed in, say, epistemic contexts is to be able to use the knowledge of the knower in question to carry out cross-identifications. The cross-identification method just explained shows how this knowledge can be brought to bear on the task.

Q. But yours is not a procedure that can answer all questions of cross-identification. If we cannot follow the two characters in their respective novels or, rather, in their respective worlds all the way to the common ground, the procedure you sketched fails to yield an identification one way or another.

C. That is not clear. When the method I described does not produce an answer, the presumption seems to be that the two characters in question are two different individuals. Although the assumptions we make in our actual conceptual practice about these matters need further investigation, it also looks likely that when the procedure I described fails, considerations of similarity are sometimes resorted to.[61] (I want to emphasize that they are at best of secondary importance only.)

However, my main thesis is independent of these details. You did not challenge me to give the last word on cross-identification, but the first word. You claimed that cross-identification is impossible. I have shown that in some cases, indeed very likely in most actual cases, it is possible to accomplish by means of principles you yourself accept.

Q. That is not good enough for me. What I am worried about are not the marginal cases where the procedure is applicable but does not yield an answer, I am concerned with the presuppositions of the whole procedure. You have yourself argued that world lines of individuals usually cannot be continued *ad libitum*. We can say more than this, however. The cross-identification procedure you employed depends on rather strong assumptions. It depends not only on John's having enough beliefs to create a sufficiently large common ground, but more importantly on his beliefs' being of the right sort. They must be such that all the worlds we are collating for the purposes of cross-identification are tolerably orderly. In each of them strong continuity properties must prevail. Otherwise we cannot trace our individuals in space-time toward the red-letter area in the way your procedure requires.

C. That does not prevent it from being applicable to many instances of propositional attitudes and also to physical or natural modalities (natural necessity and natural possibility).

Q. Your reply is not addressed to the most important problem we are facing here. The central application I have always had in mind is to logical (conceptual) modalities, that is to say, to logical (conceptual) necessity and logical (conceptual) possibility. In this application, the possible worlds we must consider are not worlds compatible with somebody's propositional attitude of some sort, but all logically (conceptually) possible worlds. Since it is logically possible that the continuity of our individuals (for instance, physical objects and persons) in space and time should fail, it will fail in some of these conceptually possible worlds. Hence no world line connects all the worlds we are reckoning with, which simply means that we have no well-defined individuals at hand. In brief, your cross-identification method fails altogether, and so do all others I can think of. Quite literally we therefore do not have a well-defined set of individuals available to us as values of our bound variables in such contexts.

C. You are mistaken if you expect me to disagree with what you just said. Just because I acknowledge the central role of cross-identification in the semantics and pragmatics of quantified modal logic and the dependence of this cross-identification on the structure of the possible worlds that are being compared with each other, I am led to acquiesce to the pragmatic impossibility of such cross-identifications in the case of logical modalities.[62]

Q. Then we agree here. But be sure to notice what an important admission you are making. If we cannot cross-identify between all logically (analytically) possible worlds, we do not have well-defined individuals at our disposal in the context of logical modalities, and if we do not have such individuals at hand, we cannot use quantifiers in such contexts. (More precisely, we cannot quantify into a context governed by an operator for a logical modality.) Hence what you are admitting here is nothing less than the pragmatic impossibility of a quantified modal logic of logical modalities. This impossibility has in fact been my main thesis all along.

C. I am perfectly happy to grant you this point, for my main interest has all along been in the direction of propositional attitudes, especially epistemic notions. Vis-à-vis logical or analytical modalities, we stand united in opposition to those philosophers of logic who believe that our individuals (basic particulars) must somehow be able to take care of themselves independently of our semantical and pragmatic problems concerning them. This type of view strikes me as metaphysical in the bad sense of the word and very shallow epistemologically. I think you will agree with me here.

However, we can still use happily even logical or analytical modalities as it were locally, that is to say, relative to sufficiently strong assumptions. These assumptions will then serve to limit us to a relatively small set of possible worlds which are tolerable orderly and tolerably similar. What emerges from our discussion is thus mostly a keener awareness of the presuppositions – I think Kant would call them transcendental pre-suppositions – of our discourse.

More than anything else, I also want to emphasize that the flaw we found in quantified modal logic of logical modalities does not reflect on the use of quantifiers in the context of propositional attitudes.

Q. Perhaps not in an equally fatal way. However, what we have found does have important consequences for the use of quantifiers *cum* proposi-tional attitudes. Notice, for instance, that by the same token as before cross-identification succeeds in, say, belief-contexts only when the beliefs in question are not too few and far between. For if they do not allow for continuity within each world and for large enough a common ground, the procedure you relied on fails. Thus quantified doxastic logic is not universally applicable as a matter of course, but only by courtesy of the rationality of the relevant believers. The same holds of course for other propositional attitudes.

Notice also what happens to questions of ontology, in the sense of the domain of individuals one is quantifying over. The failure of cross-identification for analytical (logical) modalities means that there simply is not any uniform domain of individuals that could serve as the values of our bindable variables irrespective of the context in which they occur. When discussing people's propositional attitudes, we thus cannot presuppose a constant domain of individuals, but that domain depends on the attitude. The best approximation that one can have to an ontology of one's own is presumably the set of individuals that can be cross-identified between one's belief worlds. This ontology depends on one's substantial beliefs about individuals, not only on one's beliefs as to what individuals there are.

Even if I don't want to raise now the question of the empirical indeterminacy of one's beliefs, we can thus see that the vagaries of cross-identification make the applicability of quantification theory uncertain and one's ontology relative.

C. I don't see why I should be unhappy with those conclusions. They suggest to me very interesting further applications, for instance to the connection which has often been claimed to obtain between logic and rationality, and indeed to the explication of your own ideas about the indeterminacy of ontology.[63]

Q. You are in effect accepting my main theses, then.

C. That depends on what precisely your theses are. There are in any case a number of smaller mooted issues. I have earlier criticized several of the points you used to make, especially your remarks on identity. It seems to me that the role of this notion can only be evaluated in terms of possible-worlds semantics, and when this is done, many of your claims are disproved.

Another matter in which I still find myself disagreeing with you are your references to essentialism. If I am right about the methods of cross-identification which we actually employ in ordinary discourse, then essentialism is not a live issue here. We cross-identify, not in terms of any priviledged attributes of our individuals, but by means of the continuity of these individuals in space and time. You may of course propose to call these continuity properties 'essential attributes', but they are by any token a far cry of Aristotelian essentialism. (A much better historical precedent would be Descartes' reidentification of his lump of wax.)

In particular, the truth-conditions of 'knowing who' and 'knowing what' statements which we discussed earlier do not involve 'essential properties' in any useful sense of the term. To know who John is is not to know certain particular things about him, but to know enough of him and of his behavior in space and time – enough, that is to say, to recognize his manifestations in all possible worlds compatible with what I know by tracing them back to where I know that John has been at the time.

Of course, a sufficiently large 'common ground' shared by all these epistemic alternatives must also be available, but what it happens to be has little to do with essentialism. It is simply a matter of knowing enough particular matters of fact about John and his whereabouts at different moments of time.

If cross-identification between all logically possible worlds were feasible, it is true that we would need large enough a common ground of logically (or analytically) necessary agreements. They would presumably have to involve the imputation of a sufficiently large number of in-alienable attributes to our individuals. But we have argued that for logical (analytical) modalities individuation does not work anyway. Hence we do not obtain any vindication of essentialism here, but perhaps rather an additional reason for the failure of cross-identification between all logically possible worlds, their 'common ground' probably being too small to sustain cross-identification. Again, in the case of (say) epistemic modalities the common ground is not predicated on a mysterious distinction between essential and nonessential attributes but on the commonplace distinction between known and unknown attributes.

For reasons of this sort, I find your references to essentialism misleading, if not actually mistaken.

However, my main concern lies elsewhere. One of the main things I am insisting on is the possibility and interest of a quantified logic of propositional attitudes, even if the applicability of this logic is contingent on the content of peoples' propositional attitudes. And by 'possibility' I do not mean possibility merely as an abstract model-theoretical exercise, but realistic pragmatic feasibility.

Q. Whether I agree with that depends on certain interrelated issues, especially on the epistemological status of beliefs and of your possible worlds. If possible worlds are not empirically meaningful entities, your line of thought will fail.

C. Those are already more general problems than the possibility of quantified modal logic. Furthermore, they are related more closely to your discussions with Carnap on meaning and analyticity than to your criticism of quantifying into opaque contexts. Perhaps we should save those problems for another Monday night.

NOTES

[1] Cf. 'Reply to Professor Marcus', reprinted in *The Ways of Paradox*, Random House, New York, 1966, pp. 175–182, especially pp. 175–177.

[2] See Kurt Gödel, 'Eine Interpretation des intuitionistischen Aussagenkalküls', *Ergebnisse eines mathematischen Kolloquiums*, Vol. 4, Verlag Franz Deuticke, Vienna, 1933, pp. 39–40. Translated in *The Philosophy of Mathematics*, Jaakko Hintikka (ed.), Oxford University Press, London, 1969, pp. 128–129.

[3] Cf. 'Three Grades of Modal Involvement', reprinted in *The Ways of Paradox* (1966), pp. 156–174.

[4] Cf. *op. cit.*, p. 159.

[5] Richard Montague, 'Syntactical Treatments of Modality, with Corollaries on Reflexion Principle and Finite Axiomatizability', in the *Proceedings of a Colloquium on Modal and Many-Valued Logics, Helsinki, 23–26 August, 1962, Acta Philosophica Fennica* **16** (1963) 153–167.

[6] Cf. for instance 'Three Grades of Modal Involvement', *loc. cit.*, especially pp. 156–157, 164–166. What Quine there calls necessity expressed by a semantical predicate is in effect necessity interpreted as the syntactical predicate of provability.

[7] This was asserted in so many words by Montague in a talk to the Berkeley-Stanford Logic Colloquium in the Spring of 1963.

[8] See, e.g., 'Three Grades of Modal Involvement', in *The Ways of Paradox*, especially pp. 156–157, 164–166.

[9] For the role of the SI and of EG as touchstones of referentiality, see 'Reference and Modality', *From a Logical Point of View*, Harvard University Press, Cambridge, Mass., 1953, revised ed. (1961), pp. 139–159.

[10] Cf. *Word and Object*, MIT Press, Cambridge, Mass., 1960, p. 212: "…conspicuously opaque as it is, quotation is a vivid form to which to reduce other opaque constructions."

[11] The connection between SI and EG and one's domain of individuals (one's ontology) is pointed out by Quine for instance in 'Reference and Modality', *From a Logical Point of View*, p. 150: "But referential opacity depends in part on the ontology accepted…." A case study of such dependence is Jaakko Hintikka's suggestion that the sense-datum ontology was inspired by sense-datum theoreticians' realization of the opacity of perceptual locutions, with the ensuing uncertainty as to what the individuals really are that are discussed in such locutions. This is amusingly confirmed by A. J. Ayer who introduces sense-datum terms like his "seeming-cigarette case" in order to salvage the inference from "It now seems to me that I see a cigarette case" to "I am now seeing a seeming-cigarette case", that is (nearly enough), to salvage the applicability of EG in perceptual contexts. (See A. J. Ayer, *The Problem of Knowledge*, Penguin Books, Ch. 3, section (iii).)

[12] This reference is apparently to 'Reference and Modality', in *From a Logical Point of View*, especially pp. 152–153.

[13] Cf. *Word and Object*, especially §33 and §47.

[14] With the following, cf. 'Quantifiers and Propositional Attitudes', reprinted in *The Ways of Paradox*, pp. 183–194.

[15] Cf. 'Quantifiers and Propositional Attitudes', in *The Ways of Paradox*, esp. p. 185.

[16] In *op. cit.*, p. 188, Quine recognizes the doxastic counterparts to (6) and (7) as true (in the approach he there outlines).

[17] Cf. Jaakko Hintikka, *Knowledge and Belief*, Cornell University Press, Ithaca, N.Y., 1962, Ch. 6, and (for important refinements of the view presented there) Jaakko Hintikka, *The Semantics of Questions and the Questions of Semantics* (forthcoming). Cf. also Chapter 7 below.

[18] Here the attribution of the speaker's remarks to Quine is particularly questionable, for Quine has never expounded, still less espoused, in print the line of thought that is being presented here.

[19] The speakers will repeatedly return to this question of essentialism later. See especially the critic's penultimate rejoinder below.

[20] See 'Quantifiers and Propositional Attitudes', *The Ways of Paradox*, p. 188.

[21] Cf., e.g., Wilfrid Sellars, 'Some Problems About Belief', in *Words and Objections: Essays on the Work of W. V. Quine*, Donald Davidson and Jaakko Hintikka (eds.), D. Reidel, Dordrecht, 1969, pp. 180–205; Robert C. Sleigh, 'Restricted Range in Epistemic Logic', *Journal of Philosophy* **69** (1972) 67–77. The misconception that referentially opaque contexts are essentially characterized by the possible vacuousness of singular terms occurring meaningfully in such contexts is alarmingly widespread.

[22] Cf. *Word and Object*, p. 166: "...*no variable inside an opaque construction is bound by an operator outside*. You cannot quantify into an opaque construction." (Quine's own italics.)

[23] See Jaakko Hintikka, 'Existential Presuppositions and Uniqueness Presuppositions', in *Models for Modalities*, D. Reidel, Dordrecht, 1969, pp. 112–147, where these extra premisses required by EG are also generalized to more complex situations.

[24] The reference is apparently to Jaakko Hintikka, 'Questions about Questions', in *Semantics and Philosophy*, Milton K. Munitz and Peter K. Unger (eds.), N.Y.U. Press, New York, 1974, pp. 103–158. See also the works referred to in note 17 above.

[25] Cf. Jaakko Hintikka, *Models for Modalities*, D. Reidel, Dordrecht, 1969, pp. 97, 120–121, 141.

[26] See Stig Kanger, *Provability in Logic* (Stockholm Studies in Philosophy, Vol. 1), Stockholm, 1957; Stig Kanger, 'The Morning Star Paradox', *Theoria* **23** (1957) 1–11; Stig Kanger, 'A Note on Quantification and Modalities', *Theoria* **23** (1957) 133–134; Jaakko Hintikka, *Quantifiers in Deontic Logic*, Societas Scientiarum Fennica, Commentationes Humanarum Litterarum **23**, no. 4, Helsinki, 1957; Jaakko Hintikka, 'Modality as Referential Multiplicity', *Ajatus* **20** (1957) 49–64; Marcel Guillaume, 'Rapports entre calculs propositionnels modaux et topologie impliqués par certaines extensions de la méthode des tableaux sémantiques. Système de Feys – von Wright', *Comptes rendus des séances de l'Académie des Sciences* (Paris) **246** (1958) 1140–1142; 'Système S4 de Lewis', *ibid.* 2207–2210; 'Système S5 de Lewis', *ibid.* **247** (1958) 1282–1283.

[27] Cf. Quine's review of *Identity and Individuation*, Milton K. Munitz (ed.), in *The Journal of Philosophy* **69** (1972) 488–497, especially 492–493.

[28] See, e.g., Richard Montague, 'Pragmatics and Intensional Logic', *Synthese* **22** (1970–71) 68–94, especially p. 91; 'On the Nature of Certain Philosophical Entities', *The Monist* **53** (1969) 159–194, especially p. 164.

[29] Jaakko Hintikka, 'Carnap's Semantics in Retrospect', *Synthese* **25** (1973) 372–397, especially pp. 377–381, reprinted above as Chapter 5 of this volume.

[30] Besides the papers already quoted, see Richard Montague, 'Pragmatics', in *Contemporary Philosophy*, Vol. 1, R. Klibansky (ed.), La Nuova Italia Editrice, Florence, 1968, pp. 102–122; 'English as a Formal Language', in *Linguaggi nella società e nella technica*, Edizioni de Comunità, Milan, 1970, pp. 189–223.

[31] In case documentation is needed, the conventional strictures of textbooks and treatises

against 'the referential theory of meaning' should be enough. Cf., e.g., William P. Alston, *Philosophy of Language*, Prentice-Hall, Englewood Cliffs, N.J., 1964, pp. 12–13.

[32] Gottlob Frege, 'Über Sinn und Bedeutung', *Zeitschrift für Philosophie und Philosophische Kritik* **100** (1892) 25–50, especially p. 26.

[33] Cf., e.g., Quine's use of 'Nec' as a "semantical" predicate in *The Ways of Paradox*, p. 166, or section iv of 'Quantifiers and Propositional Attitudes'. The misleading idea that a difference in the referring expressions themselves suffices as the relevant difference between the ways in which their references are given is maintained explicitly in R. M. Martin, *Logic, Language and Metaphysics*, New York University Press, New York, 1971, pp. 59–60.

[34] Cf., e.g., "... all... singular terms may be introduced by contextual definition in conformity of Russell's theory of singular descriptions", *The Ways of Paradox*, p. 171; also *Word and Object*, pp. 179–187.

[35] The recent interest in rigid designators, dubbings and suchlike is partly just a revolt against the idea that the correlation of a singular term and its references is always established through the descriptive content of the term.

[36] The same pun has (independently) been used by Michael Dummett in *Frege's Philosophy of Language*, Duckworth, London, 1973, p. 584. Dummett attributes it to Paul Benacerraf.

[37] This appears to be somewhat exaggerated. Frege did connect the concept of *Sinn* very closely with the criteria of identity of the reference, especially in the case of the sense of a proper name. (See, e.g., Dummett, note 36 above, pp. 179–180.) This concern with the criteria of identity can only manifest through questions as to how the reference of a term is to be specified (reidentified) in different circumstances, thus making the discussion reminiscent of possible-worlds semantics. However, there is no clear general framework in Frege for dealing with these questions, and later during the dialogue it will turn out that questions concerning *Sinne* will have to be distinguished rather sharply form questions of the re-identification of individuals. Hence it seems fair to conclude that Frege did not after all fully grasp the function-like character of his *Sinne*.

[38] For instance, Frege acknowledges that two different arithmetical expressions for the same natural number, for instance 2^2 and $2+2$, may have different *Sinne*, even though the identity of their references is of course for him a truth of logic. Cf., e.g., Gottlob Frege, *Grundgesetze der Arithmetik*, Vol. 1, Jena, 1893, pp. ix, 7.

[39] See Dana Scott, 'Advice on Modal Logic', in *Philosophical Problems in Logic*, Karel Lambert (ed.), D. Reidel, Dordrecht, 1970, pp. 143–173; cf. Richard Montague, 'Pragmatics', in *Contemporary Philosophy – La philosophie comtemporaine*, R. Klibansky (ed.), La Nuova Italia Editrice, Florence, 1968, pp. 102–122; Krister Segerberg, 'Some Logics of Commitment and Obligation', in *Deontic Logic*, Risto Hilpinen (ed.), D. Reidel, Dordrecht, 1971, pp. 148–158.

[40] Jaakko Hintikka, 'Surface Semantics: Definition and Its Motivation', in *Truth, Syntax, and Modality*, Hugues Leblanc (ed.), North-Holland, Amsterdam, 1973, pp. 128–147; Jaakko Hintikka and Ilkka Niiniluoto, 'On the Surface Semantics of First-Order Proof Procedures', *Ajatus* **35** (1973) 197–215. Cf. also Chapter 9 below.

[41] This is a point where a charge of circularity could apparently be raised against C., for the best way of spelling out the logic of counterfactuals is undoubtedly in terms of possible worlds. Cf. David Lewis, *Counterfactuals*, Basil Blackwell, Oxford, 1973. However, the interlocutors seem to agree that a circle of explication need not be a vicious one, provided it is wide enough to enable a logician to uncover nontrivial aspects of the structure of the concepts involved.

[42] Cf. Jaakko Hintikka, *Models for Modalities*, D. Reidel, Dordrecht, 1969, pp. 116–117;

Jaakko Hintikka, *Knowledge and Belief*, Cornell U.P., Ithaca, N.Y., 1962, pp. 132–136.

[43] The reference is apparently to Jaakko Hintikka, 'The Semantics of Modal Notions and the Indeterminacy of Ontology', *Synthese* 21 (1970) 408–424: reprinted above as Chapter 2 of the present volume.

[44] See Jaakko Hintikka, 'On the Logic of Perception', in *Models for Modalities* (note 42 above); 'Objects of Knowledge and Belief: Acquaintances and Public Figures', *The Journal of Philosophy* 67 (1970) 869–883, reprinted above as Chapter 3 of this volume; 'Knowledge by Acquaintance – Individuation by Acquaintance', in *Bertrand Russell: A Collection of Critical Essays*, David Pears (ed.), Doubleday, (Garden City, N.J., 1972), pp. 52–79, reprinted in *Knowledge and the Known*, D. Reidel, Dordrecht, 1974.

[45] Cf. "Where modal logic has thus been paraphrased in terms of such notions as possible world or rigid designator, where the displaced fog settles is on the question when to identify objects between worlds..." (Quine reviewing *Identity and Individuation*, Milton K. Munitz (ed.), in *The Journal of Philosophy* 69 (1972) 488–497, especially p. 249). Quine goes on to list two other destinations for the "displaced fog" of interpretational problems, but they can be shown to reduce mostly to this first and foremost one.

[46] Pun by courtesy of David Kaplan and Trans World Airlines.

[47] An explicit argument to this effect is given in Hintikka, *Models for Modalities* (note 42 above), pp. 130–133.

[48] It turns out that we also have to assume that either one of two locally coinciding world lines can always be continued as far as the other one. This is what (C.ind = E) in Hintikka, *Models for Modalities*, p. 130, says. This assumption does not give rise to any new problems, however.

[49] See the papers by Hintikka referred to in note 44 above.

[50] This can easily be seen in Hintikka's treatment. See *Models for Modalities*, pp. 116–117, 128–133.

[51] Cf. *From a Logical Point of View*, p. 156.

[52] Cf. Jaakko Hintikka, *Logic, Language-Games, and Information*, Clarendon Press, Oxford, 1973, pp. 233–235.

[53] Cf. Jaakko Hintikka, 'Surface Semantics: Definition and Its Motivation' (note 40 above), and Chapter 2 below.

[54] Cf. *Word and Object*, §37.

[55] Cf. Jaakko Hintikka, 'Carnap's Semantics in Retrospect' (above Chapter 5, pp. 76–101; pp. 382–387 of the original).

[56] Cf. David Lewis, 'Counterpart Theory and Quantified Modal Logic', *The Journal of Philosophy* 65 (1968) 113–126.

[57] Cf. *The Ways of Paradox*, p. 145: "I see no reason to expect a coherent application of quantification theory to temporal matters on any other basis." For Quine's preference of persisting or, as he puts it, four-dimensional objects, see also *Word and Object*, p. 171.

[58] *Word and Object*, pp. 51–52, 71–72.

[59] Cf. Hintikka, 'The Semantics of Modal Notions', pp. 26–42 above, pp. 401–402 of the original.

[60] Richard C. Jeffrey, *The Logic of Decision*, McGraw-Hill, New York, 1965, p. 196.

[61] Once again, see Hintikka, 'The Semantics of Modal Notions', pp. 26–42 above, pp. 401–402 of the original.

[62] Cf. Hintikka, 'The Semantics of Modal Notions', pp. 36–37 above, pp. 408–409 of the original.

[63] Cf. Hintikka, 'The Semantics of Modal Notions', pp. 36–37 above, pp. 409–410 of the original.

CHAPTER 7

ANSWERS TO QUESTIONS

In an earlier paper,[1] I have tried to answer the question of answerhood, that is, tried to specify the conditions on which a response to an English question counts as an *answer* to it. In this new paper, I shall strive to extend and to deepen that earlier analysis.

This enterprise has several different kinds of interest. One of them is that in so far as my analysis of the conditions of answerhood is successful, it reinforces the general approach to questions in natural languages through which it was reached. This general approach was first used by Lennart Åqvist.[2] It proceeds in two stages. First, questions are analyzed systematically as requests of information. Secondly, the informational state desired by the speaker is analyzed in terms of epistemic logic.

In order to spell out this approach explicitly, certain distinctions and explanations are needed. We shall distinguish between *propositional questions* and *wh-questions*.[3] In the former, the relevant alternatives are propositions while in the latter they are (a logician might say) values of a bound variable. Thus yes-or-no questions are propositional, and so are (illustrating the mild awkwardness of the terminology) whether-questions. In contrast, who-, what-, which-, when-, and where-questions are wh-questions. How- and why-questions, which present several special problems, are not dealt with here, except in so far as they share the logic and semantics of other wh-questions.[4]

In the logical (semantical) analysis of any direct question we shall distinguish two main ingredients. They are an *imperative* or *optative operator* whose force may roughly be expressed by

(1)   Bring it about that

and what I shall call the *desideratum* of the question. The latter is a specification of the (epistemic) state of affairs the questioner is asking to be brought about. It thus has in effect the form 'I know ---'.

What goes into the slot '---' here depends on the kind of question we are dealing with. Propositional questions may be characterized by saying that their desiderata are of the form

(2)   I know whether $p_1, p_2, ..., $ or p_k

which can be further analyzed as

(3)   I know that $p_1 \vee$
           I know that $p_2 \vee$
           --- $\vee$
           I know that p_k.

A wh-question, say

(4)   Who X'?

has as its desideratum

(5)   I know who X

where 'who X' is the indirect question corresponding to the direct question 'who X''. What precisely the grammatical process is that takes us from X to X' will not be discussed here. A transformational grammarian might say here that X' results from X through auxiliary attraction. A generalization to other wh-questions is obvious.

Thus for instance the question

(6)   Who lives here?

is analyzed (approximately) as

(7)   Bring it about that I know who lives here

and

(8)   What did Mary buy?

is analyzed as

(9)   Bring it about that I know what Mary bought.

In the former case the desideratum is

(10)   I know who lives here

and in the latter it is

(11)   I know what Mary bought.

A yes-or-no question, say 'X'?', will have as its desideratum

(12)   I know whether X

which can be analyzed as

(13)   (I know that X) $\lor$ (I know that neg $+ X$)

where 'neg $+$' indicates the negation-forming process. For instance,

(14)   Did Mary come?

will have as its desideratum

(15)   I know that Mary came or
          I know that Mary did not come.

The cognitive meaning of the desideratum of some particular (token of a) question can also be expressed by using the proper name of the questioner instead of as it were putting a first-person knowledge-statement into his mouth, as we have in effect done. The difference between these is not relevant to the purposes of this essay, and will therefore be tacitly disregarded. We shall occasionally use the possibility of moving from the one to the other, however.

It is clear that, for any semantical and logical theory of questions, their desiderata are the most important things about them. For one thing, the imperative element is essentially the same in all ordinary (direct) questions. (Certain qualifications this statement needs will be indicated later.) This is not at all surprising. Once a questioner has indicated what it is that he wants to know – which is what the desideratum specifies – all that remains is for him to ask for that to be brought about (by addressee of the question). In what follows, we shall mostly discuss the desiderata of questions and disregard the imperative element.

It may nevertheless be of interest to point out that sometimes the imperative or optative ingredient may vary or may be replaced by something altogether different while the desideratum remains largely intact. This is often what happens in questions – we shall call them *nonstandard* questions – which are *not* asked in the interest of information-gathering. For instance, an examination-question does not have the force of

          Bring it about that I know ---

where 'I know ---' is the desideratum, but perhaps rather the force of

Show that you know ---.

Apart from the switch from the first to the second person the desideratum has remained unchanged here, whereas the imperative element has changed. Some (indirect) evidence for this point will be presented later in this chapter.

It is nevertheless clear that we have not yet made much progress. We have analyzed *direct* questions in terms of certain *indirect* (subordinate) questions, viz. those having 'know' as the main verb. My theory will not really get off the ground before I have spelled out the logical (semantical) structure of these subordinate questions. This is the second stage of our approach promised above. In it, we shall use the usual notation of epistemic logic: 'K_a' for 'a knows that'; the two quantifiers '(Ex)' and '(y)'; propositional connectives '$\vee$', '$\wedge$', '$\supset$', and '$\sim$'; etc. For the advantage gained in the first stage of our theory is that the only new elements needed to specify the desiderata of direct questions are these well-known paraphernalia of epistemic logic.

Please note, incidentally, that the notation 'K_a' has turned out to be rather misleading in one respect. The subscript 'a' indicating the knower is *not* within the scope of the operator 'K'. It is for instance not subject of any opacity that 'K' may create. I shall not depart from the more or less customary notation, however.

The expressibility of the desiderata of questions in the notation of epistemic logic is clear in the case of propositional questions. But how can we analyze wh-questions by means of the same tools?

The basic answer to this question is very simple.[5] It can be best explained by means of an example. The desideratum (10) of (6) will be analyzed as

(Ex) I know that x lives here

or, more briefly put

(16) $(Ex) K_I(x$ lives here$)$.

The naturalness of this analysis is obvious. What else could it mean to know who lives here than to know of some particular person that he (or she) lives here? However, in spite of the naturalness of the analysis it needs both several explanations and certain important qualifications before we can be satisfied with it.[6]

First, although it is in most cases clear how the analysis is to be extended to other who-questions and to other wh-words, we can see that the range of the bound variable 'x' will have to be chosen differently for the different wh-words. With 'who' it ranges over persons, with 'when' over moments (or periods) of time, with 'where' over places, and so on, unlike ordinary logic where we have a single 'universe of discourse'. This does not cause any difficulties, however. The different domains can usually be specified without any trouble. Hence all that is involved here is that we must presuppose a many-sorted epistemic logic. There are no problems in principle about such a logic, however, over and above problems encountered already in the usual (one-sorted) epistemic logic.

A more important group of problems is due to the non-extensional character of knowledge-contexts. These problems can be solved, I believe, through a satisfactory possible-worlds semantics for epistemic concepts. I also believe that such a semantics has already been developed elsewhere. It would take us too far to explain it here, however. I shall be appealing to insights obtained in that area later in this paper when we are analyzing the semantics of questions, but I shall not present full arguments for these insights here. Suffice it to say that in expressions like (16) the variable 'x' must range over well-defined individuals, that is, individuals that can be re-identified in all the possible worlds as a member of which the values of this variable are considered in (16). These are shown by the sequences of nonextensional operators in the scope of which 'x' occurs in (16). Since the only such operator is 'K_I', the relevant possible worlds are the epistemic alternatives with respect to the speaker. Had there been (say) a belief-operator 'b believes that' between 'K_I' and 'x' in (16), we would have been forced to consider, not the speaker's knowledge-alternatives, but b's belief-alternatives to these knowledge-alternatives; and similarly in other cases.

This explains (among other things) why existential generalization – that is, the inference schema that leads us from

(17) $F(b)$

to

(18) $(Ex) F(x)$

– is invalid here. Even if (17) is true, 'b' may pick out different individuals in the different worlds as a member of which b is considered there. Then (18) need not be true, for then there may not be any one (one and the same) individual of which the things can be true which in (17) are said of b.

For existential generalization to go through, we need an extra premise guaranteeing that 'b' picks out the same individual in all the relevant worlds. What these are is seen in the way just indicated. The uniqueness premise will therefore be in general

(19) $(Ex)\,[S_1(b=x) \wedge S_2(b=x) \wedge \cdots]$

where $S_1, S_2, \dots$ are the different sequences of the non-extensional operators within the scope of which 'x' occurs in '$F(x)$'.[7] (I am assuming here and in the sequel that negation signs have been pushed as deep into the sentence $F(x)$ as possible.) If the only such operator is 'K_1', the premise needed is

(20) $(Ex)\,K_1(b=x)$

whose intuitive meaning is clearly

I know who b is

(assuming for the sake of an example that 'x' ranges over persons).

If 'x' occurs in $F(x)$ within the operators 'K_1' and 'B_d' (in this order), the extra premise will be

(21) $(Ex)\,K_1B_d(b=x)$.

In spite of the simplicity and naturalness of the principles employed here, there is room for subtleties and novelties. For instance, I have earlier required that whenever we are using pairs of dual modal or epistemic operators (e.g. 'necessarily' and 'possibly') or using '$\sim K_a \sim$' as an operator dual to 'K_a' (and analogously for other non-extensional operators), we must always replace the weaker one of each pair of dual operator by the stronger one in constructing the sequences $S_1, S_2, \dots$ in (19). This relatively inconspicuous feature of the approach used here has been the (unacknowledged and unrecognized) basis of several criticisms levelled at it. I have come to realize that it does in fact amount to an unnecessarily strong requirement. This superfluous force can be seen by observing that in '$\sim K_a \sim A(b)$' b is considered as a member of only one (at least one) epistemic a-alternative. Yet the correlated uniqueness premise $(Ex)\, K_a(b = x)$ requires that it have one and the same reference in all of them.

However, it cannot easily be changed without modifying certain other aspects of my approach. Although these changes would be merely technical, they are too sweeping to be made here. I shall accordingly forego them, but not without a reminder of their feasibility.

Be this as it may, we obtain in any case a semantical analysis of a class of subordinate questions in English in terms of epistemic logic and its semantics. It is easy to see that a similar analysis can be given of subordinate wh-questions whose main verb is for instance 'perceives', 'remembers', etc. It does not apply in its present form to certain other subordinate questions, particularly to those with a 'performative' main verb like 'ask', 'wonder', etc. Such questions will not be discussed here.

Our analysis can be extended to certain other constructions with nonextensional notions, some of them involving subordinate questions, for instance

> b is known (believed, hoped, ...) by a to ---
> a knows (believes, hopes, ...) of b that $- b -$
> a knows (remembers) whom (when, where, ...) to ---

We shall not be concerned with these constructions here, however.

Although the approach developed here can be applied to multiple questions (questions with several wh-words in the same clause) as well as iterated questions (questions already containing subordinate questions), there are certain interesting problems about such applications which I shall study elsewhere. They will in fact necessitate a considerable further development of our semantical framework. Certain other problems which are associated with our approach will be discussed later in the present chapter.

As far as direct questions are concerned, our analysis of their desiderata enables us to define certain useful notions about them. We shall call the desideratum of a question minus its initial epistemic operators (those introduced in the transition from the direct question to its desideratum) the *presupposition* of the question. For instance, the presupposition corresponding to (2) will be

(22) $\qquad p_1 \vee p_2 \vee \cdots \vee p_k$

and the presupposition of (6) is

(23) (Ex) x lives here

i.e.,

someone lives here.

The presupposition of a wh-question minus the existential quantifier will be called the *matrix* of the question.

It is seen that yes-or-no questions have a vacuous presupposition, which perhaps helps to understand their naturalness.

It is to be emphasized that the somewhat technical notion of presupposition defined above is not the only one relevant to the semantics of questions. The general idea of presupposition can be brought to bear on it in other ways, too. The specific sense in which we are using the term in this essay will become clearer when we proceed.

The notion of presupposition helps us to qualify our earlier analysis of the logical or semantical form of questions. The imperative or optative operator which we suggested is one of the two main parts of the logical structure of a question is not absolute but conditional on the truth of the presupposition of the query in question. Thus a little fuller analysis of the logical form of a wh-question might be

(24)   Assuming that (Ex) $F(x)$,
            bring it about that (Ex) $K_1F(x)$

If we did not make this change, it might be pointed out for instance that the question

(25)   Who is Mary married to?

entails that the speaker wants it to be made true that

(26) (Ex) K_1 Mary is married to x

which arguably implies

(27) (Ex) Mary is married to x.

In other words, part of the force of the question would be to try to marry Mary off. This mistaken implication is cut off by the new, more refined analysis.

I shall not try to explain precisely what kind of conditionalization is being presupposed in (24) and in its ilk, however.[8]

To sum up, we have to distinguish several different things from each other here:

(i)   the surface form of a direct question;
(ii)   its desideratum;
(iii)   its presupposition; and
(iv)   its matrix.

(The last of these is applicable to wh-questions only.) All these will have to be distinguished from *answers* to questions.

The notion we shall first try to capture is that of a *potential conclusive* (or *full*) answer. By the former epithet, I mean an answer which would satisfy the questioner *if* it were true and *if* he were in a position to trust the answer. By a *conclusive* answer, I mean a reply which does not require further backing to satisfy the questioner.

There are many other types of responses to a question which are natural and which may even have been intended by the questioner. However, they can usually be easily distinguished from conclusive answers. One symptom is that such a *partial* answer can typically be prefaced by "I do not know, but...". Our concept of desideratum offers another way of characterizing a conclusive answer to a question: it is one which brings out completely and not only partially the state of affairs specified by the desideratum. Partial answers serve to bring this state of affairs only in part – in some sense of 'part'.

We shall also assume that the answers we shall be dealing with are *direct* answers, that is, their status as answers is established by such an answer itself, independently of whatever inferences the questioner may draw on its basis.

It is easy to say what is an answer (direct potential conclusive answer) to the propositional question with (3) as its desideratum. Each of the propositions $p_1, p_2, ..., p_k$ is such an answer.

It is not much more difficult to spell out what an answer to a wh-question is. Here the force of the insights we obtain in epistemic logic and in its semantics comes into play for the first time very strongly. Suppose that someone asks a who-question whose desideratum is

(28) $(Ex) K_1 F(x)$.

Suppose further that the addressee of the question responds by a singular term (noun phrase) 'b'. This is of course equivalent to his replying by uttering or by otherwise giving the questioner the substitution-instance $F(b)$ of the matrix with respect to 'b'. When is this reply a (conclusive) answer to the question? Since we are dealing with potential answers we may assume that this substitution-instance is a true statement and that the questioner knows it to be an honest and well-informed response to his query. When does it on these assumptions satisfy him?

We can approach this question by asking another. What is the epistemic state of affairs brought about by this response? On the assumptions made the questioner can truly say, after having received the putative answer 'b',

(29)   I know that $F(b)$.

But this is not yet the state of affairs the questioner wanted to be brought about. This state of affairs is specified by the desideratum (28) of his question. Hence the status of the response 'b' or '$F(b)$' as a potential conclusive answer hinges on the question: When does (29) imply (28)?

But this is merely a special case of the question (discussed briefly above) as to on what conditions existential generalization is valid in epistemic contexts. Assuming for the time being that there are no non-extensional operators in '$F(x)$', we can read off from the earlier discussion the extra premise which is needed here to reinstate existential generalization and to raise thereby 'b' (and '$F(b)$') to the status of (potential conclusive) answers to the question whose desideratum is (28). It is

(30) $(Ex) K_1(b=x)$.

In other words, 'b' is an answer if and only if the questioner can truly say

(31)   I know who b is.

This is natural and perhaps even expected. If the questioner does not know who b is, he is apt to parry a reply 'b' by the further question

(32)   But who is b?

thereby showing that the reply was not conclusive as an answer.[9]

For instance, of someone replies to (6) by uttering

(33)   The richest man in town lives here

he will easily prompt the response

(34)   I do not know who the richest man in town is

or

(35)   But who is the richest man in town?

Several consequences and further suggestions ensue from this answer to the question of answerhood. For one thing, it can be seen that the question whose desideratum is (28) cannot have any true answers (in the intended sense of 'answer') unless its presupposition is satisfied. However, the truth of the presupposition does not guarantee that the additional condition (30) is satisfied for any choices of 'b'. This serves to illustrate the nature of my notion of presupposition.

One interesting thing about my solution to the answerhood problem is that it extends very nicely to certain types of nonstandard questions. Earlier, it was suggested that in examination-questions we have a different imperative operator and the second (grammatical) person instead of the first one. Now the latter change implies the corresponding change in the conditions of answerhood. It will now be required that *the addressee* of the question knows who b is in order for 'b' to be a satisfactory answer to a who-question.[10] This is of course just the condition which could have been expected to apply here. It does not help the examinee if the examiner knows who b is: he will have to know it himself in order for his reply 'b' to be a satisfactory answer to the examiner's who-question. Thus my theory works nicely here.

Another piece of evidence for my criterion of answerhood is obtained by observing what happens when for some reason the range of the variables which there tacitly are in a wh-question changes.[11] For then my criterion follows suit. For instance, in the question

Who administers the oath to a new President?

the relevant alternatives might be the different officers (offices) (Secretary of State, Chief Justice, Speaker of the House, etc.) rather than persons holding them. Then my criterion of answerhood will require that the questioner knows which office it is that an answer refers to, not that he knows who the person is who holds it. This is obviously what must be required of a satisfactory answer.

In spite of its naturalness, my answer to the answerhood problem is not only new, but is unlike its predecessors in that it is *contextual*. It does not depend only on the logical and semantical status of the question and its putative answer, and on that of their ingredients, but also on the state of knowledge of the questioner at the time he asks his question.

It has other implications as well. It shows that an attempted answer to a wh-question, say the one whose desideratum is (28), has to serve two functions. Not only must it provide the questioner with a name or other noun phrase 'b' such that '$F(b)$' (the substitution-instance of the matrix with respect to this noun phrase) is true. The reply will have to presuppose, or provide, so much information concerning a that it enables the questioner to know who (what, where, ...) b is. This double function is in fact absolutely vital in the pragmatics of questions. For instance, take the following bit of dialogue from an exceptional dramatic juncture of Anthony Powell's novel *At Lady Molly's*. Everybody is interested in Lady Molly's new guest, but the narrator to his surprise recognizes him as one of his schoolmates.

"I know him".
"Who is he?"
"He is called Kenneth Widmerpool. I was at school with him as a matter of fact. He is in the City."
"I know his name of course. And that he is in the City. But what is he like?"

Powell's narrator also intimates why the second speaker, Mrs. Conyers, does not accept poor Mr. Widmerpool's name and profession as a satisfactory answer to the question "Who is he?". This information is not enough for her to place Widmerpool socially and morally in her world, to find his 'essential properties' for her purposes.

However, there are many legitimate responses to wh-questions which are not answers in the sense just explained. The most important class of such responses are what I shall call *partial answers*.

In order to see what can be said of them, suppose someone asks a who-question with the desideratum (28). Suppose further that he receives putative the answer 'b' ('b' being a singular term). For simplicity, we shall assume that both the questioner and the addressee of the question know that b exists. What will now happen if 'b' nevertheless does not satisfy the usual requirement that the questioner can truly utter (30)? Then several questions arise, among them the following.

(i) How close does 'b' come to being a complete answer? (From this point on I shall distinguish between the kinds of answers so far dealt with, which will be called conclusive answers, and certain other legitimate responses to questions, which will be called partial answer.)

(ii) What can the questioner do in order to make 'b' into a conclusive answer?

We shall assume that 'b' is a *true* (partial) answer, i.e., that it is in fact the case that

(36) $F(b)$.

If the sum total of the questioner's knowledge at the time of the question is expressed by k, now he knows that

(37) $k \wedge F(b)$.

What the answer accomplished was to narrow down the class of possible situations ('possible worlds') admitted by k in that all those are now excluded in which the reference of 'b' does not satisfy $F(x)$. However, this reference will still sometimes vary from one world to another even among the remaining ones. (Otherwise (30) would be true.)

Here we can already see one respect in which we must qualify what has been said. It is not necessary in order for 'b' to be a (complete) answer to the question whose desideratum is (28) that the questioner knows *prior to the answer* who b is. The precise requirement is that he knows it *after* having received the answer 'b'. This makes a difference, for this answer was seen to narrow down class of possible worlds compatible with what the questioner knows. It may happen that 'b' picks out one and the same individual in the narrower class but not in the wider one, i.e., that (30) is true after the answer but not before it. It is in this sense that an answer may have to provide the grounds of its own completeness.[12]

The logical situation may be depicted somewhat as in Figure 1.[13]

I shall assume that there is a class of 'rigid designators' (singular terms picking out the same individual in each world in our language, and that they can be formed by taking an arbitrary singular term, say 'd', and a world, ω and stipulating that $|d|_{\omega}$ is in each world that individual which

the world line of $|b|_{\omega_0}$

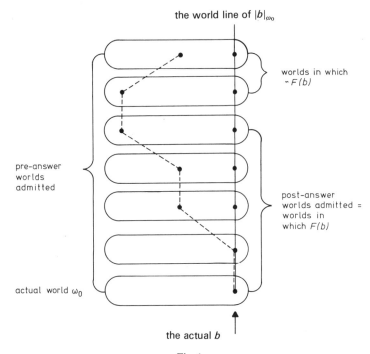

worlds in which
$\sim F(b)$

pre-answer
worlds
admitted

post-answer
worlds admitted =
worlds in
which $F(b)$

actual world ω_0

the actual b

Fig. 1.

in ω is picked out by 'd'. Furthermore, I shall assume that a reasonable probability distribution P has been defined on closed as well as open sentences.[14] Then the closeness of the partial answer 'b' to being a complete one is naturally measured by

(38) $P(b = |b|_{\omega_0} \mid (F(b) \wedge k))$

where ω_0 is the actual world. This might also be called the degree of success of the answer 'b' or its degree of conclusiveness.

However, this is not the only natural way of measuring how satisfactory an answer 'b' is. For even after the answer the questioner will not know (so to speak) which world among the post-answer ones is the actual one. Hence the best he can do is to take the maximum of the probabilities (38) with respect to different possible post-answer worlds. This maximum is

(39) $\max_{i \in I} P(b = |b|_{\omega_i} \mid (F(b) \wedge k))$

where the ω_i $(i \in I)$ are all the different post-answer worlds. Clearly (39) is a kind of measure of *subjective* satisfactoriness of the answer while (38) is a measure of its *objective* satisfactoriness.[15]

This answers our first query (i).

It is interesting to see that this answer turns completely on the second of the two requirements on a satisfactory complete answer: that is provide the questioner with a *true* substitution-instance with respect to a *known* substitution value. Now true is true is true: no one can do better than to provide a true substitution-instance of the matrix. It is the second requirement that admits of better and worse.

What about the second query (ii)?

One's first idea (already used above) is that unless (2) is true the questioner will have to parry the first answer with the second who-question

(40)   And who is b?

This is of course one possible way of trying to narrow down the class of worlds compatible with the questioner's knowledge so that $b = |b|_{\omega_0}$ holds in all of them. However, there is no need to try to carry out the narrowing down in this particular way. Many other questions concerning b may accomplish the same purpose equally well or better. Thus even if a questioner's ultimate purpose is to arrive at a *complete* answer to a wh-question by means of a question-and-answer sequence, it is not necessary that all the questions in the sequence are themselves who-questions or even wh-questions. Small wonder, therefore, that in the Anthony Powell example above the questioner's second query was not, "Who is Widmerpool?" but "What is he like?"

But could this endeavor always succeed, at least in principle? In order to answer this question, we have to go back to the limitations of our discussion so far. We have been assuming (among other things) that we are dealing with questions which do not contain any nonextensional operators. When this is the case, there is no general reason why the questioner could not be supplied so much information that (30) becomes true, i.e., why the set of his 'knowledge-worlds' could not be pared down so much that 'b' picks out one and the same individual in all of them. (We may have to make some assumptions concerning b's existence and the questioner's knowledge thereof, but this is a subordinate problem here.) However, the situation may be quite different when the question itself contains non-extensional concepts.

For instance, take the question

(41)   Who is believed by John to live here?

Its desideratum is

(42)   I know who is believed by John to live here.

This may be taken to have the form

(43) $(Ex)\ K_I B_{John}(x\ \text{lives here})$

where 'B_{John}' is a shorthand for 'John believes that'.

A little more accurately, we might write instead

(44) $(Ex)\ K_I (Ey)\ (x = y \land B_{John}(y\ \text{lives here})).$

However, for our present purposes the difference between (43) and (44) does not matter.

Now intuitively speaking one of the striking features of the question (41) is that it need not possess what I have called a conclusive answer at all. For John might not suspect any particular person; the most accurate answer that can be given to (41) might be something like 'an accountant' or 'a gipsy'. This is parallel with Quine's example where the best answer anyone can give to the question

(45)   What does John want?

is merely 'a sloop'. As Quine puts it, John might simply want relief from slooplessness.

How is this reflected in my approach? Because of the presence of an additional non-extensional operator in (42) (or (43)), the uniqueness condition (19) which yields the criterion of answerhood assumes a new form. For (42) becomes then

(46) $(Ex)\ K_I B_{John}(b = x).$

(Cf. (21) above.) This requires that 'b' pick out the same individual, not in all the speaker's epistemic alternatives, but in John's belief-alternatives (doxastic alternatives) to these alternatives. The semantical situation can be depicted intuitively as follows.[16]

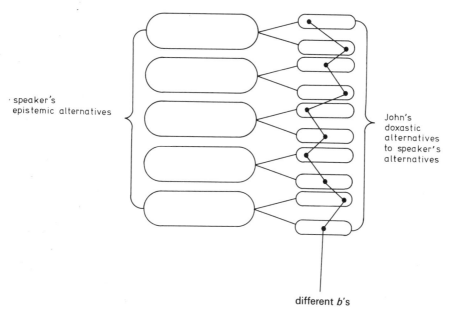

speaker's
epistemic alternatives

John's
doxastic
alternatives
to speaker's
alternatives

different *b*'s

Fig. 2.

What additional information the answerer may supply can do is to narrow down the class of the speaker's epistemic alternatives. (Cf. Figure 1 above.) However, this may not serve to bring about uniqueness of reference among the individuals referred to by '*b*' in John's doxastic alternatives to these speaker's alternatives. Hence there need not be any way of reaching an answer (conclusive direct answer) here by means of giving further information to the questioner. Now *b* cannot be chosen completely freely. It must of course refer to someone living here. But in any one set of John's doxastic alternatives to a given world it need not refer to one and the same individual at all. This may in fact be true of all of John's doxastic alternatives to the speaker's epistemic alternatives. Then there will not be (in the sense that is seen from our discussion) any conclusive answer around that can be given to the speaker's question.

It is also easily seen when this will be the case. However much the class of speaker's epistemic alternatives is narrowed down, there must remain at least the actual world in it (since we are dealing with knowledge). Hence a conclusive answer can be reached through further information in our example if and only if '*b*' picks out one and same individual in all of John's doxastic alternatives to the actual world at the same time as it picks out a person living here. But this amounts to the truth of the sentence

(47) $(Ex) B_{John}(x$ lives here$)$.

Hence there is a conclusive answer available here if and only if John in fact has a belief as to who lives here.

This is not in the least surprising. It is precisely what we would have expected in the first place. However, it is reassuring to see this (sufficient and necessary) condition on the existence of a conclusive answer to emerge inevitably on the basis of the assumptions of our approach.

This condition can obviously be generalized to other questions containing an non-extensional operator. For instance, (45) has a conclusive answer if and only if John wants some particular thing, and not just a thing of some particular sort.

Furthermore, we can likewise easily extend our discussion of partial answers and of the measurement of their relative success to questions with intensional verbs. For instance, it can be seen that the best partial answer to (41) will have the degree of success (satisfactoriness, conclusiveness)

(48) $\max_{i \in I} P(|d_i|$ lives here $| b)$

where the d_i $(i \in I)$ are all the individuals occurring in John's belief-worlds and *b* specifies the sum total of his beliefs.

This shows that we should rather speak of degrees of satisfactoriness or conclusiveness here rather than of degrees of success, for no answer to (41) can have a greater degree of 'success' than (48), which need not be equal to one.

There are further types of responses to questions which deserve serious attention and would perhaps merit the term 'answer'. Among them, there are *demonstrative* or *ostensive* answers to wh-questions. Instead of supplying a noun phrase, the addressee of a question might point and say 'This man' or 'That building'. Such responses to questions have been analysed briefly in an earlier paper of mine.[17] This analysis provides strong evidence for the distinction I have made between individuation by acquaintance and descriptive individuation.

For reasons of space, several further types of answers to questions can only be mentioned here. First of all, the analysis of subordinate questions so far given covers only one half of the subject. For I have come to realize that in principle the semantic structure of any 'knows who' statement, for instance the desideratum (10) of (6), admits of two different representations. In addition to (16), we may have the representation

(49) $(x)((x \text{ lives here}) \supset K_1(x \text{ lives here}))$.

The parallelism between this and (16) can be enhanced by rewriting (16) as

(50) $(Ex)((x \text{ lives here}) \wedge K_1(x \text{ lives here}))$.

For certain purposes, we must here interpret 'K_1' as 'I know whether' rather than 'I know that'. Then the first conjunct in (50) will not even be redundant any longer.

The generalization of this observation to other wh-questions is obvious. They all admit in principle a duality of readings, even though one or the other of these readings is often 'filtered out' by pragmatic (e.g., conversational) factors.

For instance, the (direct) question whose desideratum was said to be (28) will now also have another desideratum, viz.

(51) $(x)(F(x) \supset K_1 F(x))$

while (28) could be paraphrased as

(52) $(Ex)(F(x) \wedge K_1 F(x))$.

These observations are vital for several purposes. One of them is the semantics of multiple questions. Another is the rebuttal of certain criticisms that have been made against my approach.[18] Neither purpose will be pursued here, however, although both of them could.

Suffice it to point out that the new universal-quantifier reading of wh-questions (as we might call it) goes together with certain new types of answers to wh-questions. The answers to the question whose desideratum is (51) might be

(53) $b_1, b_2, \ldots,$ and b_k

where $b_1, b_2, \ldots,$ and b_k are intended to be all the values of the variable 'x'

which make $F(x)$ true. Alternatively, the reply might be

(54)   all the G's.

An argument which parallels our earlier discussion of the criterion of answerhood shows what conditions these responses will have to satisfy in order to qualify as (satisfactory direct) answers. The upshot is that each of the b_i $(i = 1, 2, \ldots, k)$ will have to satisfy

(55) $(Ex)\, K_1(b_i = x)$

assuming that there are no non-extensional operators in '$F(x)$'. Likewise, the reply (54) will have to satisfy the condition

(56) $(x)\, [G(x) \supset (Ey)\, (y = x \wedge (Ez)\, K_1(y = z))]$.

Since the former criterion (55) of answerhood is a generalization of the earlier one, i.e., (30), and since the latter (56) is only a further generalization, we shall not pursue the subject further in this chapter. If we pursued it, we would also be led to acknowledge certain stronger senses of 'knowing who', and likewise certain stronger senses of other (grammatical) constructions with 'knows'.

A further subject relevant to answers to questions is the use of general terms in partial answers. This may take place on either reading, on the old existential reading or on the new universal reading of questions and their desiderata. For instance, someone might respond to (6) by saying 'a gipsy' or 'some students of the local college'. The analysis of such partial answers will not produce any surprises, and will therefore not be undertaken here. They are of course especially natural responses to such questions as contain a non-extensional verb and therefore have no conclusive answers. (Cf. above for a discussion of the precise reasons why.) They can be as good partial answers to such questions as partial singular-term answers.

The challenging theoretical problem concerning the relation of the duality of readings just discovered to the notion of ambiguity will not be taken up here, either, largely because the best material contributing to its solution will come from from the study of multiple questions.

NOTES

[1] 'Questions about Questions', in *Semantics and Philosophy*, Milton K. Munitz and Peter K. Unger (eds.), N.Y.U. Press, New York, 1974, pp. 103–158. (See especially pp. 135–136.)
[2] Lennart Åqvist, *A New Approach to the Logical Theory of Interrogatives*, Filosofiska

föreningen, Uppsala, 1965. See also Lennart Åqvist, 'Revised Foundations for Imperative-Epistemic and Interrogative Logic', *Theoria* **37** (1971) 33–73, for a later reformulation of Åqvist's theory.

[3] The former are sometimes called nexus-questions. The distinction can be made best later in terms of the logical form of what I shall call the desiderata of questions. The desiderata of propositional questions are disjunctions of 'I know that' statements, whereas wh-questions have a reading on which their desiderata have the form '(*Ex*) I know that ---*x*---'.

[4] It is predictable on the basis of our theory that they should be harder to deal with than, say, who-questions. For the range of quantifiers associated on this theory with why- or how-questions, and the status of the entities they range over, is less clear than in the case of who-questions.

[5] This answer has been argued in my earlier discussions of epistemic logic. See *Knowledge and Belief*, Cornell U.P., Ithaca, N.Y., 1962; *Models for Modalities*, D. Reidel, Dordrecht, 1969, and the further references given there.

[6] For the most important amplifications needed here, see the discussion below (last few pages of this essay) of the inevitable duality of readings of wh-questions. Another qualification (likewise mentioned below) is that the quantifier involved in the desideratum may turn on cross-identification by acquaintance rather than on descriptive cross-identification.

[7] This extra premise is not only the eminently natural one on the informal semantical grounds just indicated. Given certain weak assumptions concerning the form of the truth-conditions of quantified sentences, we can prove that any satisfactory 'uniqueness premise' that can restore existential generalization *must* be equivalent with (19). For an argument to this effect, see my 'Existential Presuppositions and Uniqueness Presuppositions' in *Models for Modalities*, D. Reidel, Dordrecht, 1969.

[8] The main problem here is to spell out the idea that the way in which the addressee of a question is supposed to bring about the truth of its desideratum is not through a change in the facts, but merely through a change in the questioner's information (knowledge) about them. Åqvist rightly emphasized this point in his earlier writings, but has unfortunately (and mistakenly) given it up in favour of a misguided effort to assimilate the conditionalization needed here to the dyadic deontic operators of G. H. von Wright and Bengt Hansson.

[9] Other possible (and likely) responses will be mentioned in the sequel.

[10] By this time, the reader has undoubtedly noticed the liberty I am systematically taking with my notation: I am using *placeholders* (syntactical variables) as if they were themselves expressions of the sort they stand for. Otherwise it would not make any sense to put '*b*' into quotes here. This liberty is completely innocuous, however, and merely saves me the trouble of employing Quine's quasi-quotes.

[11] Here I am repeating an observation already made in 'Questions about Questions' (first note above), Section 28.

[12] These grounds of completeness may be provided by the reply '*b*' (or equivalently '*F(b)*'). But they may also be provided by whatever additional information the addressee supplies over and above this part of his reply. One interesting observation here is that the latter kind of information, too, can now be seen to be an integral part of a conclusive answer to a question in that it may serve to narrow down the set of the questioner's epistemic alternatives and thereby contribute to making the uniqueness condition (30) true.

[13] Note that the broken line in Figure 1 is not a 'world line' connecting the manifestations of the *same* individual in different worlds. It merely connects the individuals – usually *not* the same ones – which '*b*' picks out in different epistemic alternatives.

Note also that the post-answer worlds may be restricted further by whatever supplementary information the answerer has provided, over and above telling the questioner that $F(b)$. This does not change the figure in other respects, however.

[14] Better still, I shall assume that a suitable probability-measure has been defined on such sets of possible worlds as can be specified by conditions like the argument of (38).

[15] The questioner does not know which one of the post-answer worlds is the actual one. Hence the best he can do, from his subjective vantage point, is to take the individual which is likeliest to go together with b in these worlds as his best bet and to see how close this individual comes to being known by him to be b. This is just what (39) does.

[16] Again the line that is attached to 'b' in Figure 2 is *not* the world line of one and the same individual. It merely connects the (usually disparate) individuals that 'b' refers to in the different worlds compatible with everything the questioner knows John to believe.

[17] 'Questions about Questions' (see the first note above), pp. 151–155.

[18] The reading (51) is natural only if the operator 'K' has a success grammar in some fairly obvious sense. For instance,

$$(x)\,(F(x) \supset B_{\text{John}}\, F(x))$$

would mean that John has the *right* belief in any actual case x of $F(x)$. But this would mean that in some weak sense he *knows* who $F(x)$. In so far as the duality of the two readings is an integral part of the semantics of subordinate wh-questions, only verbs with a success presupposition can enter into an interrogative wh-construction. And this is precisely what the evidence shows. Sometimes even a verb which normally does not have a success force miraculously acquires one when it occurs in the wh-construction, as shown for instance by the sentence

John guessed who was going to win the race.

For here 'guess' clearly carries a success sense, even though it usually does not.

Although this argument needs a little further tightening, it shows that, far from wrongly predicting the possibility of a wh-construction with non-success verbs like 'believes', as George Lakoff has claimed, my theory (in its present version) aptly explains why such constructions are not possible in English.

CHAPTER 8

GRAMMAR AND LOGIC:
SOME BORDERLINE PROBLEMS

It has been claimed by generative semanticists that "the rules of grammar are identical to the rules relating surface forms to their corresponding logical forms" (Lakoff, 1970, p. 11). Even apart from such sweeping claims, a certain convergence of interest is currently unmistakable among logically minded linguists and linguistically minded logicians.

Much of this convergence of interest has taken place in the area which logicians know as modal logic (in the wide sense of the word in which it includes the logic of propositional attitudes) and in the study of the behavior of modal concepts as expressed in natural language. Thus Lakoff writes: "It seems to me that recent developments in modal logic, together with recent developments in linguistics, make the serious study of natural logic possible" (op. cit., p. 124), 'natural logic' being for Lakoff tantamount to "the empirical study of the nature of human language and human reasoning" (op. cit., p. 126).

It seems to me that in modal logic and its applications we indeed have a promising field for the interaction of logical and linguistic viewpoints. A major reason for this promise is precisely the one Lakoff mentions, viz. recent developments in modal logic, especially the construction of a satisfactory semantical theory of modality (in logicians' sense of semantics, of course). At the same time, it seems to me that much remains to be done and to be changed in this area. Some of logicians' insights have apparently been partly overlooked by linguists. Some of these insights may even serve to disprove certain claims by linguists or at least to bring to light major difficulties in them. In particular, in this direction we can perhaps discover serious flaws in some of the more sweeping theses of such linguists as Lakoff.

In the present chapter, I shall try to illustrate these points by discussing somewhat tentatively a couple of problems arising from those aspects of natural languages which correspond – in some rough sense – to certain phenomena modal logicians have studied.

First, it seems to me that the most germane idea in the last fifteen years' work in modal logic, viz. the use of 'possible worlds' to elucidate the semantics of modality, has not been brought to bear by linguists on their problems in its full strength. This idea is as simple as it is fruitful.[1] According to it, to understand a modal notion is to understand a certain relation – we may call it an alternativeness relation – on a set of possible worlds. In the case of propositional attitudes, this relation is relative to a person. For instance, in the case of necessity, the alternatives to a world W may be thought of as those possible worlds which could be realized instead of W. Then a necessary truth in W means truth *simpliciter* in all these alternatives. Likewise, the alternatives to W involved in an explication of what a person a believes – we may call them doxastic a-alternatives to W – are all the possible worlds compatible with what a believes in W. If so, it follows that it is true in a world W that a believes that p if and only if p is true in all these doxastic a-alternatives to W.

These examples show how we may obtain truth-conditions for modal statements. Putting the main point very briefly and somewhat crudely, by stepping from a world to its alternatives we can reduce the truth-conditions of modal statements to the truth-conditions of nonmodal statements. And in view of the importance of such truth-conditions it is only to be expected that on their basis we can easily explain a good deal of the behavior of modal notions.

The advantages of this approach are nowhere more clearly in evidence than in dealing with questions of reference. If all nonredundant use of modal notions entails the consideration, however tacit, of several possible worlds, then for each singular term – linguists might prefer speaking of certain kinds of nouns and noun phrases here – we *ipso facto* have to consider its several references in these different worlds. This shows at once that there is nothing strange in the failure of such so-called laws of logic as the substitutivity of identity in modal contexts. Clearly two singular terms 'a', 'b' which in the actual world pick out the same individual and hence make the identity '$a=b$' true *de facto* may fail to do so in alternative worlds, and hence fail to admit of interchange *salva veritate* in a context containing modal terms.

Likewise, the law known as existential generalization can only be expected to fail, for a singular term 'a' may very well make a statement – say '$F(a)$' – true and yet fail to allow any foothold for maintaining that '$(Ex) F(x)$' is true, i.e., that '$F(x)$' is true of *some definite individual x*.

This may happen when '*a*' picks out different individuals in the different possible worlds which we are considering in '*F*(*a*)', assuming that it contains nonredundant modal notions.

All this is old hat to most logicians and to some linguists. It could all be given an explicit logico-semantical formulation, which nevertheless would neither add much to nor detract much from the central theoretical ideas just adumbrated.

An informal remark might illustrate further the naturalness of this approach. Some of those linguists who have in fact seen the advantages of the idea of considering more than one 'possible world' have occasionally tried to get away with a simpler scheme. Instead of considering, say, all the possible worlds compatible with what *a* believes, they have tried to consider *a*'s 'belief world', that is, the world as *a* believes it to be. The only thing wrong here is that unless *a* is supremely opinionated, his beliefs do not specify completely any particular world, but rather a disjunction (as it were – usually it would have to be infinite) of descriptions of several such worlds. To specify 'the world as it is believed by *a* to be' is not to describe any one possible world, but rather a set of possible worlds. Of course these are precisely the doxastic *a*-alternatives to the actual world. Hence to specify them *is* to specify what *a* (actually) believes.

Now assuming that our possible-worlds semantics is something like the true story of the 'logical form' of our modal statements, some interesting conclusions are immediately suggested by it.

For instance, consider the role of what has been called by grammarians coreferentiality. It is exemplified by the problem of the admissibility of a derivation of

(1)   John lost *a black pen* yesterday and Bill found *it* today

from

(2)   John lost *a black pen* yesterday and Bill found *a black pen* today,

possibly by way of

(3)   John lost *a black pen* yesterday and Bill found *the black pen* today.

In so far as the derivation in question is supposed to preserve meaning,

(3) can be obtained from (1) only on the assumption that the two noun phrases "a black pen" in (1) are coreferential. (I am stealing these examples, and others, from Partee, 1970.) Consideration of more complicated examples already led Postal (1968) to realize that the reference (or coreference) in question cannot be one that obtains in the actual world. However, it is not very easy to tell precisely what else it could be. For instance, it is sometimes said that what counts here is some kind of identity relative to the "speaker's mental picture of the world". Apart from the vagueness of such characterizations, this particular formulation is demonstrably mistaken, for what matters in modal contexts is typically the 'mental picture' – whatever it may look like – not of the speaker, but of the person whose propositional attitudes are being discussed. A simple case in point is offered by

(4)   John lost a black pen yesterday and Bill believes that he has found it today.

One reason why (4) cannot be dealt with in terms of coreferentiality in the actual world or in the kind of world the speaker is assuming is that the speaker may know that Bill is mistaken in his belief and has not found John's pen – perhaps he has not found anything at all.

Yet all these problems are predictable – and solvable – as soon as it is acknowledged that in modal contexts more than one possible world is inevitably at issue. For then we cannot even speak meaningfully of co-referentiality except relative to the specification of some particular possible world or class of possible worlds. For instance, what makes the difference in (4) is the identity (i.e., the coreferentiality of the corresponding terms) of the black pen John lost yesterday with the one Bill has found today in Bill's doxastic alternatives to the world (4) is dealing with. By systematically using the possible-worlds idea, the theory of coreferentiality can be freed from the looseness of 'mental pictures' and other similar largely metaphorical paraphernalia.

Likewise, we can at once appreciate a fact which *prima facie* can be fitted into the coreferentiality framework only by mild violence, viz. the fact that "coreferentiality may hold independently of referentiality". By this paradoxical-sounding statement I mean such things as, e.g., the fact that we can say

(5)   John wants to catch *a fish* and eat *it* for supper

even when John is not assumed to be angling for any particular piece of seafood. (According to the coreferentiality theory, the occurrence of "it" in (5) presupposes coreference.) *Prima facie*, all talk of coreference is here vacuous, for "a fish" in (5) does not (on the so-called nonreferential interpretation of (5)) refer to any particular submarine beast rather than another, and hence apparently cannot be said to refer to the same (or a different) fish as any other term. Yet the sense in which the coreferentiality idea applies here is transparently clear on the possible-worlds approach: in each possible world compatible with John's wants he catches a fish and eats *that fish* for supper. The fact that in different possible worlds different specimens of fish undergo this fate does not spoil this coreference in each world, considered alone.

There remains the problem, however, of formulating the precise rules for this kind of coreferentiality in English. Part of the difficulty here is due to the fact that the account just given presupposes, logically speaking, that in such pairs of sentences as

(5a)   John was trying to catch a fish. He wanted to eat it for supper.

"it" is within the scope of the operator tacitly introduced by "was trying." This does not seem to be the case in any grammatically natural sense of 'scope'. Here it is very hard to see the connection between the 'logical form' and the 'grammatical form' of the sentences in question.

This difficulty seems to be due to the way in which quantifying expressions operate in ordinary language. What goes on there is *prima facie* quite unlike ordinary quantification theory, where the scopes of the several quantifiers are the main determinants of logical structure. What happens is, rather, that ordinary language uses – for reasons that are likely to be quite deep – for the purposes of quantification scopeless ('free') terms not completely unlike Hilbert's ε-terms (Hilbert and Bernays, 1934, 1939).[3] What matters here is not the respective scopes of these terms, for they are typically maximal (comprising as much discourse as belongs to one and the same occasion), but rather the order in which they are thought of as being introduced. There seems to be a fair amount of data available concerning the grammatical indicators of this order. However, the study of 'natural logic' seems to have been hampered here by the absence of an appropriate logical framework. Linguists and linguistically oriented logicians should here pay much more attention to such unconventional reformulations of quantification theory as Hilbert's ε-theory or the 'game-theoretical semantics' I have developed elsewhere.

One of the indicators sometimes used in ordinary language for the same purpose as logicians' brackets is simply the left-to-right order of complex terms in a given sentence. Since this is affected by the passive transformation, this transformation affects in an important way the meaning of the sentence in question. Chomsky's example (1965, p. 224) "every one in this room knows at least two languages" vs. "two languages are known by every one in this room" illustrates this point. I do not see any evidence for Chomsky's claim that an ambiguity between these is latent in the former (or in its 'deep structure'). Hence we have here one more counter-example to the alleged meaning preservation of transformations.

Here we are already approaching a group of problems which has recently exercised both philosophical logicians and linguists, viz. the ambiguity between what have been called by Donnellan (1966) the referential and the attributive uses of certain singular terms, especially definite descriptions. It is exemplified by the ambiguity of

(6)   John wants to marry a girl who is both pretty and rich.

Here it may be that beauty and wealth are among John's *desiderata* for a wife in general, or it may be that John is keen on marrying some particular girl who happens to have these desirable qualities. The former is the attributive reading of (6), the latter the referential reading. For the historically minded, it may be pointed out that the distinction between the two readings belongs to the older stock of a logician's trade. In the Middle Ages, the referential reading would have been said to yield a statement *de re*, the attributive a statement *de dicto*.

The possible-worlds semantics at once shows what the distinction amounts to under any name. Consider a statement which contains a singular term – say 'b' – and also some modal notions. These notions imply that we are in effect considering several possible worlds over and above the actual one. Now such a statement can often be understood in two different ways. It may be taken to be about the individuals – typically different ones – which the term 'b' picks out from the several possible worlds we are considering. This yields the *de dicto* reading. However, it can also be taken to be about that particular individual – considered of course as a citizen of several possible worlds – whom the term 'b' picks out in the actual one. This results in the *de re* reading. For instance,

(7)   John believes that the richest man in town is a Republican

may mean that in each possible world compatible with John's beliefs the description 'the richest man in town' picks out a Republican. It may also mean that John has a belief about a particular person, who as a matter of fact is the richest man in town, viz. the belief that he is Republican.

Letting bound variables range over (well-defined) individuals (in the logical sense of the word), as Quine and others have persuasively argued that we had better do, we may symbolize the two statements as follows:

(8) $F(a)$ (*de dicto*)

(9) $(Ex) (x = a \ \& \ F(x))$ or alternatively
          $(x) (x = a \supset F(x))$ (*de re*).

Some philosophers of language, e.g., Quine (1956, 1960), have described the ambiguity as a contrast between two interpretations of the verb in question, an opaque and a transparent one. The former is supposed to yield the attributive and the latter the referential reading. Our analysis of the situation shows that these cannot be considered two unanalyzable senses of the verbs in question. In fact, in (9) the so-called transparent (referential) sense is analyzed in terms of the opaque (attributive) one (plus quantifiers). As to the assumption of the ambiguity of the verb in question, we just do not need that hypothesis. Later it will be seen that speaking of two senses of the verb in question is misleading for another reason, too.

Likewise, the contrast between the two apparently irreducible uses of definite descriptions postulated by Donnellan seems to be completely unnecessary, for an analysis can be given of the two uses which does not presuppose any irreducible ambiguities or irreducible conflicts between different ways of using the expressions in question.

This account of the ambiguity at once suggests several conclusions which do not all agree with what the linguists have said of the subject.

First, the *de dicto-de re* ambiguity (if it may be so called) is unlike many other types of ambiguity in that the two senses coalesce in the presence of simple kinds of further information. What this information is, is shown by our semantics. The difference between a statement about the several references of a term '*b*' in certain possible worlds and a statement about the individual actually referred to by this term '*b*' disappears as soon as '*b*' picks out one and the same reference in all these worlds. Depending on what the worlds are, this may amount to a simple factual assumption concerning the people in question. For instance, the two readings of (7) collapse if the phrase "the richest man in town" picks out one and the same man in all of John's doxastic alternatives to the actual world. But this, obviously, means nothing but John's having a belief as to who the richest man in town is. And of course it is obvious that if John has such an opinion, the difference between the two interpretations of (7) indeed does not matter.

This power of simple factual assumptions (which of course usually cannot be made) to dissolve the *de dicto-de re* ambiguity by making the two senses coincide seems to me an interesting phenomenon which distinguishes this type of ambiguity from many others. (No factual assumption can apparently eliminate, say, the ambiguity of 'flying planes can be dangerous' without ruling out one of its two senses.) It is beautifully accounted for, it seems to me, by the possible-worlds semantics.

Secondly, our semantical theory shows that the *de dicto-de re* ambiguity is present only in a context where we have to consider several possible worlds (including the actual one). Typically, but perhaps not quite exclusively, these are contexts involving (nonredundant) modal notions in our wide sense of the word.

Now it has been claimed that, on the contrary, the *de dicto-de re* contrast can be present also in nonmodal contexts. Since a couple of general theoretical points are involved in this question, I shall comment briefly on it. Partee (1970) claims that such sentences as the following:

(10)   John married a girl his parents didn't approve of.

(11)   Bill caught a snipe.

(12)   The man who murdered Smith is insane.

exhibit the same ambiguity as (6) or (7).

For instance, (12) is said to be ambiguous because "either the speaker is asserting of a particular individual, referred to by the definite noun phrase, that that individual is insane; or the speaker is asserting that whoever it is that murdered Smith is insane – i.e., the definite noun phrase gives a characterization of an individual not necessarily otherwise known, and the sentence asserts that whatever individual is so characterized is insane."

Several comments are in order here. First, even if the quoted explanation were the whole story, the conceptual situation would be different from the *de dicto-de re* contrast which arises in modal contexts. For we already saw that what matters there is not what the speaker asserts, but what the person thinks whose propositional attitudes are being discussed. For instance, what matters in (6) is the individualization (or lack thereof) of John's wants, not of the relative specificity of the speaker's thoughts. This difference already creates an asymmetry between (6)–(7) and (10)–(12).

Second, the real question is not what the speaker happens to think when he utters something, but whether the semantics of the uttered sentence forces him – and his audience – to make certain distinctions whenever he spells out his meaning explicitly.

A speaker who utters (6) may be indifferent to whether John has a particular girl in mind or not. However, when the meaning of what he says is made explicit, a decision is unavoidable. The question is whether the same holds of (10)–(12).

The objective counterpart to this decision in our possible-worlds semantics is the question whether an individual (the girl John wants to marry) or a possible world (one compatible with everything John wants) is chosen first. (In other words, the question is whether 'a' or 'wants' has the wider scope in (6).) Since there are no modal terms in (10)–(12), whatever ambiguity they exhibit cannot come about in the same way as in (6), that is, cannot be the result of an interaction of a model operator with a quantifier.

The question whether (10)–(12) exhibit an ambiguity is thus not a question about the semantics of modal terms. It is rather a question concerning such action words as 'marries', 'catches', 'murders', etc. What is at issue is whether the semantics of those verbs involves an operator which is like modal operators in that it can commute with a quantifier-like operator such as 'a' or 'the'. Since I am in this chapter dealing with modal concepts, not with action theory, I shall not discuss this problem here, except for emphasizing its independence of the semantics of modality.[4]

It may nevertheless be in order to point out one likely but fallacious source of the idea that (10)–(12) exhibit the same ambiguity as (6)–(7). In the quotation I have been criticizing, the writer (Barbara Hall Partee) moves from the question as to what *the speaker* asserts to the question as to what *the sentence* asserts. This seems to me to signal a confusion between such sentences as (10)–(11) and the corresponding sentences in which the assertoric element is made a part of the statement:

(13)   I assert that John married a girl
         his parents did not approve of.

(14)   I assert that John caught a snipe.

Since 'asserts' is for our present purposes a *bona fide* modal term, the usual modal *de dicto-de re* contrast applies to (13)–(14) in the way I have examined. Certain linguists' belief in the applicability of the same contrast to (10)–(11) seems to me to be partly due to a confusion of the logic and semantics of (10)–(11) with that of (13)–(14).[5]

The illicit presupposition on which this fallacy is based is spelled out neatly by Mrs. Partee when she suggests as a reason for the ambiguity of such sentences as (10)–(12) the (undoubtedly true) observation that when they are imbedded in an opaque context, they exhibit the referential-attributive ambiguity. Hence, the argument seems to go, they cannot on their own be partial to one reading (presumably to the referential one). This mistake involved here is again demonstrated by our possible-worlds semantics. It shows that the possible univocity of such nonmodal sentences as (10)–(12) is not due to their having the referential rather than the attributive reading. Rather, the very distinction referential vs. attributive does not apply to nonmodal contexts, barring a further analysis of the main verbs in (10)–(12). Hence Mrs. Partee's argument mistakenly presupposes that her opponents are assuming the referential reading of nonmodal sentences, whereas the true moot point is whether the distinction applies to such sentences in the first place.

Another point which the possible-worlds semantics serves to bring out is that the referential-attributive contrast has much less to do than people commonly assume with the relative emphasis on the naming of a particular object in contrast to describing it. Rather, the importance of the descriptive element in the *de dicto* interpretation is secondary, derived from a deeper feature of the situation. According to the *de dicto* interpretation, the statement in question deals with the several individuals which a noun or noun phrase picks out in several different possible worlds. Since they are not (manifestations of) the *same* individual, we often – but not always – have to rely on their descriptive characteristics to pick them out from among the members of the world in question. They are not automatically picked out by the general criteria we have for identity of one and the same individual in different worlds.

Although the descriptive content of a noun phrase is therefore often quite important for its *de dicto* uses, it is not uniformly so. As soon as it can be assumed for any reason whatsoever that a singular term picks out a definite individual from each of the worlds we are considering, however different these individuals may be, we have an opening for the attributive reading, even though the singular term in question has little descriptive content. It has been claimed (Partee, 1970b) that "names are almost always used referentially, since they have virtually no descriptive content". Questions of frequency aside, there nevertheless is no difficulty whatsoever in finding examples of the attributive use of names. For instance, consider the following:

(15)   Utterson believes that the murder was committed by
         Mr. Hyde, although he does not know who Mr. Hyde is.

Here a *de dicto* reading is the only natural one. Since Utterson is assumed not to know who Mr. Hyde is, his belief can scarcely be said to be about any particular person. (In different worlds compatible with his knowledge and presumably even with his beliefs, Mr. Hyde will be a different person.)

Notice, moreover, that (15) does not amount to saying that Utterson has a belief about whoever *is called* Mr. Hyde, for he is not at all interested, say, in Hyde's namesake in Manchester with a perfect alibi. Hence, we cannot in this way give "Mr. Hyde" in (15) a normal descriptive content.

By the same token, a wide class of sentences in terms of names admit of a *de dicto* reading, assuming that they contain words for knowledge, belief, memory, wishing, hoping, wanting, etc.

Such observations strongly suggest, incidentally, that much of the terminology in this area is misleading. This is the case with the terms 'referential' and 'attributive' as well as (though to a lesser degree) '*de re*' and '*de dicto*'.

Mistaken emphasis on the descriptive element in the attributive (*de dicto*) use of nouns and noun phrases has apparently led to a misclassification of some interesting examples. For instance, we read that the following sentence "seems unambiguously non-referential":

(16)   Since I heard that from a doctor, I'm inclined to take it seriously.

Insofar as the *de dicto-de re* distinction is here applicable at all, the presumption seems to me to be that a *de re* (referential) reading is being presupposed here rather than the *de dicto* (nonreferential) one. For whoever utters (16) is surely likely to have in mind some definite person from whom he or she heard whatever he or she is there said to have heard. In other words, (16) is naturally taken to be equivalent to something like

(17)   Since the person from whom I heard that is a doctor,
        I am inclined to take it seriously.

which shows that we are likely to be dealing with a *de re* reading here.

A point which I can raise but not answer here concerns a possible moral of the *de dicto-de re* ambiguity for such claims as Lakoff's concerning the near-identity of grammar and 'natural logic'. This claim is trivial as long as it only asserts the identity of *some* grammatical and logical phenomena. Moreover, there are surely features of grammar (in any reasonable sense of the word) which have little logical interest. Hence Lakoff's thesis has a bit only if it is taken to claim that all or at the very least all really interesting features of the logical behavior of natural language can be turned into "rules relating surface forms to their corresponding logical forms".

Another restraint that is needed to make Lakoff's claim relevant is the following. The thesis must presuppose some idea what the rules of grammar are independently of the requirement that they match (or can be interpreted as) rules of logic. For if there is no such independent criterion, Lakoff's thesis can be satisfied trivially, simply by taking some suitable formulation (if any) of the relevant aspects of logic and postulating grammatical relations and rules to match these. The real question, it seems to me, is not whether this is possible, but whether such an attempt to satisfy Lakoff's thesis is likely to produce results that have some independent grammatical significance.

My modest proposal here is to use the *de dicto-de re* ambiguity as a test for such theses as Lakoff's. If they are correct, this ambiguity must be possible to account for in the usual way in grammatical terms. If my diagnosis of the situation is correct, we have here a widespread and clear-cut phenomenon whose explanation in grammatical terms would be of considerable interest. Because from a logical point of view we can see the unity of the different manifestations of the ambiguity, according to Lakoff's thesis we presumably ought to be able to give to it a unified grammatical treatment.

I have no proof that such a treatment is impossible. As far as I can see – and here I may very well be mistaken – there nevertheless are some definite difficulties confronting any attempt to account for the ambiguity in a satisfactory manner in ordinary grammatical terms. In an old-fashioned terminology, we might say that here linguistic form perhaps does not match logical form.

As I said, I have no strict impossibility proof here, and I do not believe that such a proof is possible until some explicit restraints are imposed on the grammar which is supposed to account for the ambiguity. However, some indications of the nature of the problem can be given. Part of the aim would have to be to derive all sentences of the form

(18)   *a* knows (believes, remembers, hopes, wishes, intends, etc.) that *p*

where nouns or noun phrases occur in *p* in more than one way. One way is presumably some more or less straightforward imbedding of *p* in the 'knows that' context. However, it is far from clear what the other derivation might look like. Moreover, it does not suffice to provide just one alternative derivation, for when several nouns or noun phrases occur in *p*, we often face (*ceteris paribus*) a choice, for each of them, whether to interpret it *de dicto* or *de re*. (Thus *n* nouns or noun phrases occurring in *p* may create a 2^n-fold ambiguity.)

Incidentally, this suggests that it is misleading to attribute (as Quine among others has done) the ambiguity in question to the verb which serves to express the propositional attitude in question, unless we are prepared to countenance such strange consequences as, e.g., that the number of readings of the verb in question depends on the number of nouns and noun phrases in the imbedded clause. Hence Quine's analysis of the situation appears very suspect.

A fairly obvious candidate for the role of an intermediate stage of the desired derivation would be something of the form

(19) a knows (believes, etc.) of b that – he –.

or of one of the similar parallel or more complicated forms. It is in fact true that (19) is prejudiced in favor of the *de re* interpretation much more firmly than the corresponding construction

(20) a knows (believes, etc.) that – b –.

Hence the choice of (19) rather than (20) may very well serve to signal that the speaker is opting for the *de re* interpretation.

However, it is not clear whether (19) itself is ambiguous in the same way as (20). An example of the attributive reading of a sentence of the form (19) is perhaps offered by the following:

(21)   It is believed of Jack the Ripper that he killed more than thirty women.

thought of as being uttered in a context where complete ignorance of – and complete doxastic disinterest in – the identity of Jack the Ripper is being presupposed. (Would anyone find (21) at all strange if uttered in such circumstances? I doubt it very much.) If so, the alleged possibility of deriving (20) from (19) scarcely serves to explain why (20) is ambiguous.

The fact, registered above, that the two senses involved in a *de dicto-de re* ambiguity will coalesce as soon as a simple factual assumption is satisfied also seems to militate against any simple-minded attempt to account for it in terms of two different derivations of the ambiguous sentence. It is hard to see how this latter type of duality can be made to disappear by changing certain facts about the world.

The problem is thus to account in grammatical terms for the two features which distinguish the *de dicto-de re* ambiguity from typical structural ambiguities. These features are (i) the collapse of the different senses into one wherever certain simple kinds of factual information are present and (ii) the dependence of the number of senses on the number of singular terms (nouns and noun phrases) in the sentence in question or in some part of it.

It is perfectly possible to account for these interesting phenomena in a sufficiently sophisticated logical and/or grammatical theory. For instance, there is no difficulty in explaining (ii) in Montague's formal grammars. However, in such cases the question of independent grammatical interest of the account can be raised.

Moreover, certain widely accepted grammatical theories do not seem to admit of an adequate account of (i)–(ii). For instance, if ambiguities of this kind are to be explained by reference to the pretransformational (i.e., deep structure) base component and if this base component is to be obtained in the simple way assumed, e.g., by Chomsky (1965, pp. 67–68, 120–123, 128), I cannot see any hope for explaining (ii) by means of alternative ways of obtaining the base component. Furthermore, it is even unclear what an account of (i) would look like in terms of typical contemporary grammatical theories.

What is likely to even be more important here is that there does not seem to be any independent grammatical reason for postulating a derivation of (20) from (19). Yet we saw that such reasons are needed to prevent Lakoff's thesis from degenerating into a triviality. I cannot help finding it very unnatural to think of (20) as being derived by so circuitous a route as (19). Of course, this may be merely due to my ignorance of grammatical theory. But even if this should turn out to be the case, the onus of proof is very much on generative semanticists. If they cannot supply one, or some alternative account of the situation, we have here a counterexample to their claims.

A final word of warning is perhaps needed here concerning the further complications into which the possible-worlds semantics leads us. Or perhaps – hopefully – we rather ought to speak of the complexities it helps to unravel. I have spoken rather casually of this or that individual's making an appearance in the different possible worlds we are considering. In reality, the criteria by means of which we actually do this – that is, cross-identity or tell of members of different possible worlds whether these are the same or different – are not unproblematic, at least not for philosophical purposes. Although our possible-worlds semantics enables us to pose some very interesting questions concerning them, it is not even completely clear what structural properties the 'world lines' have that connect the different 'manifestations' or 'roles' of, or 'counterparts' to, one and the same individual in several possible worlds with each other. One such structural question is of particular concern to the subject matter of this chapter. This is the question whether a 'world line' may split when we move from a world to its alternatives. If this question is answered affirmatively, we can no longer speak light-heartedly of *the* individual (considered as a member of a number of alternative worlds in several possible worlds which corresponds to (is identical with) a given member of the actual world. For if splitting is admissible, there may be in some of the alternative worlds several 'manifestations of' or 'counter-parts to' this individual. What that would mean is that the whole *de dicto-de re* contrast becomes messier. Or, more accurately speaking, the *de re* reading becomes considerably less sharp.

Can we rule out the splitting of world lines (of the kind just men-tioned)? This question is of considerable importance to many philos-ophers of logic and of language, but unfortunately there is nothing re-motely like a consensus concerning the answer. Rather plausible argu-ments both *pro* and *con* can in fact be found in the literature.

Here I cannot survey these arguments. It may nevertheless be worth-while to recall the fact – which I have pointed out elsewhere (Hintikka, 1969, pp. 112–147) – that a prohibition against splitting is essentially tantamount to the most plausible version of the famous principle of the substitutivity of identity which Quine and others have made the corner-stone of their interpretation of the logic of modal notions. If the prohibi-tion against splitting cannot be upheld, Quine is in serious trouble even on a relatively charitable interpretation of his views on modality and reference. (For an elaboration of this point, see Chapter 6 below.)

In contrast, allowing world lines to split would not tell in the least against the possible-world semantics as such. It would merely show that some of the phenomena that can be studied by its means exhibit com-plications that at first do not meet the eye.

The only constructive suggestion I want to offer here is that what looks like splitting is often an indication of something quite different. It often indicates that more than one overall principle of cross-identification is at work.

Elsewhere (Hintikka, 1969, pp. 112–147; 1972; see also Chapters 3 and 4 above), I have studied a few such contrasts between different methods of cross-identification in some detail. I do not think that I exaggerate if I say that they turn out to have a tremendous philosophical interest. The reason why I mention them here is that recognizing the frequent presence of different principles of cross-identification is highly relevant to the theory of reference as it has been employed by linguists, especially to some of the puzzle examples that have been bandied around in the literature. Suffice it here to point out that the logic of McCawley's well-known example becomes crystal clear from this point of view. I mean of course the sentence

(22) I dreamt that I was Brigitte Bardot and that I kissed me.

Here it is abundantly clear that in the speaker's dream-worlds (worlds compatible with what he dreams) there were two counterparts of him. It is also clear that they are counterparts in a different sense. What precisely the two respective senses are is not specified by the example and may be difficult to spell out in detail. It is fairly clear, nonetheless, that the distinction participant-observer, employed by some analysts, does not give us much mileage here, although it perhaps points to the right direction. However, the outlines of the two cross-identification principles used in the example are clear enough. One of the speaker's counterparts is the person whose experiences he has in the dream-world, the other is the one who is like him by some less exciting criteria, maybe by such criteria as appearance and social position.

Such a dream example is perhaps not entirely representative of the overall situation, however. I have argued elsewhere that in our actual conceptual practice we operate with two main types of cross-identification methods. They have interesting linguistic manifestations in that the distinction between them is reflected in many natural languages by the contrast between wh-constructions (subordinate questions with 'knows', 'remembers', 'perceives', etc. as the main verb) and the direct-object construction (knowing someone, remembering something, etc.).

Within each type of method there remains a fair amount of smaller-scale variation. (The variability of our criteria of knowing who is nicely illustrated by the familiar reference-book title 'Who is Who'.) Many of the details of this finer variation and much of the interaction between the two main types of methods remain to be investigated.

It may be the case, as Lakoff has urged, that for this purpose the usual simple-minded method of referential indices, first proposed by Chomsky, is insufficient, though no hard proof to this effect has been given. (Lakoff's analysis seems to me misleading in any case in that he speaks of a person's splitting into several in another possible worlds. The presence of two different methods of cross-identification is nevertheless a phenomenon which ought to be sharply distinguished from the splitting of individuals under one and the same method.) However, they do not reflect in the least on the possible-worlds semantics, which on the contrary gives us excellent methods of analyzing the situation. And since the possible-worlds semantics which I have informally sketched here can easily be turned into an explicit treatment of this part of logic by means of an explicit axiomatization, I cannot agree with Lakoff's claim that "symbolic logic… is of no help here" (1968, p. 5), though Lakoff may provide a way out for himself by speaking of "symbolic logic of the traditional sort". Traditional or not, a satisfactory logical account here does not fall with the use of referential indices.

Since I have been criticizing many of the specific things logically minded linguists have recently said, let me end by reiterating that I find their direction of interest not only worthwhile but also distinctly promising. The corrections I have tried to offer to their claims are calculated to illustrate this promise rather than to detract from it. I am especially deeply indebted to the authors whose detailed remarks I undoubtedly appear to be criticizing most, viz. to George Lakoff and Barbara Hall Partee.

NOTES

[1] Probably the best brief account of this approach is still to be found in the original papers by Saul Kripke (1963a, 1963b, 1965). Cf. also my *Models for Modalities* (1969), Kanger (1957), Kaplan (1969) and the writings of Montague, collected in Montague (1974).

[2] This account is in need of a major qualification, however, for as it stands it implies that we all believe all the logical consequences of what we believe, that having inconsistent beliefs entails believing everything, plus all the awkward parallel conclusions for other propositional attitudes. The problem arising here is discussed by Barbara Hall Partee in Partee (1973). I have outlined a solution to the problem in other papers, especially Hintikka (1970a, 1970b). The former is reprinted as Chapter 9 below.

[3] I recall that Paul Ziff used to make the same – or at least closely related – point in discussion already some twelve years ago.

[4] Notice that there is no ambiguity in the truth-conditions of (10)–(12). For instance, (10) is

true if and only if John's bride actually was not approved of by his parents, quite independently of the specificity of the speaker's knowledge of who that girl is.

Notice also the interesting difference between what is claimed by Partee about (10) and what in fact happens in (6). Here, it is suggested, it makes a difference whether *the speaker* has in mind a particular girl or not. This is entirely different from *John's* having a specific girl in mind in the state of affairs described by (6). The ambiguity that is claimed to reside in (10) is therefore not the same one that surfaces in (6).

[5] What has probably misled many people here is the important fact that surprisingly often modal notions are tacitly being considered in apparently nonmodal contexts. This fact would deserve further attention, and it partly excuses the kind of mistake I have been criticizing.

REFERENCES

Chomsky, N., *Aspects of the Theory of Syntax*, M.I.T. Press, Cambridge, Mass., 1965.

Donnellan, K., 'Reference and Definite Descriptions', *Philosophical Review* **75** (1966) 281–304.

Hilbert, D. and Bernays, P., *Grundlagen der Mathematik*, Vols. 1–2, Springer, Berlin, 1934, 1939.

Hintikka, K. J. J., *Models for Modalities: Selected Essays*, D. Reidel Publishing Co., Dordrecht, 1969.

Hintikka, K. J. J., 'Knowledge, Belief, and Logical Consequence', *Ajatus* **32** (1970a) 32–47.

Hintikka, K. J. J., 'Surface Information and Depth Information', in K. J. J. Hintikka and P. Suppes (eds.), *Information and Inference*, D. Reidel Publishing Co., Dordrecht, 1970b.

Hintikka, K. J. J., 'Knowledge by Acquaintance – Individuation by Acquaintance', in *Bertrand Russell, A Collection of Critical Essays*, D. Pears (ed.), Doubleday and Co., Garden City, N.Y., 1972, pp. 52–79 *(Modern Studies of Philosophy)*.

Kanger, S., *Provability in Logic*, Stockholm Studies in Philosophy, Vol. 1, Stockholm 1957.

Kaplan, D., 'Quantifying In', in *Words and Objections: Essays on the Work of W. V. Quine*, D. Davidson and K. J. J. Hintikka (eds.), D. Reidel Publishing Co., Dordrecht, 1969. Reprinted from *Synthese* **19** (1968) 178–214.

Kripke, S. A., 'Semantical Considerations on Modal Logic', *Acta Philosophica Fennica* **16** (1963a) 83–94.

Kripke, S. A., 'Semantical Analysis of Modal Logic: I, Normal Modal Propositional Calculi', *Zeitschrift für Mathematische Logik und Grundlagen der Mathematik* **9** (1963b) 67–96.

Kripke, S. A., 'Semantical Analysis of Modal Logic: II, Non-Normal Modal Propositional Calculi', in *The Theory of Models*, J. W. Addison, L. Henkin and A. Tarski (eds.), North-Holland, Amsterdam, 1965.

Lakoff, G., *Linguistics and Natural Logic*, Studies in Generative Semantics, Vol. 1., Ann Arbor, Mich., 1970. (Also appeared in a modified form in *Synthese* **22** (1970–71) 151–271. References in the text pertain to the earlier version whose relevant theoretical theses have been somewhat modified and weakened in the newer version.)

Partee, B. H., 'Opacity, Coreference, and Pronouns', *Synthese* **21** (1970) 359–85.

Partee, B. H., 'The Semantics of Belief-Sentences', in *Approaches to Natural Language*, K. J. J. Hintikka, J. M. E. Moravcsik and P. Suppes (eds.), D. Reidel Publishing Co., Dordrecht, 1973, pp. 301–36.

Postal, P. M., 'Cross-Over Phenomena', in *Specification and Utilization of Transformational Grammar*, Yorktown Heights, N.Y., 1968.

Quine, W. V., 'Quantifiers and Propositional Attitudes', *Journal of Philosophy* **53** (1956) 177–87; reprinted in V. W. Quine, *The Ways of Paradox and Other Essays*, Random House, New York, 1966.

Quine, W. V., *Word and Object*, M.I.T. Press, Cambridge, Mass., 1960.

Thomason, R. (ed.), *Formal Philosophy, Selected Papers of Richard Montague*, Yale University Press, New Haven and London, 1974.

CHAPTER 9

KNOWLEDGE, BELIEF, AND
LOGICAL CONSEQUENCE

One of the most lively debated questions in the logical analysis of the notions of knowledge and belief today might be called the problem of *conservation laws* for these notions.[1] The term is apt because one of the more or less equivalent formulations of the problem is to ask whether knowledge and belief (in some suitably strong and possibly idealized sense) are invariant with respect to logical equivalence. This invariance may in turn be taken to amount to the validity of the rules of inference

$$(1) \qquad \frac{p \equiv q}{K_a p \equiv K_a q} \qquad\qquad \frac{p \equiv q}{B_a p \equiv B_a q}$$

where '$K_a p$' is to be read 'a knows that p' and '$B_a p$' 'a believes that p'.

Perhaps a more usual formulation pertains to the corresponding implicational rules of inference

$$(2) \qquad \frac{p \supset q}{K_a p \supset K_a q} \qquad\qquad \frac{p \supset q}{B_a p \supset B_a q}$$

Their import may be expressed, somewhat roughly, by saying that whenever someone knows (or believes) anything, he knows (or believes) all its logical consequences.

It is obvious that the rules of inference (2) imply (1). The converse is true if we assume in addition the relatively unproblematic distributive principles

$$(3) \qquad \vdash K_a(p \wedge q) \supset K_a q$$
$$\vdash B_a(p \wedge q) \supset B_a q$$

For if $\vdash p \supset q$, then $\vdash p \equiv (p \wedge q)$, hence by (1) $\vdash K_a p \equiv K_a(p \wedge q)$, and hence by (3) $\vdash K_a p \supset K_a q$. For belief, the argument is analogous.

One consequence of the assumptions (2) (or (1) and (3)) for the concept of belief is that no one can believe the impossible. For p's being logically inconsistent means that $\vdash p \supset (q \wedge \sim q)$, which by (2) implies

$$(4) \qquad \vdash B_a p \supset B_a(q \wedge \sim q).$$

If we assume – as it seems natural to do – that no one can believe an explicitly contradictory proposition on the form $q \wedge \sim q$, then (4) implies that no one can believe an inconsistent statement, however hidden its inconsistency may be. What has been dubbed 'Alice's Law' (viz. the thesis that one cannot believe what is impossible) is thus a natural concomitant of the doxastic part (1) or (2), and it is indeed implied by (2) if we assume in addition that

(5) $\vdash \sim B_a(q \wedge \sim q)$.

This assumption comes very close to ruling out believing the impossible while knowing it to be impossible, for the impossibility of a proposition which is the explicit form $q \wedge \sim q$ surely cannot escape anyone's attention who understands what he is saying.

At first blush, the assumptions (1)–(2) undoubtedly look blatantly unrealistic. Surely each of us, at the very least anyone who has ever been trying to trace the logical implications of an intricate set of assumptions, has often believed and even known things whose distant consequences are beyond the ken both of his knowledge and of his belief. We do not like to say that Euclid already knew all that there is to know about elementary geometry (apart from the imperfections of his axiomatics). However obvious a logical implication from p to q may be, some sufficiently dense person may in principle fail to recognize it, and hence might believe (know) that p without believing (knowing) that q.

The first answer usually given to these objections to (1)–(2) is that "some idealization is necessary in doxastic and epistemic logic: we cannot get a consistent system and at the same time take account of the vagaries of infants or idiots". The problem is nevertheless more serious than this, for there does not seem to be any guarantee that even the most acute mathematician can see all the logical consequences of the axioms he is studying without a great deal of mental exertion.

Or is there perhaps such a guarantee? There would be if certain widely discussed and widely held philosophical doctrines were correct. Insignificant-looking problems in epistemic and doxastic logic thus turn out to have a significant connection with much wider issues. It has sometimes been held that all logical inference is analytical or 'tautological', that all information that the conclusion of such an inference gives us is 'objectively' contained already in the premises, and that all increase of information in a logical inference is therefore purely psychological.[2] If these interesting claims were true, there would not be any reason to modify the rules of inference (1)–(2). In every 'objective' sense, a man who believes that p already believes that q whenever $\vdash (p \supset q)$, if these claims are right. What prevents him from assenting to q can only be a psychological block or an ignorance of the meanings of his own symbols. If this were the case, the idealization involved (1)–(2) would not only be admissible but inevitable.

However, I have all along been suspicious of these claims, and recently I have sought to disprove in some detail their theoretical basis.[3] It simply is not true that there are no objective senses of information in which logical inference can add to our information. Hence (1)–(2) do present a genuine – and serious – problem. To this extent at least, the recent surge of papers dealing with them is justified.

Several different lines of thought may be attempted here. One is to stick to (1)–(2) but to reinterpret the metalogical notions of provability, disprovability, etc. in some new way. This is the course I followed in my book *Knowledge and Belief*.[4] The upshot of the ensuing discussion[5] seems to be that although the details of my account can be tightened up so as to bar all specific criticisms, the reinterpretation tends to limit seriously the applicability of this approach. Something else thus seems to be needed, in other words, a different approach to (1) and (2) seems highly desirable. If leaving these laws unmodified results in too unrealistic a treatment, it lies close at hand to try to restrict (1) and (2) in some suitable way.

What would such a course look like? *Prima facie*, it may seem hopeless to impose any sharp boundaries between admissible and inadmissible uses of (1)–(2). What causes the breakdown of these rules is after all the fact that one cannot usually see all the logical consequences of what one knows or believes. Now it may seem completely impossible to draw a line between the implications one sees and those one does not see by means of general logical considerations alone. A genius might readily see quite distant consequences while another man may almost literally 'fail to put two and two together'. Even for one and the same person, the extent to which one follows the logical consequences of what one believes varies with one's mood, training, and degree of concentration. How can anyone hope to impose strict, uniform limits on these logical insights which so obviously are not only ephemeral but also idiosyncratic?

By way of an answer, a general methodological point can be made. Of course we cannot set sharp limits on people's logical acumen or lack thereof. What one can do is to isolate those objective, structural factors which contribute most to the difficulty of perceiving relations of logical consequence. Making them the only relevant factors may involve some idealization, but it may also result in an interesting theoretical model of people's 'deductive behavior' which facilitates the description and analysis of the inferences they draw as well as their failures to draw certain inferences. A quick comparison may not be entirely misleading. No one is likely to behave precisely so as to maximize one's expected utility. But the 'expected utility hypothesis' postulating such behavior has given rise to extensive and interesting theories of human behavior in certain situations.[6] It may be hoped that a logical theory which isolates the most salient obstacles to perceiving deductive relationships will perform similar services to a student of the logical inferences people actually draw and fail to draw.

Now what are the crucial factors that limit our 'deductive omniscience'? Many plausible-looking candidates spring to mind: the number of steps of inference, the length of the propositions involved, and so on. Important as these parameters may be, most of them are by no means peculiar to human information processing, and are not invariant with respect to relatively trivial changes from one deductive system to another. Something more central to our spontaneous strategies of information processing has to be found.

It seems to me that some of the deepest remarks on the peculiarities of human information processing have been made by John von Neumann. In his Silliman Lectures[7] he introduces the concept of *arithmetical depth*. He does this primarily for languages dealing with numerical computations. In them, arithmetical depth indicates the maximal nesting of the basic operations in a composite function. Can this notion be extended to the languages in connection with which (1)–(2) have been considered? These are typically first-order (quantificational) languages with operators like K, B added, but without function symbols. Now it is well known how quantifiers can be replaced by the so-called Skolem functions.[8] When they are considered as primitives, von Neumann's definitions applies. If we then go back to the original first-order proposition, the nesting of functions becomes the nesting of quantifiers, and arithmetical depth is converted into the number of layers of quantifiers in our first-order expression.

Apart from certain niceties in the notion of nesting (such as the question: When precisely is an operation independent of earlier ones and hence irrelevant to nesting and when does it depend on it so as to contribute to nesting?), this will then be the extension of von Neumann's notion to quantification theory: the number of layers of quantifiers in a proposition at its deepest or, which amounts to the same, the length of the longest chain of nested quantifiers. We shall call this the *quantificational depth* or simply the *depth* of the proposition in question.[9]

In addition to arithmetical depth, von Neumann considers what he calls the logical depth of a function. Since this notion is tied to the breakdown of functions into operations that a computer can actually perform, and thus to the peculiarities of one particular way of realizing the functions in question on a computer, it need not concern us here.

What von Neumann emphasizes is that "whatever language the central nervous system is using, it is characterized by less logical and arithmetical depth than what we are normally used to" (p. 81). "Thus logics and mathematics in the central nervous system, when viewed as languages, must structurally be essentially different from those languages to which our human experience refers" (p. 82).

Thus the crucial parameter which according to von Neumann apparently presents the greatest resistance to such information processing as takes place in our central nervous system is, in the case of (modalized or unmodalized) first-order languages, the depth of its expressions. In order to catch "the logic in our nervous system" we therefore have to pay special attention to this parameter.

Even apart from von Neumann, the importance of quantificational depth is easy to appreciate. For simplicity, we may consider closed sentences in some suitable first-order language, i.e., sentences without individual constants and other free singular terms. In other words, all the individuals the sentence invites us to consider are introduced by the quantifiers. (That each of them asks us to consider an individual is seen from the very meaning of quantifiers: '(Ex)' means 'for at least one individual, call it x, it is the case that', and '(x)' 'for each individual, call it x, it is the case that'.) Then the quantificational depth of a sentence s

will be the maximal complexity of the configurations of individuals considered in it at any time, measured by the number of individuals involved. Of course, it is only to be expected that the complexity of the configurations involved in a sentence is one of the prime factors limiting our insights into its logical relations to other sentences. The deeper sentences a chain of inferences involves, the harder it presumably is (*ceteris paribus*) to perceive.

It may be shown that in a certain natural sense such increase of depth is frequently involved in quantificational (first-order) deductions, even in the sense that to derive q from p one has to go by way of propositions deeper than either p or q. In the light of von Neumann's observations on the "logic in our central nervous system", it is not surprising that relatively few non-trivial quantificational inferences can be found in ordinary discourse, as some perceptive logicians have rightly emphasized. It is also significant that the tremendous subtlety and power of first-order deduction is virtually hidden by most introductory textbooks of logic.[10] Furthermore, the naturalness of the so-called natural deduction methods is obviously due to the fact that in them the depth of one's expressions (although not the depth, suitably defined, of the whole argument) is kept as small as possible. The importance of our unconscious strategy of minimizing depth for understanding the behavior of quantifying expressions of ordinary language has not been fully realized by linguists, although it is vital for understanding the behavior of quantifying expressions in ordinary language.

The main non-trivial example of quantificational reasoning which has traditionally been considered by philosophers of mathematics is found in axiomatic geometry. It is probably not accidental that there "the logic of the central nervous system" is helped by the 'logic' of our perceptual apparatus.

When free singular terms are admitted to our sentences, the important parameter will be the sum of the number of these terms and the quantificational depth of a sentence. This again indicates the maximal complexity of the configurations one has to consider in order to understand the sentence. However, all the interesting problems come up already in the case of closed sentences, and I shall therefore restrict my attention to them.

In first-order languages, the depth of sentences is therefore one of the most important obstacles to perceiving their logical relations, probably the most important one. This observation may be brought to bear on our problem concerning (1)–(2). The obvious way of doing so is to restrict (2) to those cases in which the implication from p to q can be proved without going beyond the depth of p.

This restriction is of course relative to the method of proof involved. If this method is the one that relies on distributive normal forms and on the elimination of trivially inconsistent constituents, the restriction amounts to requiring that $p \supset q$ be a surface tautology at the depth of p. This is a well-defined restriction, which I already have put forward earlier as a solution to the problems of 'deductive omniscience' (or lack thereof).[11] It seems to me to accomplish very well the purpose a restriction was to serve in the first place.

The main *prima facie* disadvantage it has is its apparent dependence on one particular method of deduction. Moreover, this method of deduction is so laborious as to be practically useless. It can nevertheless be shown that the restriction on (2) we just obtained is essentially the same as one would have obtained by considering what can be proved by the standard deductive techniques without increasing the depth of one's expressions (plus the total number of free singular terms involved in the deduction). Hence the restriction mentioned seems to have a great deal of intrinsic interest, as might indeed be expected on the basis of the role distributive normal forms play in the logical structure of first-order languages.

Another apparent problem about the proposed restriction on (1)–(2) is that it seems to be a purely syntactical one, without a clear-cut intuitive semantical backing. I have made an attempt to provide such a backing to the important 'surface concepts' like surface tautology in my paper, 'Surface Semantics: Definition and Its Motivation', in *Truth, Syntax, and Modality*, Hugues Leblanc (ed.), North-Holland, Amsterdam, 1973, pp. 128–147. However, an even more persuasive account is emerging from the highly promising unpublished work by Veikko Rantala and myself on the semantics of what we call *changing worlds*. (The change intended is of a special sort, viz such change as interferes with our examination of the world, but this does not make the idea any less intuitive.) By means of these 'changing worlds', a very natural semantics can be constructed to back up my precise restrictions on (1) and (2) in a very natural way.

Other reasons can be given for this type of restriction on (1)–(2). One is the fact – as it seems to me to be – that we spontaneously apply something very much like probabilistic concepts also in the area of deductive relationships.[12] (We may, for instance, speculate how likely it is that this or that putative theorem can be proved, and choose our deductive strategies accordingly.) Now these quasi-probabilities cannot obey all the usual laws of probability calculus, for they require that the probability-measure (on the sentences of our language) be invariant with respect to logical equivalence, and that all logically inconsistent sentences be assigned zero probability. These assumptions are remarkably similar to (1) and (5). They will have to be given up if probabilistic notions are to be applied to deductive relationships. However, we clearly want to preserve most of the other axioms of probability calculus. (What will otherwise remain of the idea of probability, anyway?) This is impossible (or at least extremely difficult) if the number of deductive steps, the maximal length of a deductive branch, or any similar parameter is used as an index of the difficulty of perceiving a deductive relationship (viz. the one established by these deductive steps or these interrelated branches of deduction). In this respect, the restriction I am proposing to impose on (1)–(2) is superior to its more obvious-looking competitors. We may perhaps say that it leaves propositional relationships intact, affecting only quantificational ones. Since the latter play no role in the axioms of probability calculus, the changes needed in these axioms are minimal.

Although the restriction on (2) which can be formulated in terms of distributive normal forms is clumsy to apply, this particular way of formulating the restriction serves to throw some interesting light on Purtill's suggestions (in the paper referred to in note 1 above). In order to save (1)–(2) unmodified, he proposes a strong sense of belief in which

(6)   *a* believes that *p*

implies

(7)   *a* understands *p*

and

(8)   *a* is disposed to act as if it were the case that *p*.

Here 'acting' will mean, on the intended interpretation, non-verbal behavior – that is, not only sincerely *saying* that p is the case but also actually taking some non-verbal measures not incompatible with the truth of p.

Purtill suggests that no such non-verbal behavior can be consistent with the truth of an inconsistent proposition, and that no one can therefore believe what is impossible in the intended strong sense of belief.

By the same token, no form of behavior can fail to be consistent with a logically true proposition. Thus we seem to have

(9) $\vdash B_a p$

whenever p is logically true. But (9) implies (together with certain relatively unproblematic assumptions) the doxastic part of (1)–(2). For if $\vdash (p \supset q)$, then by (9) $\vdash B_a(p \supset q)$, and hence by a well-known principle of doxastic logic $\vdash (B_a p \supset B_a q)$. For knowledge, the situation would be parallel. However, this defence of (1)–(2) does not work.

One highly interesting observation we can make by means of distributive normal forms is that Purtill's assumption is in fact incorrect and that it often makes perfectly good sense to speak of acting (non-verbally) as if a logically inconsistent sentence were true. In order to see how this is possible, we have to recall the structure of constituents.[13] A brief intuitive explanation is to say that a constituent $C^{(d)}$ of depth d is as full a description of a (kind of) possible world as one can give without considering more than d individuals in their relation to each other. This description takes the form of a ramified list of all the different sequences of individuals (of length d) that one can find in a world in which $C^{(d)}$ is true. By 'ramified', I refer to the fact that this list specifies which sequences are possible completions of an initial segment of a given sequence. A constituent thus has the structure of a finite set of trees. At each node of each tree, it is specified what properties the corresponding (kind of) individual has and how it is related to individuals lower in the same branch. The different branches from bottom to top specify the different kinds of sequences of individuals that one can come upon in a world in which $C^{(d)}$ is true.

A finite set of such trees may fail to describe a possible world, for obvious reasons. All the sequences have to be drawn from one and the same supply of individuals. This creates obvious similarities between the several parts of the trees. For instance, the same result (apart from the order of the trees and branches) must be obtained by truncating the trees at any one level, that is, by cutting off the tops, the bottoms, or any intermediate layer of nodes. Constituents failing certain obvious tests of this kind I have called *trivially inconsistent*.

The remarkable fact is that the inconsistency of some constituents cannot be perceived in this way. Such a constituent tells a story as to what kinds of individuals one might come upon one after another in the world, a story which cannot be disproved by comparing the different parts of the story with one another but which nevertheless cannot describe any actualizable world. The inconsistency of a constituent of this kind can only be seen by considering longer sequences of individuals than the ones considered in it – sequences whose length can be very great, indeed so great that it cannot in general be predicted on the basis of the given constituent by recursive methods.

Given such a constituent, it makes perfectly good sense to speak of someone's acting as if it were true. For instance, the constituent might say that individuals of two different kinds (defined by specifying what further kinds of individuals there are in relation to them) exist in the world. Then one can perfectly well make preparations for meeting both of them, unaware that they cannot co-exist in the same world, although each kind of individual can exist in a suitable possible world. To gain some feeling for the situation, we may think of someone asserting that a's father was an only child and that a has first cousins on his father's side. Whatever the case may be, no one will be able to find both these individuals – a's father who is an only child *and* one of a's first cousins on father's side – in the same world, although there is no impossibility in either's existing alone. And surely one can think, say, of a hopeful legatee who acts as if he should inherit both these relatives of his. In general, acting on the truth of a first-order proposition is in any case to act on the assumption that one can only come upon certain ramified sequences of individuals in the world, and not upon others. Even if there are hidden discrepancies in the list of acceptable sequences, this does not make any essential difference to the kinds of preparations one can – or perhaps has to – make for the eventuality that the constituent in question should turn out to be true: they are similar in both cases.

Notice that this sense of 'acting on' is quite a concrete one. It means acting on a specific expectation as to what kinds of individuals, and in what combinations, one may encounter in examining the world, hence in a sense what possible experiences one might have in a world as described by the constituent in question.

It seems to me that this possibility of being disposed to act on the truth of an inconsistent proposition undercuts Purtill's defense of the unmodified rules (1)–(2). I do no see any difficulty whatsoever in someone's believing the impossible (though not any old impossibility) even in Purtill's strong sense.

It also seems to me that another aspect of Purtill's definition of the strong sense of belief can be turned to a defense of my restriction on (1)–(2) rather than of the unrestricted form of these rules. That is the requirement (7) to the effect that the believer has to understand the proposition in question. I am not sure whether this requirement can be considered as a sign of a strong sense of belief, for one can scarcely be said to believe a proposition in any normal sense of the word unless one understands it.

This may of course depend somewhat on the elusive notion of understanding. When can one be said to understand a proposition? There may be some temptation to try to identify understanding p with capturing all its logical consequences. If we could assent to this identification, we could leave (1)–(2) unmodified, for whoever believes that p (sc. with understanding) will surely believe any logical consequence of q, for he could not then have 'understood' p without being aware of these consequences. However, already in the case of non-trivial first-order propositions, this involves a most unrealistic standard of understanding. Surely one can understand perfectly well (say) the axioms of elementary geometry without knowing all the theorems.

A much more interesting (although still somewhat idealized) standard of understanding can be based on our earlier observations. Surely the most concrete sense imaginable of understanding what a first-order proposition p says is to know which sequences of individuals in which combinations one can expect to hit upon if it is true – sequences no longer than those already considered in p. Now this is just what the distributive normal form of p (at the depth of p) spells out as fully as possible. The elimination of trivially inconsistent constituents, which I shall assume to have been accomplished, does not spoil this interpretation.

But if so, one can defend the restriction I proposed to impose on
(1)–(2) in an interesting way. The question really is not when one can
believe p without believing q while $\vdash (p \supset q)$. The question really is when
this can happen while one fully understands p (and perhaps also to the
same extent q). In the former sense, people may indeed fail to see the
most elementary logical connections, whereas in the latter case it is
much less obvious that they can fail to believe that q in the case of any
relatively simple consequence q of p. If the concept of understanding is
now delineated along the lines just suggested, understanding p implies
knowing (in principle) its distributive normal form minus trivially inconsistent constituents, and this is enough to perceive all surface tautologies of the form $p \supset q$ at the depth of p. But this means that whoever
believes that p *and understands* p will believe all surface consequences
of p (at the same depth). This of course amounts to saying that the
restricted forms of (1)–(2) are valid. If I am right, they are valid as soon
as we merely add the requirement of understanding, suitably interpreted,
to our concept of belief.

Notice that I am not saying that nobody will be found who will sincerely
say that he fails to believe that q even when he believes that p and when
$(p \supset q)$ is a surface tautology at the depth of p. What I have done is to
provide a sense of understanding in which such a failure *ipso facto*
shows that he does not fully understand what he is saying.

These observations provide in my opinion interesting further reasons
for restricting (1)–(2) in the way I have proposed. We may perhaps say
that although knowledge and belief are not invariant with respect to
logical equivalence, they are invariant with respect to those logical
equivalences necessary for understanding what is being believed.

NOTES

[1] The contributions to this debate which originally prompted the present chapter are
Richard L. Purtill, 'Believing the Impossible', *Ajatus* **32** (1970) 18–24; Kathleen G. Johnson
Wu, 'Hintikka and Defensibility', *Ajatus* **32** (1970) 25–31.
[2] This was one of the most characteristic theses of logical positivists. See, e.g., A. J. Ayer,
Language, Truth, and Logic, Gollanz, London, 1936, Chapter 4, 'The A Priori'; Carl G.
Hempel, 'Geometry and Empirical Science', *American Mathematical Monthly* **52** (1945)
7–17, reprinted in *Readings in Philosophical Analysis*, Herbert Feigl and Wilfrid Sellars
(eds.), New York, 1949, pp. 238–48; Hans Hahn, *Logik, Mathematik und Naturerkennen*
($=$*Einheitswissenschaft*, Vol. 2), Vienna, 1933.

[3] See the following papers of mine: 'Are Logical Truths Analytic?', *Philosophical Review* **74** (1965) 178–203; 'Are Logical Truths Tautologies?' and 'Kant Vindicated' in *Deskription, Analytizität und Existenz*, Paul Weingartner (ed.), Salzburg and Munich, A. Pustet, 1966, pp. 215–33 and pp. 234–53, respectively; 'Are Mathematical Truths Synthetic A Priori?', *Journal of Philosophy* **65** (1968) 640–51; 'Information, Deduction, and the A Priori', *Nous* **4** (1970) 135–52; 'Surface Information and Depth Information' in *Information and Inference*, Jaakko Hintikka and Patrick Suppes (eds.), D. Reidel, Dordrecht, 1970, pp. 263–97. All but the last of these papers are reprinted in my book, *Logic, Language-Games, and Information*, Clarendon Press, Oxford, 1973.

[4] Contemporary Philosophy Series, Cornell University Press, Ithaca, N.Y., 1962. (See especially pp. 29–39.)

[5] Leonard Linsky, 'Interpreting Doxastic Logic', *Journal of Philosophy* **65** (1968) 500–02; Wu, 'Hintikka and Defensibility' (above, note 1).

[6] See, e.g., R. Duncan Luce and Patrick Suppes, 'Preference, Utility, and Subjective Probability', in *Handbook of Mathematical Psychology*, Vol. 3, Luce, Bush, and Galanter (eds.), New York, John Wiley & Sons, 1965.

[7] John von Neumann, *The Computer and the Brain*, Yale University Press, New Haven, 1958. (See especially pp. 23–28, 80–82.)

[8] For instance, $(x)(Ey) F(x, y)$ is true in a model if and only if there exists a function $f(z)$ such that $(x) F(x, f(x))$ is true in that model. This function $f(z)$ is an example of Skolem functions.

[9] A minor qualification is needed here because some of the apparently nested quantifiers may not really be connected with each other. (This corresponds to a situation in which one of the Skolem functions inside does not really depend on some of the outer variables.) The necessary minor adjustment is indicated e.g. in my article 'Information, Deduction, and the A Priori', *Noûs* **4** (1970) 135–52, note 11, reprinted in *Logic, Language-Games, and Information* (note 3 above).

[10] Examples may convey a feeling of this triviality of textbook logic. Hao Wang has shown that most of the propositions of the purely logical part of *Principia Mathematica* fall within the scope of extremely simple decision methods. Almost all logical truths (of first-order logic) that are found in textbooks are 'surface tautologies' in the sense of my paper 'Surface Information and Depth Information' (note 3 above) and probably all of them admit of proofs in which the increase is very small, at most 1 or 2.

[11] See the papers listed in note 3 above, especially the last one, as well as '"Knowing Oneself" and Other Problems in Epistemic Logic', *Theoria* **32** (1966) 1–13.

[12] Some such probabilistic notions are developed in the papers listed above in note 3.

[13] The following explanation is similar to the one given in 'Information, Deduction, and the A Priori' (note 3 above). Constituents are studied systematically in my paper, 'Distributive Normal Forms in First-Order Logic' in *Formal Systems and Recursive Functions*, J. N. Crossley and M. A. E. Dummett (eds.), North-Holland, Amsterdam, 1965, 47–90, reprinted in *Logic, Language-Games, and Information*, Clarendon Press, Oxford, 1973.

CHAPTER 10

THE INTENTIONS OF INTENTIONALITY

1. INTENTIONALITY AND CONCEPTUALITY

The contrast flaunted in the title of this colloquium, "Explanation and Understanding",[1] is predicated on an important assumption. This assumption is best known as Brentano's thesis. It says, roughly, that there is an irreducible conceptual difference between two kinds of phenomena which I shall refer to as intentional and nonintentional phenomena. The nonintentional or physical phenomena are subject to explanation, the intentional ones to understanding.

Corresponding to these two classes of phenomena, we have intentional and nonintentional concepts. If Brentano is right, neither of these two classes of concepts reduces to the other. According to him, every intentional phenomenon "is characterized by what the scholastics of the Middle Ages called the intentional... inexistence (*Inexistenz*) of an object (*Gegenstand*), and what we could call... the reference to a content, a direction upon an object..., or an immanent objectivity."[2] This directedness is what according to his lights distinguishes the intentional from the nonintentional.

Brentano identifies the contrast between the intentional and the nonintentional phenomena with the distinction between the mental and the physical. This identification is highly dubious, however. There are lots of mental events, for instance twinges of pain, which do not seem to involve any directedness to an object or to a content.[3] They point to no way beyond themselves. Brentano tried to argue that even such mental events are accompanied by a presentation, a *Vorstellung*, and are therefore intentional.[4] But this term is dangerously obscure in that it does not distinguish images or mental pictures from conceptualizations. And it is in my judgement only the second, conceptual interpretation that really counts here. According to the lights of Husserl and other leading phenomenologists, the notions of intentionality and conceptuality are intertwined. The world of intentions is the world of concepts, and vice versa.

Brentano seems to think that the fact that we for instance experience pain as localized is enough to show that it is accompanied by a *Vorstellung* and is therefore intentional. But even if this were admitted, does it make the experience of pain itself intentional? Using a well-known Wittgensteinian ploy, one can try to argue that insofar as we can speak intersubjectively of our pain-experiences, they must be accompanied by public criteria by means of which they could presumably be conceptualized.[5] But does it follow from this that the raw sensations of pain and pleasure are themselves intentional in the intended sense? I don't see that it follows. It is much wiser to say with Husserl that, although intentionality is a universal medium of all conscious experience, there are within it experiences that are not themselves intentional.[6] In other words, it seems that the best course to follow here is to 'bracket' Brentano's assumption and to count as intentional, not all and sundry mental events, but only those characteristic of conscious, conceptualizable human experience. They seem to be precisely what Husserl referred to as 'acts'. Husserl in any case unmistakably identified the intentional with the conceptual. He went so far as to hold that all 'meanings' relevant to intentionality can be expressed in language. The vehicle of intentionality *apud* Husserl are the noemata, and every noematic 'meaning' is according to him conceptualizable. "Whatever is 'meant as such'", he writes,[7] "every meaning in the noematic sense (and indeed as noematic nucleus) of any act whatsoever *can be expressed conceptually (durch 'Bedeutungen')*."

This viewpoint is not without consequences for the dichotomy mentioned in the subject matter in this colloquium. Presumably an account of human behavior given exclusively in terms of pleasurable and painful experiences would account as an explanation. (Similar accounts could be given, say, of the behavior of lower animals.) However, as soon as a conceptual element is imported into the account, we surely have to practice understanding and not only explanation. Or so it seems.

2. Intentionality and Intensional Logic

In recent years, several studies have been carried out concerning the logical structure of various particular concepts which are intentional by any reasonable token, such as belief and knowledge.[8] It may be time to survey some of the vistas opened by these studies so as to see what they imply for the distinction between intentional and nonintentional. In this paper, a suggestion will be made concerning the nature of this important distinction. I shall not examine systematically the question of the reducibility of one half of the dichotomy to the other, but rather the ways of spelling out the dichotomy and of relating it to certain important philosophical problems.

3. INTENTIONALITY AS DIRECTEDNESS

Conceived of in the way as we have done, there are few questions more important than this problem of characterizing the nature of intentionality. For the question is then: what is characteristic of conscious, conceptualizable human mental life and mental experience? This question is intimately related to the salient philosophical questions: What is man? and: What is thinking?

It is of course quite possible that none of these questions can be given a brief nontrivial answer. But even if that were the case, it would be important to examine and to criticize the answers that actually have been given to them and especially to our question of the nature of intentionality. We have already seen the answer Brentano gave. Answers of the same general type still enjoy a wide currency. To come extent, they are encouraged by the etymology of the term 'intentional'. According to this type of answer, intentionality equals *directedness*. Intentional phenomena, we found Brentano affirming, are characterized by their directedness to a content or to an object, and they contain in a sense this object as existing or, rather, inexisting in it. On views of this sort, an act or other phenomenon is intentional if it has an object to which it is directed ('aimed at', one is tempted to say) and if this object is somehow present in the act itself. Of course, this is not so far removed from what 'intending' originally meant, although its career as a philosophical term (which Brentano reminds us of in so many words) is perhaps not so easily predictable as its etymology suggests.[9] In the field where this colloquium is supposed to move, views of this sort are represented by frequent assimilations of intentional, *verstehende* accounts of actions to the so-called teleological explanations.

4. INTENTIONALITY AS INTENSIONALITY

This putative solution to the problem of intentionality is mistaken, I shall argue. To it I shall contrast a different answer to the same question. Formulated in blunt terms, this solution says that a concept is intentional if and only if it involves the simultaneous consideration of several possible states of affairs or courses of events (in brief, involves several 'possible worlds', to use this metaphysically loaded term). In other words, possible-worlds semantics is the logic of intentionality, and intentional is what calls for possible-worlds semantics.

Several minor explanations are in order here. The word 'simultaneous' refers of course to logical parity rather than to contemporaneity in the literal sense of the word. By 'involves' I refer to the semantical explication of a concept, not to the overt features of its use. The 'possible worlds' contemplated here are not grand histories of the world but usually only what a theoretical statistician à la Savage might call 'small worlds',[10] that is to say, alternative courses of events which are rather short in duration and which concern only a minuscule part of the universe, for instance alternative courses that a single experiment might take. What is crucial is only that several such alternative courses must needs be considered within the same 'logical specious present'. We shall also find that the word 'possible' in my phrase 'possible world' has to be taken with a grain of salt, too,[11] and that the possible-worlds semantics in question has to be of the right kind and even so will exhibit different degrees of intentionality.

With these provisos, however, my thesis seems to be intelligible enough to be discussed at some length. Since we shall need a handy label for this thesis, I propose to dub it the thesis of intentionality as intensionality. (As you can see, I am also not above exploiting etymology for my own purposes.) In spirit, the thesis is perhaps not so far removed from Hazlitt's dictum: "Man is the only animal that laughs and weeps; for he is the only animal that is struck with the difference between what things are and what they ought to be." According to it, intentionality is not a matter of relations obtaining within the world. Its gist lies in comparisons between several possible worlds. It is an interworldly business, not an intraworldly one.

5. ARTISTIC CREATION NOT DIRECTED

Perhaps the most persuasive counterexample to the identification of the intentional with the purposive is offered by acts of artistic creation. In the eyes of the Greeks, they would not have offered any challenge to the identification, for most of the ancients seem to have been committed to the idea of an artist as an imitator, even if the paradigms he imitates are perhaps not perceptible.[12] We moderns tend to emphasise the relative or absolute novelty of an artist's conception. Even if the process of concretely realizing this conception is purposive, the genesis of the conception itself cannot be. But this dichotomy of conception vs. realization is already a dangerous admission to the identification of the intentional with the purposive, for it is in effect an attempt to maximize the scope of the purposive in the aesthetic area. The crucial feature of artistic creation is that what is most truly novel in it does not come about through a goal-directed process. To paraphrase Picasso's inimitable formulation, a creative artist does not seek: he find (finds without seeking, that is).[13] But this very non-purposiveness of artistic acts is often found paradoxical and perplexing, for unfortunately we prefer more familiar teleological models of human action. The recalcitrant element in artistic creation which cannot be accommodated in this teleological model is frequently subjected to various mystifications, ranging from theories of the unconscious to interpretations of an artist as a 'medium' of a genius 'possessing' him. (It is a sobering thought to note how repulsive such speculations would have appeared to Plato.[14]) These mystifications must not cloud the paramount fact that artistic creation, which is by any token one of the freest and most human activities one can hope to indulge in, just is not purposive (conceptually speaking). No prototype of a truly novel artistic conception 'inexists' in the act that gives rise to, nor is this act 'directed' to it. Its outcome can be a surprise even to its originator. Yet artistic creation surely ought to be counted as intentional in the sense which was intended by Husserl and with which we are here concerned. It is a form of free, conscious activity which typically even involves a clear intention on the artist's part, though not an intention to produce any particular, already defined *objet d'art*.

And such artistic creation is indeed intentional in the sense of my thesis. The very descriptions that emphasize the spontaneity of artistic creation involve concepts that are intentional in my sense. Perhaps the most characteristic descriptions involve the notion of surprise whose analysis involves especially clearly a contrastive comparison between several 'possible worlds' – those that someone expected and the one that did in fact materialize so as to surprise him. Nor are intentional concepts of this kind unrelated to our aesthetic evaluations, for such evaluations inevitably involve tacit or even explicit comparisons between the details of a work of art and what its creator might have executed instead. All aesthetic evaluations involve comparisons between the actual and the possible, and all artistic creation involves choices between alternatives of which only one can be actualized.[15]

6. Is perception intentional?

The contrast between the different interpretations of intentionality is especially acute in the area of perception. Over and above the intrinsic interest of this group of problems, it is lent a historical importance by Husserl's frequent use of acts of perception as paradigms of (intentional) acts in general.

At first blush, it might seem that perception is not intentional at all in any reasonable sense, and certainly not in the sense of intentionality as directionality. What happens in perception seems to be determined completely by physical stimuli and physiological processes, not by our purposive strivings and searchings. Perception seems to be a purely passive matter which scarcely merits the term 'act' even in its extended Husserlian sense. Even Immanuel Kant, who otherwise emphasized the role of human activity and human planning in his philosophy, spoke of sensation as *giving* us intuitions.[16] And rightly so, it might appear. One does not choose what one sees, nor is seeing a process with an end or aim. As Aristotle observed, 'I am seeing' implies 'I have seen': there is no end or aim which is realized through seeing.[17] Should the authority of Aristotle be insufficient, we may recall Quine listing perception as an unequivocally nonintensional concept.[18]

7. Noesis as the source of the intentionality of perception

Yet there is a deep truth in the insistence by phenomenologists like Husserl that perception is an intentional act. Only they carried out this idea wrongly, partly because they could not completely disentangle themselves from the wrong idea of intentionality as directedness. Husserl did not correctly diagnose the intentionality of perception as intensionality. On at least one plausible interpretation of what Husserl says, based largerly on the formulations he uses in the *Ideen*, Husserl in effect retained the nonintentional character of 'pure' perception, and introduced the intentional element only secondarily, in the form of an act of *noesis* superimposed on the perceptual rawmaterial.

Of course this is not precisely Husserlian terminology. However, what his jargon amounts to is in effect just what I said. Husserl locates the 'given' in what he calls sense data (*Empfindungsdaten*) or hyletic data or simply *hyle*. This terminology already illustrates the difficulty in Husserl's position. For most of the philosophers who have employed the sense-datum terminology, sense-data are *what* is experienced. For someone like Moore, they are what judgements of immediate experience are *about*. Husserl makes it clear that his sense-data are not *what* is experienced. However, they are components of perceptual acts. These are the experiences we have whenever our senses are stimulated. However, sense-data alone are "not by themselves experiences *of an object*" (Føllesdal's exposition of this line of interpretation,[19] my italics) and hence are not by themselves intentional according to Husserl's criteria.[20] However, hyletic data "normally occur as components of more comprehensive experiences, acts, which in addition to the hyle contain experiences of an intentional kind, the noeses. The noesis 'informs' the hyle, so that this multitude of visual, tactile and other data is unified into a set of appearances of one object"[21] and only thereby made intentional in Husserl's sense.

Thus quite literally only an additional noesis or thought-element (*Auffassungsmoment*) makes the hyletic data intentional. Thus in a sense, which is problematic but not Pickwickian, raw sensation (unedited perception) is *not* intentional according to this reading of Husserl.

What this amounts to in more mundane terms can be roughly explained by saying that our sense-impressions only become intentional when they are organized by means of one's expectations, memories, etc. These (and the like) are what the noesis relies on that makes perception intentional. The objects of our senses are reidentified from moment to moment largely by means of the continuity of the beliefs we attribute to them.

8. CONSCIOUS ILLUSIONS AS COUNTEREXAMPLES TO HUSSERL

As a corollary, we can conclude that when one's beliefs concerning what one perceives are correct, one perceives correctly. In other words, illusions (incorrect perceptions) are false beliefs induced by senses. They are discrepancies between what sensation usually leads us to believe and what further experience (e.g., measurement) will show. For instance, in the case of a pair of Müller-Lyer lines "I may be aware that I am having an illusion and expect that the two lines will come out the same length when measured by a measuring rod. In this case I am, at least so far, correctly perceiving an object." [22] But these corollaries to the views of the phenomenologists already offer clear indications of the insufficiency of their line of thought. The views of illusions under scrutiny are not addressed to one of the most important 'phenomenological' problems we face here. They have the effect of neglecting the crucially important phenomenological distinction between not having a perceptual illusion at all and having it knowingly (and being able to compensate for it in thinking). Yet this is surely a vitally important distinction here. To be able to correct a sensory illusion *in thought* just is not the same thing as to be able to correct it in *perception*. There is a very real difference between seeing or not seeing a curved surface *as* the front side of a threedimensional object, even if one knows that it is not; [23] seeing or not seeing a chair through a peephole in an Ames experiment when one knows in either case perfectly well there is none there; [24] perceiving or not perceiving a causal connection between the movements of two lightspots in a Michotte experiment even when one is aware that there cannot be; [25] and so on. Such distinctions are persuasive proofs that there is a kind of truth and falsity and therefore a kind of intentionality in a perfectly good sense even in spontaneous, unedited impressions largely independently of what current beliefs (memories, expectations, etc.) we associate with them. They correspond or fail to correspond to facts independently of what we know or believe these facts to be.

Nor can Husserl be excused by saying that the expectations and memories we associate with an object may be unconscious and that the talk of a noesis which structures the hyle into an aimed act is partly just another way of speaking of the effects of the unconscious editing and organizing process to which our sensory input is subjected by the central nervous system. Such an interpretation would destroy an even more important cornerstone of the system of phenomenology, viz. the accessibility of all noemata to phenomenological reflection. [26] In order to avoid this disaster, Husserlian phenomenologists must consider the noesis which structures ('informs') the hyletic data as falling within the purview of one's consciousness. Husserl goes in fact further and says in so many words that even the hyletic data can always be 'grasped':

> However, we can always grasp them directly as they are themselves, without being interested in the fact that with them something different, more specifically, something objective and spatial, appears to us. (*Husserliana*, Vol. IX, p. 163, lines 17–19.)

This shows that according to Husserl we can in some sense attend also to the hyletic data. What is even more important, it shows that the hyle can according to Husserl be attended to in abstruction from the three-dimensional objects which appear to us. This is the view I want to criticize here.

9. THE TRUE PHENOMENOLOGY OF PERCEPTION

To Husserl's (apparent) interpretation of the intentionality of perception I want to contrast another one. According to the former, sense-data enter our consciousness as an unstructured mass which is given a form (and the most primitive sense-experience which can show up in one's conscious-hence made object-directed) by the mind's activity, largely through comparisons with past and future sense-experiences.[27] According to the latter, ness is (in normal perception) already experience *of* certain objects, their properties, their interrelations, etc. In other words, one's unedited sense-impressions are already structured categorially. This is of course the outcome of complicated physiological processes which are conditioned by past experience and future expectations. However, the point is that these formative processes and their background information leave a trace in the conscious end product.[28] On this view, the most primitive layer of sensation we can reflectively behold is already directed, *i.e.*, organized so as to be *of* definite objects.

All this is compatible with saying that the noema of a perceptual object is not unlike a complex of expectations concerning this object.[29] However, on the view I criticized above (whether it is in the last analysis Husserl's or not) these expectations are superimposed on sensory raw-materials by a nonperceptual *noesis*. On the view advocated here, they are built right into the data of sensation themselves. If we want to describe truthfully our most spontaneous sense-experiences, we already have to use the language of those expectations. One does not perceive a hemispheric surface, and expect it to go together with the rest of a soccer ball because one recalls past experiences of it. One literally perceives a soccer ball, period.[30] The backside of a tree one sees is not brought in by apperception, but is already part and parcel of one's unedited perceptions. The examples given earlier of 'illusions' which persist even when one perfectly well knows that they are illusory shows how badly this kind of description is needed if one is to capture the true quality of one's sensory impressions.

I cannot argue here for this view of the phenomenology of sense-perception as fully as it deserves. It seems to me to be what such psychologists of perception as J. J. Gibson and David Katz have been arguing for.[31] Some reasons for this connection between the contemporary psychology of perception and my interpretation of the intentionality of perception are indicated in my paper 'Information, Causality, and the Logic of Perception'.[32] The relationship between the views put forward here and those defended by the psychologists of perception is especially close when a psychologist like Gibson emphasizes the informational character of perception.[33] But even apart from this special link, the object-directedness of perception has been strongly emphasized by several leading psychologists.[34]

All this is not incompatible with saying that we can occasionally have 'pure' (unstructured, not object-directed) sense-data and that they can for instance be studies in psychological and sense-physiological experiments. If anything, the need of elaborate experiments argues for the view presented here rather than what I have taken to be Husserl's view. For if we could always grasp the hyletic data directly, apart from their object-presenting function (cf. the last quote above in Section 8), such special setups were redundant. We could always attend to the sense-data directly. The truth seems to be quite different in that it takes special and unusual situations (e.g., colored spotlight on the wall of an otherwise completely dark room) to break the object-directedness of our spontaneous perception.

10. PERCEPTION IS INTENTIONAL BECAUSE INFORMATIONAL

But why do I say that this view is based on a conception of intentionality different from Husserl's? Because it is a direct corollary to perception's being intentional in my sense of intentionality as intensionality. In this sense the intentionality of perception means that it involves a comparison

between several possible states of affairs. And it is indeed obvious what
these states of affairs are in the case at hand. Perception is intentional
because it is informational,[35] and all talk of information involves several
different possible states of affairs or courses of events in that it involves
a distinction between states of affairs compatible with this information
and those incompatible with it.[36] Since to specify what one perceives at
a given moment of time is (I have argued) to specify the information one's
senses then convey to one about the object of one's perception, this specification involves several unrealized states of affairs, i.e., is intentional in
my sense. And of course sensation cannot convey even putative information about its objects in this way unless the contents of sensation are to
be specified in terms of the same realistic concepts as apply to its objects.
Thus perception's being object-directed (in that its contents have to be
described by speaking of its objects) is just the other side of the coin from
its being intensional, i.e., specifiable only by means of several different
'possible worlds'. Husserl thus used the right word in a wrong sense.
Perception involves in-formation, not in the etymological sense of form-
giving, but in the modern sense of telling the perceiver something about
his environment – or at least appearing to do so.

11. THE INTENTIONALITY OF PERCEPTION IMPLIES ITS CONCEPTUALITY

The intentional and informational character of perception is not uncon-
nected with the role of conceptualization in perception. On my view, the
intentionality of perception presupposes that sense-impressions are dealt
with by the perceiver as conveying information and that they do not operate merely as signals for triggering responses. This of course requires a
certain level of conceptualization of the part of the perceiver. However,
it does not require that this conceptualization is something over and above
our primary sense-impressions. Rather, the conceptualization is built right
into these unreconstructed sense-impressions themselves. This is reflected
by the fact (already argued for above) that to describe my sense-impressions is to specify which states of affairs are compatible with them and
which ones are not. For, as was also alluded to, these states of affairs have
to be described in realistic terms – in the same terms as we ordinarily use
of speaking of perceptible objects, not in terms of special imponderable

entities like sense-data or sense-impressions. But the appropriateness of such a description depends on the concepts the perceiver has available to him. In this way, one's concepts enter into the very sense-impressions one has, not as the result of a further noesis performed on them, but as a part and parcel of their very texture. It is in this way that perception can be partly cultur-dependent, it seems to me.[37] All these observations are consequences of the analysis of (spontaneous) perception in terms of the class of states of affairs it admits of, and this analysis is little more than spelling out the claim that perception is intentional in the sense of the thesis of this paper.

12. EXEGETICAL PROBLEMS

It is in order to add a few interpretational warnings to what was said above about Husserl. My account of his views is closely geared to what he says in the *Ideen*, but it must be added that Husserl himself indicates that the account given there is only a provisional one.[38] It seems that he was bothered by doubts not unrelated to the problems I discussed, and introduced various qualifications to the oversimplified account outlined above.

The main qualification we sometimes seem to find in Husserl is that we cannot separate the hyletic data from the noematic sense and consider it in isolation. In a passage to which Professor Føllesdal has drawn my attention, Husserl writes:

> We cannot place side by side two components in intuition, sense and filling. We can only obtain the difference by contrasting the empty and the filled sense, that is, through a synthesis of intuition and empty consciousness. Perhaps we might put it thus: the abstract identical in several different acts of consciousness which is called sense is an essence (sense-essence) which particularizes in its special way, indeed in two basic modes, in the mode of intuition ... and in the mode of non-intuition, the empty mode.[39]

It nevertheless appears that Husserl did not reach anything like full clarity in the problems confronting him. The quotation just given is not very easy to bring in step with passages such as the one quoted toward the end of section 8 above. Passages like the one just quoted also do not rule out the possibility that Husserl is only saying that we cannot meaningfully speak of hyletic data in their virgin state, unsullied of any *noesis*. If this is what he means, what is involved is merely a consequence of the fact that hyletic data are according to Husserl only conceptualized (made intentional) through a superimposed noesis. Since language presupposes conceptualization, we cannot speak of the hyletic data until they are subjected to the *noesis*. And even then we cannot really speak of them alone, only of the intentional experiences to which they belong as components.

If so, Husserl is not really modifying the dichotomy hyletic data vs. sense but only signalling the limitations of our language and conceptual thought in speaking of it. He is not saying that there are no unstructured hyletic data. He is only saying that we can speak of them only insofar as they have already been structured by the noesis (and even then only at the second remove, that is, only in so far as they are components of our experiences of those objects which are the only rightful subject matter of conceptualized discourse.) So understood, Husserl's second thoughts do not belie my criticism of him, they merely introduce a cautionary footnote as to how this criticism ought to be formulated.

Husserl is so elusive a thinker that I cannot put forward this interpretation with complete confidence, although it seems to me the likeliest account of his position. In particular, it seems to me that Husserl was too deeply committed to such contrasts as matter (hyle) vs. form, *Empfindung* vs. *Wahrnehmung*, etc., to be able to accommodate fully the idea that the most primary ingredients of our sensory consciousness are already 'informed', already perceptual and not mere complexes of sensations.

It may also be that two different ideas are run together in Husserl's concept of hyletic data to the detriment of this notion. In addition to the alleged formlessness of these data in Husserl, they are also closely related to what is 'given' to us in the sense of being what can 'fill' a noema, that is, roughly, what meets or fails to meet the expectations which are built into this noema. I cannot suppress the suspicion that Husserl may have thought that the role of the hyletic data in 'filling' noemata somehow implies their nonintentionality.

Hence the contrast between the hyle and the filling-component mentioned above in note 39 is nevertheless relevant. Husserl never actually says that filling is done by the hyletic data. But the two must somehow be bound inextricably together, even though Husserl never spells out their connection.

It is to be noted, though, that there is in any case one clear difference between the two in that the filling in Husserl belongs squarely with the object and therefore appears to be already conceptualized. However, just in so far as Husserl considers the filling to be done by what is most primitively given to us, the fillings become difficult to speak of and difficult to conceptualize, in brief, become like hyletic data.

If anything, my point is thus strengthened by making this hyle-filling duality explicit. For then we have to ask: Are the expectations (or expectation-like *Unsättigkeiten*) that can be 'filled' expectations concerning our sensations, or concerning the objects of these sensations? The whole tenor of Husserl's thought argues for the latter answer. But if so, the fulfilling data must already be articulated in the same terms as the expectations they meet. Thus Husserl faces a dilemma he never seems to resolve satisfactorily. Either he must disassociate 'fillings' and the hyle, or else admit that the hyletic data are already object-directed (intentional). Both horns of the dilemma appear unacceptable to him.

Even apart these problems of interpretation Husserl's ubiquitous matter-form terminology exposes him to devastating criticism. There just is no matter-form contrast in normal perception, in so far the phenomena of our conscious experience are concerned. Whatever 'form' there is in one's perception is present already in the most spontaneous sensuous 'materials' that can surface in one's awareness. Speaking of 'matter' and 'form' in perception thus appears not only empty or problematic, but positively misleading.

Although important questions are being begged by these brief remarks, they may nevertheless suffice to indicate my overall interpretation of Husserl's position, provided only that a due allowance is made for its ambiguities.

13. DIRECTEDNESS AND CONCEPTUALITY

Another comparison between my interpretation of intentionality and the views of the phenomenologists is possible. My thesis of intentionality as intensionality shows what the precise relation is that obtains between intentionality and conceptuality. Conversely, this application serves to bring out the nature of my thesis more fully. Again a comparison with the idea of intentionality as directionality is instructive. This idea in fact seems to have its strong point in this area, for it seems to bring out precisely the connection between intentionality and conceptuality which we are looking for. Briefly, concepts are the *meanings* (Frege's *Sinne*) of our linguistic acts and more generally the generalized meanings or noematic *Sinne* (in Husserlian terminology) of all our conscious acts. Acts as it were aim at objects. In linguistic acts, these objects are the *references* of our expressions. Now a noematic meaning is what establishes the *direction* of this aim. A noema is the vehicle of directedness. It "determines what the object of an act is, if the act has an object", as Føllesdal says, "just as the meaning of a linguistic expression determines which object the expression refers to". [40] As Føllesdal also puts it, according to Husserl "to be directed is simply to have a noema."

It is hard to find anything specific in such formulations with which one can disagree. Yet such remarks tend to convey a wrong idea of the relationship between intentionality and meanings which we are considering. What is wrong with such accounts of meanings as vehicles of directedness is that they are partly metaphorical. They do not really say how the determination of the object of an act through its noematic *Sinn* takes place. And in so far as something is said, or suggested, concerning the nature of this determination, the ideas associated with it are insufficiently abstract and insufficiently generalized to pass the muster as an answer to our question. A noema, conceived of as the 'vehicle of directedness', far too easily becomes like a concrete aid to a rifleman's aiming in that it becomes a single entity, however abstract. Frege would say of noemata in general the same he appears to tell us of his *Sinne*, *viz.* that they are what he calls 'complete' entities. [41] Husserlian *noemata* and Fregean *Sinne* are thus easily reified into *individuals* in logician's general sense of the term. (It may very well be that a detailed analysis of Husserl shows that, appearances notwithstanding, this is not a part of his full-fledged doctrine; but it is in any case how he is easily read.) A noema may be an *abstract* entity; but it is a on the view under discussion still definite entity in the etymological sense of the word, an one-tity.

14. INTENSIONS AS FUNCTIONS

This is simply a category mistake, it seems to me. The deep true idea in Husserl no less than in Frege is of course *not* that a *Sinn* (noematic *Sinn*) is an *argument* which functionally determines an object (e.g., a reference), for the two different noemata would only rarely be directed to the same object. Rather, the true idea is that the *Sinn* is itself the *function* which

accomplishes this. It includes, Frege said without following up the consequences of his statement, besides the reference also the way in which
this reference is given.[42] And of course all such talk of 'ways of being
given' must in the last analysis be understood functionally. Meanings of
expressions and meanings of acts are simply the functions which determine their references or objects, respectively.[43] Although neither Husserl
nor Frege appreciated the point, this is the only general thing one can
say of the logical status of noemata or *Sinne*. No matter how interested
one may (for perfectly valid reasons) be in the specific recipes for determining the values of such functions or in other aspects of their concrete
realization, one must not forget their categorical status as functions.

But what are these meaning functions functions of? What are their
arguments? Again one may in special cases try to look for specific candidates for this role. The question before us here is, however: What are all
the different things which these functions depend on as their arguments
or components of such arguments? On the general semantical level on
which we are here moving, the only plausible answer is the apparently
trivial one: everything. In particular cases, they depend on some special
features of the possible world where the reference is located, but they
cannot depend on anything more than this world as a whole. Concepts,
meanings, are therefore functions from possible worlds to references (objects), for the whole idea of 'possible world' is that it comprises everything
(at least everything that is relevant to the particular question we are asking).

This, however, is precisely the general answer given by possible-worlds
semantics to the question of the status of the concepts.[44] Concepts, as
meanings, are according to possible-worlds semantics functions from possible worlds to references (extensions). This is their logical type, and it is
of course literally worlds apart from the logical status of individuals ('entities').

What we have just done is that we have as it were deduced this view by
criticizing the flaws of the Husserlian and Fregean answers and by cor-
recting their shortcomings. It exhibits the connection between conceptuality and intentionality which I promised to show to you. Concepts, being
functions from possible worlds, are intrinsically intentional in that they
involve a multiplicity of possible worlds (as their arguments), which in
turn was precisely my definition of intentionality. Even if all uses of a
concept do not have to involve all possible worlds (if such totality as

much as makes sense), any nontrivial use of a concept implicitly involves more than one possible world.

Thus a closer analysis of the very idea of intentionality or conceptuality as directedness (directedness to an object) leads us back to my thesis of conceptuality as intentionality in the sense of involving several possible worlds at one and the same time. Moreover, once we see this, all emphasis is shifted away from directedness as a special relation of an act to an object *in this world*. The same function which in our world gives us one object will give us another object in another one. The relation of this function to its values is no more remarkable in one world than in another. This shows in further detail in what sense intentionality is an interwordly affair, not an intrawordly one.

On earlier occasions, I have in effect criticized illicit reifications of intensional objects (e.g., sense-data in the Moore-Broad-Price sense) into alleged denizens of the actual world, while in reality their peculiar status lies entirely in crossworld comparisons.[45] Somewhat analogously, I am now criticizing what looks to me like an illicit reification of intentionality, not into intrawordly objects, but intrawordly relations.

15. THE PRIMACY OF POSSIBLE WORLDS

Perhaps the most important systematical implications of the thesis of intentionality as intensionality are seen by noting what follows from it concerning possible-worlds semantics itself. The thesis can be taken to imply that the only 'raw materials' we are allowed to use in constructing the semantics of intentional concepts are possible worlds. Everything else must be constructed or, to use a perhaps more familiar jargon, constituted from the materials presented to us by a suitable set of possible worlds.

But what else could there be which it might be tempting to try to postulate as existing independently of the possible worlds? Several answers are possible, but only one such rival answer is important. There is a strong temptation, motivated both by philosophical arguments and by considerations of logico-mathematical elegance, to think of the particular entities, the individuals in the logical sense of the word, as somehow being primary with respect to possible worlds whose members they may be, and in this sense as independent of these worlds. Several logicians have in fact presented semantical treatments of intensional logic by starting out from a fixed set of individuals which can then make their appearance in different possible worlds.[46] Admittedly not all the results they obtain are necessarily any worse off if this starting point of theirs turns out not to be the ultimate starting-point of semantical and philosophical analysis. However, the philosophical weight of their results is apt to be diminished by reductions to more basic elements. And such a reduction is not only possible but (for many philosophical purposes) indispensable.

To the alleged primacy of individuals we can contrast a view which admits that each possible world comes to us already analyzed categorially into individuals, their properties, their relations, etc. However, according to this view the identity of such entities, especially the identity of individuals from one world to another is not fixed by any absolute logical principles but is at least partly constituted by our comparisons between the two different possible worlds whose denizens the two respective individuals are.[47]

In order to have vivid terminology at our disposal, let us imagine that the manifestations (roles, embodiments) of the same individual in different worlds are tied together by a line, the *world line* of this individual. (David Kaplan has jokingly called them TWA's, that is, trans world heir lines). Then I can formulate my claim by saying that the world lines of individuals are not fixed by immutable laws of logic or God or some other equally transcendent power, but that they are as it were drawn by ourselves – of course not by each individual alone but by tacit collective decision embodied in the grammar and semantics of our language.

Certain caution is nevertheless necessary here. David Lewis has suggested that the world lines joining to each other 'counterparts' (his term) in different worlds are based on the similarity of the counterparts in question, this similarity being something like a weighted average of many different kinds of similarity considerations.[48] This is a misleading view, I want to argue (and will do so in greater detail in my Quine paper). It is misleading because by far the most important vehicle of trans world comparisons is given to us by various continuity principles. This diminishes greatly the psychological and sociological arbitrariness of our cross-identification principles, but it leaves these principles largely at the mercy of the laws of nature which serve to guarantee the continuity of our 'natural' individuals (e.g., physical objects) in space and time. Moreover, the precise kind continuity in question can in principle still be chosen differently. (Is the identity of persons based on bodily continuity or on the continuity of memory?) Hence this reliance on continuity does not eliminate our choices in drawing the world lines.

16. THE BEHAVIOR OF WORLD LINES

The question of the primacy of world lines vs. the primacy of 'prefabricated' individuals is by any token an important philosophical problem concerning possible-worlds semantics. Now we can see that it is closely related to the general thesis of intentionality as intensionality and that the thesis implies a definite answer to this question.

It is also seen that the thesis is indirectly but strongly supported by whatever evidence there is for the primacy of world lines and for their being due to our (i.e., the language community's) constitutive decisions. Here I cannot survey exhaustively recent work in possible-worlds semantics and its applications to philosophical and semantical problems so as to spell out all the evidence in this direction. It is nevertheless in order to indicate what kinds of evidence one can find.

From the assumption of prefabricated individuals, certain restraints follow on the behavior of world lines. Clearly, on this assumption world lines never split in two or merge into one. On the assumption of the primacy of possible worlds there is nothing that would prevent such splittings and mergings. Even that bugbear of the critics of possible worlds, quantification into intensional contexts, makes sense as soon as the world lines have been drawn, no matter whether or not they are allowed to diverge and converge.[49] Hence the phenomenon of world lines splitting or merging offers potential evidence for a decision between the competing assumptions.

This evidence is faily unambiguous. It seems to me clear that, for certain epistemic notions at least, splitting must occasionally be allowed.[50] Merging is not even ruled out in many actual treatments of intensional logic.[51] Hence there are good reasons to distrust ready-made individuals and prefer to think of them as fabricated from the raw materials of possible worlds.

This result is all the more surprising as it involves (as you can easily see on a closer scrutiny) the occasional failure of the most solid-looking version of the logical principle which is known as the substitutivity of identity and which has been alleged by several philosophers to be a *conditio sine qua non* of any satisfactory interpretation of identity.[52]

17. DIFFERENT KINDS OF WORLD LINES

But even more striking evidence is forthcoming. If world lines are in the last analysis man-made, it ought to be possible in principle to draw them in (at least) two different ways. This expectation is dramatically confirmed by the (by now well-established) results to the effect that in our actual conceptual and linguistic practice we are all the time operating, not with one system of world lines, but with two different ones.[53] One of them is established by the methods which were already alluded to and which rely essentially on continuity. It is said to establish *descriptive* cross-identification. The other mode of cross-world comparisons identifies individuals having the same perceptual relations (or other direct cognitive relations, as the case may be) in different worlds to the person in question – meaning the person whose acts are being considered. This I will call (taking a cue from Russell) cross-identification by acquaintance. The genuineness of the distinction, and the reality of its both halves, is attested to by their linguistic counterparts. The logic of descriptive cross-identification is to all practical purposes the logic of subordinate interrogative wh-questions with an epistemic main verb like 'knows', 'remembers', 'sees', etc. The logic of cross-identification by acquaintance is the logic of direct-object constructions with the same verbs (or, rather with some of them). This linguistic distinction thus serves, when its semantics is laid bare, as strong evidence for the primacy of possible worlds and therefore also for the thesis of intentionality as intensionality.

18. ACTS *de dicto* AND ACTS *de re*

A third major way in which possible-worlds semantics helps to adjudicate the rivalry between different conceptions of intentionality is based on the insight that not all acts of knowing, believing, remembering, etc., have to be directed to a particular individual or perhaps rather on the new insights into the semantical roots of this time-honored distinction. It is in fact honored in terminology and not only in time, for it was already in the middle of the middle ages dubbed the distinction between acts *de dicto* and *de re*.[54] Let's suppose that you can be truly be said to believe that the present Prime Minister of Denmark is a social democrat. Then you might either have a particular Danish politician in mind of whom you believe this. (In fact, the identification of this person as the P.M. of the happy nation of Denmark might be mine, and no part of *your* beliefs.) In such circumstances, your belief is *de re*, the *res* in question being the person whom the belief is *about*.

However, the identification may be a part of the specification of the content of your belief. Then you need not have any particular politician in mind, but would be willing to express your belief by saying, "Whoever the Prime Minister of Denmark is, he is a social democrat". (You might for instance believe that no other party is capable of forming a cabinet right now). Then your belief is *de dicto*.

The possible-worlds semantics of this distinction is clear enough. In the example at hand, a *de dicto* belief is about the different politicians who are in their respective possible worlds the P.M. of Denmark. These possible worlds are all the worlds compatible with everything you believe. Hence these persons are usually different, and are all joined by one and the same world line only when you have a belief as to who the present Prime Minister of Denmark is.

In contrast, in a *de re* belief an individual member of the actual world is chosen satisfying the condition of being the P.M. of Denmark. Then we hang on to this individual and follow him along his world line to your different belief worlds. The individual constituted by this world line is the one whom your belief is about.

Thus the distinction is clear enough, and it has even attracted a great deal of attention on the part of contemporary linguists. It nevertheless presents a formidable challenge to the whole phenomenological conception of intentionality. For *de dicto* acts just do not seem to be directed to a particular object in any natural sense of the world.

19. HUSSERL AND *de dicto* ACTS

I find it very hard to tease out from Husserl's text any very satisfactory answer to the question as to how he proposed to deal with such in a sense undirected but yet unmistakably intentional acts.[55] The nearest I have come is the suggestion that acts *de dicto* are not directed to individual objects but rather to *facts*, in our example to the fact of the Danish Prime Minister's being a social democrat.[56] But this suggestion is most unsatisfactory. It destroys the obvious parity of acts *de re* and *de dicto*. It is also very hard to reconcile with the fact that an act *de dicto* is turned into an act *de re* when the believer acquires an additional opinion concerning the identity of the reference of the *dictum* in question. (In the example above, this means your forming a belief as to who the P.M. of Denmark currently is.) If the respective objects of an act *de dicto* and an act *de re* are entirely different, such a change would involve a major 'explosion' of the noema *apud* Husserl. However, reflection betrays no sign of explosion at all in such cases.

Furthermore, this apparent Husserlian attempt to solve the *de dicto* problem merely shifts the problem instead of solving it. For the cross-world identity of facts is quite unclear as compared with the cross-identification of individuals. How can a *de dicto* act your belief in our example be directed to one and the same fact, if this 'fact' involves different person's being the Prime Minister? Surely the fact of A's being the P.M. is different from the fact of B's being the P.M. Hence it is not clear that Husserl's stratagem would save the directedness of *de dicto* acts even if it were viable.

It is also hard to reconcile the alleged role of facts as the objects of certain acts with what Husserl says of the structure of noemata. There are any number of things he says of the determinable X which simply are categorially different from what he would be expected to say if facts could be objects of acts.

Hence the undeniable reality of *de dicto* acts is a further argument against intentionality as directedness, for such acts are undirected but yet intentional. Again, my thesis of intentionality as intensionality works out very well, for act *de dicto* certainly involve a multiplicity of different worlds. Indeed, the very distinction between what is *de re* and what is *de dicto* collapses if we are merely dealing with the actual world.

20. PERCEPTUAL INDIVIDUATION INTRINSICALLY *de re*

If a historical conjecture is admissible here, I wonder whether Husserl's oversight here might possibly be due to his use of perception as a paradigm of acts. The distinction *de dicto* vs. *de re* cuts right across the distinction between cross-identification by acquaintance and descriptive cross-identi-fication. It applies to both. But in the case of cross-identification by acquaintance, especially in the case of perceptual cross-identification, a new aspect of the conceptual situation emerges. In a sense everything that is perceived at all is *perceptually* cross-identified. This is essentially the point discussed above in connection with the intentionality of perception. Normal perception is *about* individuals; its content is spontaneously artic-ulated into objects with more or less definite locations in perceptual space. Since it is this space that serves as the frame of reference in perceptual cross-identification, all the objects of normal perception are perceptually cross-identified. One does not always see *what* or *whom* it is that one is seeing, but one cannot help seeing *it* (direct object construction). There are no perceptual acts *de dicto*, only acts *de re*, if one goes by perceptual cross-identification. In this sense, all acts of perception are directed to particular (perceptually cross-identified) objects.

Hence the mistaken but plausible thesis of intentionality as directedness is made especially seductive if one uses perception as one's paradigm case, as Husserl in fact did to a considerable extent.

More exegesis is needed to see whether this diagnosis of Husserl's over-sight is correct. But independently of it, we have obtained additional, strong evidence for the thesis of intentionality as intensionality.

21. The Form-Matter Contrast Vindicated

The contrast between two kinds of individuation methods, the perceptual and the descriptive, can be used to put Husserl's ideas into a new perspec-tive in still other ways. I emphasized earlier that cross-identification is not fixed by any absolute but is in principle carried out by ourselves. In this respect there is an important difference between the two kinds of individu-ation methods. Not only is perceptual individuation *de re*. It is determined by factors over which we cannot exercise any conscious control. As can be deduced from what I said in criticizing Husserl's theory of perception, one's perceptual individuals are in a sense given together with one's pri-mary, consciously *un*edited perceptions. One is free to use other methods of individuation besides this perceptual one, and one can try to dispense with it altogether, but one cannot change it at will. This mode of individu-ation is as it were built right into the way one's perceptual apparatus functions. No separate noesis is required for perceptual individuation.

In contrast to perceptual individuation, descriptive cross-identification typically relies on such clues as can (in principle and by hindsight) be recovered by memory and thinking from the sensory flux. It involves comparisons between different possible states of affairs or courses of events, which often may be thought of as different perceptual situations. Such comparisons are not given together with the possible situations themselves. Descriptive cross-identification is in fact very much like Husserlian constitution of objects which he describes in terms of a noesis acting on sensory materials or 'hyletic data'.

Husserl is thus right in the deep sense that the constitution of the objects which our experience is about is neither automatic nor given together with our sense-impressions. However, he fails to distinguish between the two different modes of cross-identification, and in effect applies to the perceptual one what only holds true of the descriptive mode. Thus in so far as Husserl took his insight to imply that sensation somehow has only the role of supplying the hyletic materials to be operated on by a noesis, he was badly mistaken. As I emphasized, unedited perception is in a perfectly good sense as fully articulated and as intentional as, say, thinking. It comes closer to truth to say that perceptual individuals and perceptual data, even though they are in themselves fully structured into solid three-dimensional objects and states of affairs, supply materials for the construction (constitution) of descriptively cross-identified individuals.

Husserl's mistake on this score is dramatized by the spontaneity of perceptual individuation, i.e., its being part and parcel of the rock bottom materials of sensory awareness. But now it also turns out that Husserl's form-matter contrast is not so much wrong as misplaced. Only the matter in question is not sensory raw-material, but sets of possible worlds. In the last analysis, they are such stuff as our ontology is made of, if by 'ontology' we mean the class of descriptively individuated objects of our propositional attitudes.

22. CONSTITUTIONAL PROBLEMS

These brief references to the actual development of possible-worlds semantics will have to suffice here. Since I suggested that this semantics is virtually tantamount to a general theory of intentionality, it is nevertheless in order to try to make good this claim and to show how possible-worlds semantics helps us to understand better the problems that have figured in earlier discussions about the nature of intentionality. Even though we cannot carry out more than a cursory discussion of a few selected topics, the brief glimpses of the nature of possible-worlds semantics offered above perhaps suffice as a basis of comparisons between my theory and certain views that have come up in the phenomenological literature.

For one thing, we can now see what precisely is involved in the constitution of the objects of our acts.[57] Speaking of 'constitution' easily evokes idealistic associations. They would be misplaced here, however. No doubts are thrown by possible-worlds semantics on the reality of the actual world or of its inhabitants, nor is it incompatible with this semantics to adopt the same realistic attitude to other possible worlds. Constitution is not a domestic matter, as it were, but a matter of foreign policy, that is to say, a matter of cross-world comparisons. What is brought about in constitution is literally neither here nor there – neither in one world nor in another. Constitution does not create inhabitants of any possible world, only methods of comparing entities in different possible worlds for their identity. In this sense, the possible-worlds theory of intentionality is compatible with a strong form of realism.

Notice that the point I am making here is a generalization of what was said earlier in connection with the problem of perception (section 15). It was pointed out there that we must distinguish sharply between on the one hand the problem of splitting up one given sensory manifold into individuals and on the other hand the problem of an individual's identity between different sensory contents. It was argued that only the second problem matters phenomenologically. This is just a special case of my general thesis that the crucial problem of constitution (making one's act to be directed to one particular individual) is a matter of interworld comparison.

23. THE NOEMATIC OBJECTS OF ACTS

The false appearance of idealism in connection with the constitution of world lines is brought about by the fact that in traficking with intentional concepts we are (according to my main thesis) dealing with individuals as members of more than one state of affairs or course of events. What a logician calls individuals and what he needs for instance as values of his bound variables are therefore often not elements of this or that particular world but individuals considered as members of several possible worlds. But such a consideration of individuals as members of different possible worlds already presupposes cross-identification. In such cases, the individuals needed in one's logic and semantics are more like world lines than their nodes.

Since these world lines are in principle, to borrow a phrase from Hobbes, "drawn and described by ourselves", the logician's individuals relied on in using intentional concepts are *in the specific sense which appears from these remarks* constituted by ourselves. (To repeat myself, such a constitution is of course not up to an individual's decisions but is codified in the conceptual rules of the whole speech community.) What makes this interesting but in itself ontologically innocuous observation striking is the fact that in a sense the only viable candidates for the role of the *objects* of our acts of knowledge, belief, etc., are these cross-identified individuals. In this sense, the objects of our knowledge and belief are therefore *selbsttätig* (as Kant would have said), that is, man-made. However, we have already seen that this observation does not militate against the realistic tendency of possible-worlds semantics.

It is thus the need of cross-identification that necessitates the constitution (in the Husserlian sense of the world) of the objects of our propositional attitudes. In the same way as we according to Husserl can intend one definite object only by means of a noema, in the same way we can on my view have knowledge of one definite object only if we can re-identify it in several possible worlds. In fact, I submit that the two processes, the cross-identification of individuals and their Husserlian constitution, are at bottom identical.

It is to be noted that in thus speaking of the *objects* of certain acts the term is not to be understood in the sense of the phenomenological distinction between an act and its object (in the actual world), but rather in the sense of that component of the noematic *Sinn* which establishes the identity of this object, the 'gegenständlicher Sinn' in Husserl's terminology. There thus obtains a close relationship between my notion of a world line and Husserl's notion of the 'gegenständlicher Sinn'.

24. Constitution not ontological

This serves to bring out the sense in which the very Brentano dichotomy, the whole contrast between the intentional and the nonintentional is not ontological in character. Ontology is a matter of 'the furniture of the world', that is, of what there is in the actual world or for that matter in this or that possible world. Such questions are not affected by the constitution of world lines. One reason why this plain truth is frequently overlooked is philosophers' tendency to reify world lines into alleged denizens of one particular world. Elsewhere, I have criticized a few of the many ensuing confusions.

25. THE TRANSCENDENCE OF OBJECTS

Although the connections are perhaps a shade less clear, it is also worth pointing out several other relationships between Husserlian ideas and possible worlds semantics. Husserl's idea of the transcendence of certain objects is closely related to the inexhaustible multiplicity of the possible worlds which are compatible with our beliefs and as a member of which such objects can occur. Our experience can narrow down this class but not boil it down to one world only, if we are dealing with a truly transcendent (in Husserl's sense) object. The same class of worlds can change in other respects in the light of further experience without changing the identity of the object in question. That is to say, its world line can often be continued to new worlds. But not always. When it cannot be so continued, the result is what Husserl calls an explosion of the noema.

26. THE PERCEIVING SUBJECT

More subtly, the notion of cross-identification by acquaintance is related to Husserl's ideas of *Ichbeziehung* and of the possible role of *Körperlichkeit* in our acts.[58] Since cross-identification by acquaintance depends on the point of view (in a literal or almost literal sense) of the person whose acts are being considered, for him such cross-identification is inevitably ego-bound. It presupposes an ego which is located in space and time (at least in perceptual space and time). However, this does not yet presuppose bodily existence in any very strong sense. And it is of course restricted to individuation by acquaintance, especially to perceptual individuation.

27. INEXISTENCE RECONSTRUCTED

Most importantly, we can now see in what sense the object of an intentional act can be said to 'inexist' in it. Since such an act involves several possible worlds, the object must be the same (well-defined) in all these worlds. In other words, a correct exhaustive description of the act involves a specification of what it means for this object to exist in all these different worlds. It seems perfectly appropriate to interpret 'intentional inexistence' as amounting to this kind of involvement of its identificatory conditions in an act.

28. CONCLUSION

In fact, possible-worlds semantics yields even such further pieces of evidence for its promise as a general theory of intentionality as I cannot present here. Even without them, it seems to me that we can conclude that recent developments in possible-worlds semantics have proved to have profound implications for the notion of intentionality itself, and not just for a number of particular intentional concepts.

NOTES

[1] International Colloquium on Explanation and Understanding, Helsinki, 25–26 January, 1974. The present essay is a considerably enlarged version of the paper read at that Colloquium. In expanding and rewriting it, I have greatly profited from discussions with Professor Dagfinn Føllesdal and from his unpublished (as well as published) writings. He nevertheless is not responsible for my errors, the more so as he in so many words disagrees with some of my conclusions concerning Husserl. I have also profited from comments by Professor Yrjö Reenpää and from the unpublished writings of Professors Ronald McIntyre and David Smith.

[2] Franz Brentano, *Psychologie vom empirischen Standpunkt*, Ducker und Humblot, Leipzig, 1874, Vol. I, Book 2, Chapter 1, sec. v., p. 85; translated in Roderick M. Chisholm (ed.), *Realism and the Background of Phenomenology*, The Free Press, Glencoe, Illinois, 1960, p. 50.

[3] In the sequel, I shall nevertheless argue that the sense-impressions involved in normal perception are not of this kind.

[4] Cf. Brentano, op. cit., sec. iii.

[5] Ludwig Wittgenstein, *Philosophical Investigations*, Blackwell's, Oxford, 1953, pp. 89–103 and passim.

[6] Edmund Husserl, *Ideen zu einer reinen Phänomenologischen Philosophie*, sec. 85, Husserliana ed., Martinus Nijhoff, The Hague, 1950, pp. 207–208; first ed., 1913, p. 171; Boyce Gibson translation, p. 226.

[7] Husserl, op. cit., sec. 124 (Husserliana ed., p. 305; first ed., p. 257; Boyce Gibson translation, p. 320).

[8] Cf. my books *Knowledge and Belief*, Cornell University Press, Ithaca, N.Y., 1962; *Models for Modalities*, D. Reidel, Dordrecht, 1969.

[9] Cf. Herbert Spiegelberg, 'Der Begriff der Intentionalität in der Scholastik, bei Brentano und bei Husserl', *Philosophische Hefte* (ed. by M. Beck) 5 (1936) 72–91.

10 Cf. L. J. Savage, *The Foundations of Statistics*, John Wiley, New York, 1954, pp. 9, 82–87.

11 What I have in mind in this qualification is seen from my paper, 'Surface Semantics', in *Truth, Syntax, and Modality*, Hugues Leblanc (ed.), North-Holland Publ. Co., Amsterdam, 1973, pp. 128–147.

12 This seems to have been an instance of a deeper (and wider) tendency to think of all rational activities in goal-directed concepts. Cf. the first two chapters of my book, *Knowledge and the Known*, D. Reidel, Dordrecht and Boston, 1974.

13 Cf. also the less striking formulations of the same point in *Picasso on Art: A Selection of Views*, Dore Ashton (ed.), The Documents of 20th-Century Art, The Viking Press, New York, 1972, pp. 27–31.

14 Cf. my *Knowledge and the Known*, p. 36.

15 Even more convincing evidence is obtained when it turns out that many problems concerning an artist's activity and its objects turn out to be but special cases of general problems in the semantics of intensional concepts. The problem of the identity of the object of an artist's creation (e.g.: Would he have created the same work of art if he had executed it differently in such-and-such respects?) is for example a special case of the more general problem of cross-identification. For a glimpse of this problem, see Chapter 6 above.

16 *Critique of Pure Reason*, beginning of the Transcendental Aesthetic (A 19 = B 33).

17 See Aristotle, *Metaphysica*, IX, 6, 1048b, 23–35.

18 W. V. Quine, *World and Object*, MIT Press, Cambridge, Mass., 1960, p. 9.

19 Dagfinn Føllesdal, 'Phenomenology', Chapter 21 in *Handbook of Perception*, Vol. 1, ed. by E. C. Carterette and M. P. Friedman, Academic Press, New York, 1974.

20 Cf. *Ideen*, sec. 85: "What forms the materials into intentional experiences and brings in the specific element of intentionality is... *noesis*." The 'materials' in question are described by Husserl as 'sensory data', 'hyletic or material data', or in older terms, "*sensuelle, wohl aber sinnliche Stoffe*". (See pp. 173–174 of the original; p. 210 of the Husserliana edition; and p. 228 of the Boyce Gibson translation). Husserl's formulation clearly presupposes that it is *only* through a *noesis* that these 'materials' become intentional.

21 Føllesdal, op. cit.

22 Føllesdal, op. cit.

23 Cf. Wolfgang Metzger, *Psychologie: Die Entwicklung ihrer Grundannahmen seit der Einführung des Experiments*, Dietrich Steinkopf, Darmstadt, 1954, p. 32. (Referred to and discussed by Eino Kaila, *Die perzeptuellen und konzeptuellen Komponenten der Alltagserfahrung*, Acta Philosophica Fennica, Vol. 13, Helsinki, 1963, pp. 65–69.) Another phenomenon which serves to illustrate my point here is the illusion of seeing three-dimensional Necker cube with the wrong orientation even when one's touch information gives the right orientation. See, e.g., R. C. Gregory. *The Intelligent Eye*, Weidenfeld & Nicholson, London, 1970, p. 40. Kaila discusses similar inversion phenomena; see op. cit., pp. 44–46.

24 Cf. William H. Ittelson, *The Ames Demonstrations in Perception*, Princeton and London, 1952.

25 See A. Michotte, *The Perception of Causality*, Methuen, London, 1963.

26 As is well known, Husserl goes as far as to say that for noemata "*esse* consists exclusively in its 'percipi'..." (*Ideen*, Husserliana ed., p. 246, first ed., p. 206, Boyce Gibson tr. p. 265).

27 Thus for instance Quine speaks of visual impressions as "colors disposed in a spatial

manifold of two dimensions" (op. cit., p. 2). This quote also illustrates the fact that on the view I am criticizing spontaneous sense-impressions need not be devoid of structure by any means. What is at issue is whether they are already impressions of definite objects (intentional in Husserl's sense) and hence whether they must be described in the same terms as these objects.

[28] Cf. Kaila, op. cit., pp. 71–73.

[29] Cf. Dagfinn Føllesdal, 'An Introduction to Phenomenology for Analytic Philosophers', in *Contemporary Philosophy in Scandinavia*, R. E. Olson and A. M. Paul (eds.), The Johns Hopkins Press, Baltimore, 1972, pp. 417–429, especially p. 423.

[30] Cf. note 23 above.

[31] See J. J. Gibson, *The Senses Considered as Perceptual Systems*, Houghton Mifflin, Boston, 1966. Most of David Katz' writings are also relevant here. There is a brief summary of some of his assumptions in Chapter 2 of his *Gestaltpsychologie*, Basel, 1948.

[32] See Chapter 4 above, appearing also in *Ajatus* 36 (1975), comprising the proceedings of the 1973 Colloquium on Perception in Helsinki, Finland.

[33] J. J. Gibson, op. cit., especially Chapters 1 and 13.

[34] For instance, it is emphasized that colors are not normally seen just as colors as such, but as somehow connected with the objects of perception, that is to say, as colors *of* objects (surface colors), film colors, colors *of* transparent regions of space (volume colors), colors *of* light sources (luminous colors), colored illuminations *of* objects or *of* empty space, etc. (See Jacob Beck, *Surface Color Perception*, Cornell University Press, Ithaca, N.Y., 1972, especially Ch. 2, and David Katz, *The World of Colour*, Kegan Paul London, 1935.) Nor is this object-relatedness restricted to visual perception. It is perhaps even more remarkable in the sphere of touch. There are even analogues in the tactile-haptic area to several to the different modes of color perception. (See David Katz, *Der Aufbau der Tastwelt*, Barth, Leipzig, 1925, and J. J. Gibson, *The Senses Considered as Perceptual Systems*, Houghton Mifflin, Boston, 1966, Chapter 7.)

[35] Cf. J. J. Gibson, op. cit., Ch. 13 and passim.

[36] Cf. here Hintikka, 'Information, Causality, and the Logic of Perception' (note 32 above).

[37] Cf. here Marx Wartofsky's contribution to the volume mentioned in note 32 above. The psychological literature on the experiential, conceptual, and cultural conditioning of perception is too vast to be surveyed here.

[38] Further materials concerning Husserl's views on perception are contained especially in his *Phänomenologische Psychologie* (Husserliana, Vol. IX), *Analysen zur passiven Synthesis* (Husserliana, Vol. XI), *Vorlesungen zur Phänomenologie des inneren Zeitbewusstseins* (Husserliana, Vol. X), and *Ding und Raum: Vorlesungen 1907* (Husserliana, Vol. XVI). See also Elisabeth Ströker, 'Zur phänomenologischen Theorie der Wahrnehmung', forthcoming in the volume mentioned above in note 32, and Føllesdal's comments on Aron Gurwitsch in his 'Phenomenology' (note 19 above).

[39] Translation modified from Føllesdal's; see *Husserliana*, Vol. XI, p. 363, lines 18–27. One problem with this passage is the Husserl is there speaking in so many words of the *filling component* of a perceptual noema not of sense data. Now clearly the two are related extremely closely to each other in Husserl. (Perhaps they are at bottom identical?) Yet it seems to be impossible to extract from Husserl any clear statement concerning their precise relationship. By any token, they nevertheless are sufficiently close to each other in Husserl for us to rely on the quoted passage here, presupposing of course sufficient general caution in interpreting Husserl.

[40] Føllesdal, 'Phenomenology' (note 19 above).

[41] Cf. Michael Dummett's discussion of Frege's principle "the concept *horse* is not a concept" in Dummett, *Frege: Philosophy of Language*, Duckworth, London, 1973, especially pp. 210–212. Note also that Fregean senses could not operate as the references of our terms in opaque (oblique) contexts (as they do on Frege's doctrine) if they were unsaturated.

[42] Frege, 'Über Sinn und Bedeutung', *Zeitschrift für Philosophie und philosophische Kritik* **100** (1892) 25–50; see p. 26. Husserl's term '*Gegebenheitsweise*' is also highly suggestive, even though it refers only to a certain component of the noema.

[43] Cf. Chapter 6 above.

[44] This point was emphasized particularly vigorously by Richard Montague; see *Formal Philosophy: Selected Papers of Richard Montague*, Richmond H. Thomason (ed.), Yale University Press, New Haven, 1974.

[45] See my 'On the Logic of Perception', Ch. 8 of *Models for Modalities* (note 8 above).

[46] The writings of Saul Kriple, Richard Montague, and Dana Scott offer good examples of this. Of them, Kripke has given the most sustained motivation for this view; see his 'Naming and Necessity', in *Semantics of Natural Language*, D. Davidson and G. Harman (eds.), D. Reidel, Dordrecht, 1972, pp. 253–355. Of some of the difficulties into which this treatment leads, cf. my paper, 'On the Proper Treatment of Quantifiers in Montague Semantics', in *Logical Theory and Semantic Analysis: Essays Dedicated to Stig Kanger*, Sören Stenlund (ed.), D. Reidel, Dordrecht, 1974, pp. 45–60.

[47] Cf. my papers 'Quine on Quantifying In' (note 43 above) and 'The Semantics of Modal Notions and the Indeterminacy of Ontology', in *Semantics of Natural Language* (note 46 above), pp. 398–414, reprinted above as Chapter 2 of this volume.

[48] David K. Lewis, 'Counterpart Theory and Quantified Modal Logic', *Journal of Philosophy* **65** (1968), 113–126.

[49] Cf. my 'Quine on Quantifying In' (Chapter 6 above).

[50] The perfectly unproblematic phenomenon of seeing double gives us an example of splitting world lines, when perception is treated 'informationally' along the lines indicated earlier in this paper.

[51] As one can easily see, merging is ruled out if and only if the formula (x) (y) (possibly $(x = y) \supset x = y$) is valid. In many treatments of different modal logics, it is not.

[52] The principle says that from $F(a)$ and $a = b$ you can infer $F(b)$ for any sentence $F(x)$. Of its interpretation, see once again my 'Quine on Quantifying In' (Ch. 6 above).

[53] For the following, see my 'On the Logic of Perception' (note 45 above), 'Objects of Knowledge and Belief', *The Journal of Philosophy* **67** (1970), 869–883, and 'Knowledge by Acquaintance – Individuation by Acquaintance', in *Bertrand Russell: A Collection of Critical Essays*, David Pears (ed.), Doubleday, Garden City, N.J., 1972, pp. 52–79.

[54] Cf. my *Models for Modalities* (note 8 above), pp. 97, 120–121, 141.

[55] See also Ronald McIntyre, 'Intentionality and *de re* Modality' (preprint).

[56] Cf. sec. 94 of the *Ideen*; also *Logische Untersuchungen* 5, *xvii* (Vol. 1, p. 402 of the first edition, p. 579 of the Findlay translation); 1, *xii* (p. 48 of the first ed., p. 288 of the translation); 5, *xxxvi* (pp. 472–3 of the first ed.; pp. 631–2 of the translation).

[57] Cf. R. Sokolowski, *The Formation of Husserl's Concept of Constitution*, Phenomenologica, Vol. 18, Martinus Nijhoff, The Hague, 1970.

[58] Cf., e.g., Ströker, op. cit. (note 38 above), sec. C, and the references given there.

CHAPTER 11

CONCEPT AS VISION: ON THE PROBLEM OF REPRESENTATION IN MODERN ART AND IN MODERN PHILOSOPHY

The problem of pictorial representation will be discussed here largely by reference to one single movement, the original cubism of Picasso and Braque. The crucial importance of this movement in the history of modern art is generally recognized, but its status is still puzzling and even controversial. This puzzle centers precisely on the relation of cubist art to the idea of representation. One's first impulse is to think of cubism as a step, perhaps the most important step, in the development of modern painting towards increasingly complete abstraction. A look at the apparently unrecognizable shapes of many cubist paintings seems to be enough to confirm this interpretation.

It is of course undeniable that in a purely historical respect cubism did represent a step towards abstract, nonrepresentational art. No less a critic than Harold Rosenberg has (among others) argued that this historical development was grounded in the intrinsic nature or, as Rosenberg calls it, the 'logic' of cubism. "Logically, Cubism implies abstract, nonrepresentational art, and art history since 1920 has again and again taken the path of this logic," Rosenberg writes.[1]

One does not have to disagree with this view of the historical role of cubism in order to find it a seriously incomplete account of the nature of cubism and of the aims of its first and foremost practitioners. The perspective opened by the pronouncements of the most important early cubists and of their best interpreters is in fact almost diametrically opposed to what one might expect on the basis of the idea of cubists as the openers of the floodgates of abstraction. On the contrary, these pronouncements emphasize that the aim of cubists was to restore to painting the sense of concrete, solid reality which had been lost by the impressionists and by the symbolists. A representative example of this emphasis is offered by Douglas Cooper's authoritative book *The Cubist Epoch*.[2] In his discussion of cubism, Cooper uses such phrases as "the new spirit of realism" (p. 30), "impulse toward realism" (pp. 18, 38), "accurate representation of reality" (p. 38), "realistic – indeed materialistic – intentions" (p. 58), and so on. The achievement by Braque and Picasso in creating (in 1906–12) the original cubism is described by Cooper (p. 62) by saying that "of course the major effort of Braque and Picasso went into solving the strictly pictorial problems arising out of their intention to find a wholly new and precise way of recreating tangible reality on canvas."

On the face of things, all this sounds almost unbelievable. How can paintings whose subjects one cannot always divine, let alone see, be labelled 'realistic'? How can Cooper possibly speak of the "accurate representation of reality" in connection with painters who distorted the shapes of people and objects into weird complexes of geometrical elements, of cubes, planes, triangles, etc.?

Notwithstanding this initial surprise, a closer look at what the cubists were actually doing soon shows that there is something to what Cooper says – indeed, a great deal of truth. The main cubists were really imbued with a spirit of concrete reality and plasticity. There are few portraits in the history of art which convey as strong a sense of solid reality as for instance Picasso's famous portrait of Gertrude Stein. What is perhaps more pertinent here, Picasso's cubistic portrait of Vollard is not any less of a likeness – certainly not a less recognizable likeness – of the painter's patron than Picasso's subsequent realistic picture of the same sitter. (See illustrations 1 and 2.) If anything, the cubist portrait conveys a stronger sense of concrete presence than the more conventional one. Nor is this sense of reality (if not of ordinary realism) restricted to human images. Cooper illustrates his point very well by juxtaposing two landscapes which were painted by Braque, the original cubist, and by the mere pseudo-cubist Dufy, respectively, the same year, 1908. They even depict closely similar scenes, possibly the very same one. Everyone can see – literally and metaphorically – that Braque is really representing a landscape, albeit in an unconventional way, whereas Dufy's canvas merely presents us with a composition of coloured areas only faintly reminiscent of a landscape.

This evidence of cubists' paintings is to my mind more persuasive than their own pronouncements of their aims. Nevertheless these, too, bear witness of the same point. Cubism is the only honest painting, Picasso once said.[3] He also expressed his great admiration for Velasquez: "'Las Meninas', what a picture! What realism! There you have a true painter of

Fig. 1. Picasso, Ambroise Vollard (1910).

Fig. 2.   Picasso, Ambroise Vollard (1915).

reality!"[4] Juan Gris said in 1925 that cubism was originally simply a new way of representing the world.[5] Moreover, Cooper's credentials as an interpreter of the intentions of cubists are impeccable, for he was a close friend of several of them.

Cooper's thesis cannot make any claims to novelty, either. Similar views had been voiced earlier by the most sophisticated theoreticians of cubist art, for example by John Golding[6] and Edward F. Fry.[7] For instance, Fry says that cubism "revitalized and extended" the tradition of Western art "by redefining its realistic premisses" (*Cubism*, p. 41). Of the early interpreters of cubism, Maurice Raynal spelled out more clearly than anyone else that the cubists were carrying out a "quest for truth".[8] It is also salutary to recall that the leading cubists, Picasso and Braque, never really crossed the boundary that separates representational art from the non-representational.

All this is not belied by the fact that in order to defend his thesis of the realistic intensions of the cubists Cooper has to restrict the purview of true cubism rather narrowly.[9] Not only must he dismiss many apparent cubists as merely decorative 'cubifiers'. He has to restrict his attention mainly to the work of Picasso and Braque in 1909–1914 and to its direct effects. Since their work was the most influential, the most original, and the most interesting aesthetically among all the so-called cubists, this restriction is not crucial, even though it may be historically misleading to label much of what usually counts as cubism in the history of modern art as so many misinterpretations or vulgarizations of the 'true' cubism of Picasso and Braque.

Thus we have a nice paradox in our hands. Cubists were realists in some sense, but in what sense? They were trying to convey a sense of reality, but they were not doing it by depicting real objects, at least not in the way in which they appear to our senses. But if they were not representing real perceptible people, real landscapes, or real still lives, what were they depicting? What is the reality that is involved in the realistic intentions of the cubists?

To these questions we can formulate a partial but illuminating answer in terms of an analogy between what we can find in modern art and what we can find in modern philosophy. One of the most important ideas that we can find in several different parts of recent philosophy is an emphasis on the concept of meaning. One aspect of this emphasis is a contrast between *meanings* and *objects meant*, that is to say, between on one hand the directedness or sense that enables us to refer to an object and on the other hand of this object itself. The best known form of this contrast is the distinction the German logician Gottlob Frege drew (in the case of linguistic meaning) between *Sinn* and *Bedeutung*, between sense and reference, as these terms are sometimes translated.[10] For instance, in the case of a word which refers to a particular object we must distinguish this object (the reference) from that thing about the word (its sense) that enables us to pick out the reference. Thus two senses might determine the same reference.

The most systematic early development of ideas of this kind is found in the phenomenology of Edmund Husserl, the main ideas of which he developed in 1901–1913, in particular between 1905 and 1913, that is to say, at the very same time at which cubism was born.[11] (Of course this simultaneity was not the result of any mutual influence whatsoever.)

Husserl generalized Frege's distinction between sense and reference from the area of linguistic meaning to all conscious human thought-acts.[12] (Dagfinn Føllesdal has shown convincingly how Husserl's theory is both historically and systematically a further development of Frege's views.[13]) Husserl was especially interested in what he called the *intentionality* of the acts of the human mind, that is, in the fact that they can as it were point to something beyond themselves, to be directed to it. According to Husserl, this intentionality presupposes a distinction which generalizes the Fregean distinction. Frege's references he called simply *objects*, and those meanings which enable an act to be directed to an object he called by the Greek word *noemata* (singular: *noema*). Although the object-noema distinction is applied more freely than Frege's distinction between reference and sense (*Bedeutung* vs. *Sinn*), the extension is hardly even a generalization, for Husserl thought that all noemata can in principle be expressed by linguistic meanings, which are precisely *Sinne* in Frege's sense.

Phenomenology was conceived of by Husserl as a study of noemata. An oversimplified but not unfair brief description of the famous "phenomenological reduction" is to say that in it we disregard ("bracket") objects and focus our attention to noemata. These meaning entities are the main vehicles of human thought, and can be reached by such a phenomenological reflexion. They are not subjective impressions or images or other psychological factors, but objective entities, however abstract. This abstractness has sometimes been confused with subjectivity, but wrongly so. In fact Husserl was highly critical of psychologism in logic.

After these preliminary explanations, we can give a concise answer to the question as to what it was that the cubist painters were doing. They were not painting objects, for most of their canvases do not look in the least like objects. *They were representing noemata, not objects.* Or perhaps one should rather say that cubist paintings are a sort of concretizations of noemata. In the same way as phenomenology is supposed to be a philosophical study of noemata, cubism is the art of the noemata.

Such parallelisms between entirely different kinds of intellectual (including artistic) movements are not without dangers, and often they are not very illuminating. In the case at hand, however, the analogy is more than skin-deep. It can be used to throw light on several different aspects of the cubists' art. For one thing, the analogy brings out the sense in which cubist art is conceptual (in *one* natural sense of this word which has recently been greatly abused). For what are the noemata supposed to be like? They are the meaning entities, the conceptual tools by means of which we can mentally grasp an object – or at least point to it or "intend" it. This noema is then a noema of that object. Such a noema may be compared to the totality of memories and expectations which we associate with it, the sum total of our ideas about it.

The statements of cubists and of their most perceptive interpreters show that their art was conceptual in this very sense of dealing with our conceptions of objects, not with the external appearance of these objects. Perhaps the bluntest expression of this attitude is the statement by Picasso Gertrude Stein reported: "I do not paint things the way they look, but the way I know they are." [14] The same idea is expressed clearly by Maurice Raynal in the article 'Conception et vision' already referred to. [15] Of these contrasting poles, concept and vision, Raynal writes, true art (that is, cubist art) follows the former. "In painting, if one wishes to approach the truth, one must concentrate only on the conceptions of the objects, for these alone are created without the aid of those inexhaustible sources of error, the senses." Raynal compares the cubists aptly with Giotto, who, when he "painted that picture in which, behind the men seen in the foreground, there is a fortified town, he showed the town in bird's-eye view. He thus described it as he had conceived it – that is to say, complete, all its parts at once. In this picture he respected neither per-spective nor visual perception; he painted the town as he *thought* it and not as the people in the foreground might have *seen* it" (emphasis in the original). It would be difficult to express more clearly than this that the cubists were painting noemata, not objects, without recourse to these terms.

Thus we have reached an answer to the question as to how cubism could have been realistic in intention even though it was strongly anti-naturalistic and anti-illusionistic. In fact, a paradox reminiscent of what I posed earlier about cubism can be formulated about phenomenology, too. Husserl, too, formulated his aims in realistic terms; he, too, wanted to get "zu Sachen selbst", at the real things.[16] Yet the upshot of his methods, especially when superficially understood, has often been an emphasis on one's subjective ideas of things instead of these things them-selves.

The analogy between cubism and phenomenology becomes somewhat less surprising when we recall what the two movements were principally reacting against. In the case of Husserl, we have a reaction towards the sensationalism and positivism of Ernst Mach, who tried to restrict science in the last analysis to the description of sense-impressions and their regularities.[17] This is the philosophical counterpart to impressionism in painting, and of course impressionism was a part of what the cubists were reacting against. Both the impressionists and Mach were focusing their attention on our direct senses-impressions, not on their objective sources. The former were trying to capture these impressions on canvas, the latter was studying their regularities. In contrast to this preoccupation both the cubists and the phenomenologists wanted to shift their emphasis "zu Sachen selbst".

We have to watch our terminology here. Mach's position is often called phenomenalism, which of course is to be distinguished sharply from phenomenology.

The similarity between cubism and phenomenology is striking enough to have caught the attention of more than one earlier critic. Probably the first to have called attention to it is Ortega y Gasset.[18] The most careful statement on record of the analogy is by Guy Habasque.[19] The similarity can be looked upon from different directions, however, and in earlier discussions of the relation between cubism and phenomenology the emphasis has typically been on the mental operations involved in the two activities, cubist painting and phenomenology, respectively, rather than on the semantics of the representational or intentional situation. This emphasis has perhaps not been very conducive to further developments of the analogy. Without wanting to deny the importance of 'the phenomenological reduction' for the practice of phenomenology, this importance seems to me best explicable in terms of the objective meaning entities, the noemata, which the reduction is calculated to uncover, rather than the mind-twisting that is supposed to help us to reach them. It has been argued recently, and quite persuasively, that the very meaning of the phenomenological reduction can only be understood in terms of the semantical and ontological status of noemata, not vice versa.[20] For this reason, I am here concentrating on these meaning entities rather than on the technique allegedly needed to reach them.

In modern art, too, one may ask whether the conceptual character of cubism is due more to the specific representational problems the cubists were addressing themselves to rather than to general philosophical preferences. For instance, in a brief early statement (in 1908–09) Braque spoke freely of the representation of emotions, and subjective impressions, if not quite of sensations.[21] What is significant there is that this artistic 'interpretation' or 'translation' of emotions takes place (according to Braque) by such concrete means as "volume, line, mass, weight". These representational problems are in any case easier to study and much more important for the actual work of a painter than the elusive mental experiences which he may have while doing this or that.

What is particularly interesting about the analogy between cubism and phenomenology is that it explains at once certain features of the actual techniques of the cubists. It is in fact here that the analogy is likely to be closest. For assume that the cubists were dealing with the noemata of objects, not with objects as such. What are such noemata like according to Husserl? The following is one recent answer. "To take an example from perception, let us consider the act of seeing a tree. When we see a tree, we do not see a collection of colored spots... distributed in a certain way; we see a tree, a material object with a back, with sides, and so forth. Part of it, for example the back, we cannot see, but we see a thing with a back. That seeing is intentional, object-directed, means that the near side of the thing is regarded only as a side of a thing, and that the thing we are seeing has other sides and features which are co-intended to the extent that the full thing is regarded as something with more than one side. The noema is the complex system of determination which unifies this multitude of features into aspects of one object."[22]

What this means is that the noema of an object is largely independent of the way it happens to be perceived. My conception, my noema, of a tree is not tied to any particular perspective, in the sense that it comprises many things that are not perceived at a given time and perhaps cannot ever be perceived at one and the same time. Here it might be especially helpful to think of a noema as a complex of expectations. When I see a tree, I expect that it has a back and sides, and I may also have definite expectations (say) of its hidden branches. (These expectations may be due to earlier experiences.) I expect certain definite things to happen to my visual impressions of the tree when I change my position (the perspective from which I am looking at the tree), and I expect certain things to remain constant when the lighting conditions change. All this illustrates what can and cannot belong to the noema of the tree.

Of course, if I have new experiences, for instance if I walk around the tree, my noema of that particular object may change. I may for instance come to associate a certain definite color to its back which I did not initially see. But that does not make either the old or the modified noema dependent on any particular occasion or on any particular perceptual perspective. Husserl expresses this partly by making a distinction between such things as the shapes and colors of objects and the particular impressions we receive of them. The former he calls *perspected variables*, the latter *perspective variations*. They are linked together in a noema. This noema specifies the perspected variables but is largely independent of their perspective variations, for instance independent of variations caused by perspective, lighting, etc.

This is precisely what we find also in cubist painting. Just as a Husserlian noema may contain at one and the same time expectations as to what an object or a person would look like from many different perspectives, in the same way cubists often depicted the same subject from several different angles at one and the same time. (Cf. illustration 3.) How integral a part this was of the cubist method is illustrated by a discovery Edward F. Fry made.[23] He discovered a study by Braque for the very first

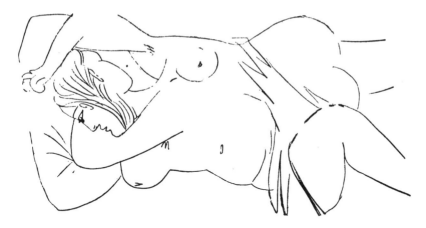

Fig. 3.   Picasso, Reclining Woman (1941).

cubist canvas Braque painted, the well-known, heavily stylized nude of the year 1908. In this study, the same nude is depicted from three different angles and in three different poses at once. (See illustration 4.)

More generally cubist art is characterized by its neglect of perspective and of consistent lighting. These two revolutions are sometimes thought of as being motivated by a quest of greater compositional freedom, independently of the representative aspects of the painting in question. This may have been part of the story, and certainly these aspects of the cubist method inspired others to venture further in the direction of abstraction. What we have seen nevertheless shows that far from being concessions to abstraction the giving up of perspective and of the assumptions of uniform lighting were partly an attempt to reach a more intense realism. We can also see how right those critics have been who have pointed out that these two innovations, dispensing with consistent perspective and dispensing with coherent lighting, stem from precisely the same source. The first of these critics seems to have been Jacques Rivière.[24] Rivière also expressed effectively the deeper reasons for the overthrow of perspective and consistent lighting by the cubists. Lighting, he says, "is the sign of a particular instant.... It has the effect

Fig. 4.   Braque, Drawing (study for the Grand Nu, probably 1907).

of profoundly altering the forms themselves.... It can therefore be said that lighting prevents things from *appearing as they are*" (emphasis in the original). Likewise, "perspective is as accidental as lighting.... It indicates not the situation of the objects, but of the spectator."

Perhaps the best thing about the analogy between cubism and phenomenology is that it points beyond itself and so betrays its own limitations. In fact, neither the general concept of meaning nor its particular explication in the phenomenological concept of noema is unproblematic or even clear. According to a widespread vulgarization of phenomenology, the upshot of the phenomenological reduction is to direct one's attention to one's own mental contents and mental acts. This is very misleading, for noemata are abstract entities which are not like images and which cannot be perceived in any sense of the word, not even by any 'internal sense'.[25] Husserl himself warned in so many words against thinking of noemata as images or pictures.[26] Phenomenology thus certainly is not of the nature of inward gazing at or contemplation of image-like noemata. But what it really is is much harder to establish.

In fact, in the last couple of decades another kind of meaning analysis has developed which addresses itself to similar problems from a somewhat different-looking vantage-point. This approach is often referred to by the metaphysically loaded term 'possible-worlds semantics'.[27] In reality its basic ideas are not very far from Frege and Husserl. Frege said that in his notion of *Sinn* or sense more is involved than the reference.[28] It includes also the way in which the reference is given (*die Art des Gegebenseins*).

Now possible-worlds semantics arises when it is realized that all such talk of 'ways of being given' is functional, that the only reasonable way of understanding Frege's statement in the last analysis is to interpret the sense or *Sinn* as the *function* which gives us the reference, by means of which we as it were can find this reference. This is already one of the main ideas of possible-worlds semantics. It is not so far from Husserl, either, for what Husserl was interested in was precisely those 'vehicles of directedness', the noemata, which enable us to intend or refer to objects. This is precisely what the meaning functions do on the possible-worlds conception. This theory of meaning entities as those functions which give us the references as their values is thus apparently only a small step beyond Frege and Husserl. It merely seems to spell out the logical type of those meaning entities.

Yet in spite of this similarity with Frege and Husserl the step to possible-worlds semantics is quite long. For one thing, neither Frege nor Husserl came close to taking this step. In some sense which is perhaps not very easy to pin down, precisely, both of them considered their meaning entities somehow as objects, not functions, however abstract these objects may have been. For possible-worlds semantics these meaning entities are not objects, but functions.

But what are the arguments of these functions? What are they allowed to depend on? Here it turns out that possible-worlds semantics is really a general form of a theory, rather than a complete, closed doctrine. For its answer to the question of the arguments of meaning functions is the safest possible one: Everything. The meaning function which gives us the reference of (say) a term as its value may depend on this or that aspect of the situation or world in which the reference is located, but it cannot depend on anything more than the whole world itself. At the abstract level on which possible-worlds semantics is moving, the only general answer to the argument question is therefore: the whole possible world in question. It is for this reason that possible-worlds semanticists say that meanings are functions from possible worlds to extensions or references. Given a term and a world, they yield as a value the object the term refers to in that world.

This leaves of course all sorts of further problems unexamined. The most important questions in possible-worlds semantics are in fact these further ones, the ones that try to probe a little deeper into the nature of the meaning functions.

One problem we face is due to the fact that one cannot grasp a meaning function as the abstract entity it is in the eyes of a logician. For him, a function is a class, usually an infinite class, of pairs of correlated arguments and values. Such a class is not usually apprehended directly, but only by means of some 'algorithm' or 'recipe' for obtaining the value from the argument. This already complicates the situation, and partly explains why it was so hard for Frege and Husserl to reach the abstract interpretation of meanings as functions just outlined.

Curiously enough, cubists were sometimes accused of a 'mistake' which is parallel to the mistake of considering meaning functions in the abstract, as mere classes of pairs of arguments and values. Jacques Rivière (op. cit.) once claimed that the "first mistake" of the cubists was to try to represent an object from all the different angles at one and the same time. This is of course not the same thing as representing it in all possible situations, but the analogy is nevertheless amusing. (There are also echoes of the use of possible worlds as arguments of meaning functions in

Rivière when he accuses the cubists of failing to carry out any 'selection' among the ingredients of the world.)

An especially important group of questions that arises here concerns the *constant functions* which in different circumstances or situations (in different 'possible worlds') pick out *the same object* or individual. Such meaning functions define what it is to be one and the same individual. In the Husserlian jargon, they *constitute* the objects we think and speak about. Questions of this sort are what philosophers call questions of individuation. In thinking of them, it may be of some illustrative help to think first of the different possible worlds as existing separately and then think of the embodiments of one and the same individual in them as being connected by a 'line', the *world line* of that individual. (David Kaplan has coined a nice pun and called them trans world heir lines or TWA's.) They are as it were graphical representations of the meaning functions which tell us how to find the same object or individual in different possible situations.

It is immediately obvious that this problem of individuation is closely related to the problems of pictorial representation. For a picture which represents certain objects or individuals will have to present us with some clues or others that enable us to tell what or who these objects or individuals are. It will have to present us a way of grasping the world line of that object or individual.

Now possible-worlds semantics allows for several different answers to the question as to how such individuation takes place. The easiest answer would be that we recognize objects by their identical looks both in pictures and in real life. However, according to the cubists this answer just does not work. For we saw that they were not depicting objects and individuals by means of their appearances or looks, but by means of the properties they are known or thought to have. But what properties?

Both in art and in philosophy one's first idea is to say here: by means of certain especially important properties. Philosophers call them essential properties. They are the properties a given individual or object cannot lose without thereby losing its identity, becoming another object or individual.

Now there is obviously a touch of essentialism to cubism. Its tendency to simplify and to reduce the depicted objects, not to say caricature them, is an indication of this. "We are looking for the essential", the early cubists Albert Gleizes and Jean Metzinger wrote in 1912 in the first book devoted entirely to cubism.[29] The early dealer in and interpreter of the cubists, Daniel-Henry Kahnweiler even borrowed terms from philosophy to make essentially the same point. He said that cubists were distinguishing between "primary and secondary qualities" of objects.[30]

This is a happy phrase, for the primary qualities of the cubists are perhaps not so very far removed from the primary qualities of philosophers. We already saw Braque mention as his most important representational means "volume, line, mass, weight", which are all among philosophers' primary qualities.[31]

However, it seems to me that neither in art nor in philosophy is essentialism the essential thing. Although no complete solution to the individuation problem can be given or even indicated here, there is one very important partial aspect of the situation which deserves emphasis and which is particularly interesting in the case of cubism. In the realm of the logical and philosophical individuation problem, it is the insight – if it is an insight, for the point is not uncontroversial[32] – that the individuation principles are not absolute in the sense that they are not fixed by Logic or Nature or by some equally inescapable power. The world lines are in principle "drawn and described" by ourselves. This does not mean of course that they are arbitrary. They may be grounded in our innate nature and also in the laws of nature. The point is that all this still in principle leaves room for more than one way individual objects are 'constituted', for more than one individuation method. In fact, elsewhere I have shown that in our actual conceptual and linguistic practice we often rely on two different individuation methods, that is, in a sense consider two different kinds of individuals at one and the same time.[33]

This specific doctrine gains some additional interest from being a kind of natural sequel to a most important overall change in philosophers' and logicians' attitudes to the logic of our own language. The two contrasting conceptions concerning it have been labelled by van Heijenoort 'logic as language' and 'logic as calculus',[34] but these terms do not fully explain what is involved. In the conception of 'logic as language' we have a view to the effect that our language and its logic is the inescapable medium of all communication. We can modify it by small steps, but we just cannot seriously contemplate an altogether different system of logical rules and of representational relationships between language and reality. We just cannot get outside our language according to this view.

This type of conception was represented by Frege. In our days, it is the tacit presupposition of much of W. V. Quine's philosophy of language.[35]

In contrast to this, the conception of 'logic as calculus' allows us as it were to step back and have a detached view from the outside of the whole of our own language, as if it were an artificial calculus to be freely interpreted.[36] The possibility of such bird's-eye view includes the possibility of allowing changes in the representational relationships between our language and the reality. In technical jargon, it allows the development of a *model theory* of our language, for the basic idea of this theory (sometimes also called *logical semantics*) is just to study a language by letting its interpretation vary systematically. This interpretation is of course just what the representational relationships I mentioned establish. It is no accident that the development of logical semantics and of model theory has been one of the most important large-scale changes in modern logic and in contemporary philosophy.[37] The growth of possible-worlds semantics is one aspect of this development.

The key idea of this whole development can be taken to be just the idea of freely varying the representational relationships between language and reality. The possibility of constituting our individuals in more than one way is a small but important instance of this general tendency.

Now here we have another analogy with cubism which in my view is even more important than the analogy between phenomenology and cubism. For the most important feature of the cubist revolution consisted precisely in the giving up of one preferred method of pictorial representation, viz. the naturalistic and illusionistic one. This is analogous to the step from 'logic as language' to 'logic as calculus' which also involved giving up the idea of one preferred and indeed inescapable mode of representation. What the cubists did was to substitute for the traditional illusionistic and naturalistic system of representation others which were at least partly created freely by the painter himself. This is the explanation for the apparent abstractness of many cubistic pictures. It is not that these pictures do not represent. Rather, they represent their objects by means of conventions, by means of a 'language' which the spectator has not yet learned. Once one realizes this 'key', one finds much more method in the apparent madness of cubist paintings. There are in fact clear-cut

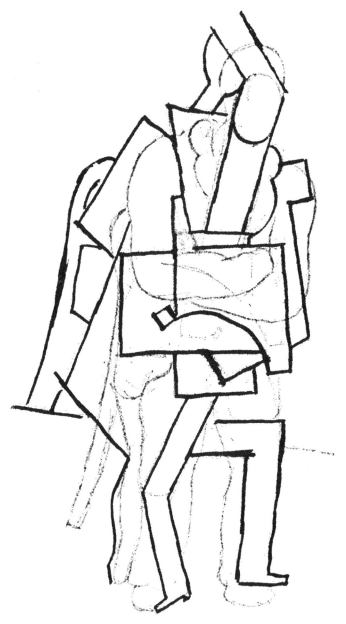

Fig. 5.   Picasso, Seated Man with Arms Folded (1915).

Fig. 6.   Velasquez, Las Meninas (1956).

representational principles underlying the pictures of the cubists. For
instance, in analytic cubism the painter as it were split the surface of the
object into small facets and then turned most of them into one and the
same plane represented in the picture (illustration 1). On other occasions

other rules were followed. Picasso's drawing of a sitting man vividly shows these rules at work (illustration 5). It is also fascinating and instructive to see how Picasso takes one set of representational conventions, for instance the ones Velasquez had used, and transposes them into his own system, or, more accurately, into one of the many systems he is using.[38] (See illustrations 6–8.)

Fig. 7.   Picasso, Las Meninas (17 August, 1957).

That one of the main novelties of the cubists was the rejection of naturalistic representation is of course a commonplace. What is not appreciated equally often are the realistic motives of this rejection. They are nevertheless unmistakable. One example among many may suffice here. In his inimitable ironic way, Picasso emphasized this point in one of his revealing discussions with Kahnweiler.[39] They had been discussing Michelangelo's 'Last Judgment' and Picasso had emphasized the impossibility of painting such a picture "honestly" and without presenting mere "charm" by using naturalistic means. "Look at Michelangelo's

Fig. 8.   Picasso, Las Meninas (19 September, 1957).

'Last Judgment'", Picasso said. "Is it truly worked out? Is it truly worked out right down to the nostrils of Christ's nose? Of course not! It is just charm, decoration. When you reduce all that to its basic elements there is enough left to make a nice tie. To produce a big picture like that would need the help of every painter since the beginning of time and even so it would not be finished yet."

Kahnweiler's reaction was to ask: "So you think one cannot do a 'Last Judgment'?" Picasso replied, "Not at all, I know how I would do one [sketching with his finger on the pedestal]. You see God here at the top [drawing a 'mandorla']. As you know, they often used to represent Him by an oval. Underneath, a sword [drawing a horizontal stroke] for Divine Justice. Then some scales. At the bottom on the left the damned. On the right the elect. [He drew some circles.] You see!"[40]

We can conclude with Kahnweiler: "I began to see what he was leading up to. He meant that Cubism was the only honest painting and that honest painting could be conceived only in the form of language with invented signs and no attempt at imitation." Picasso assented to this and reiterated, "Cubism is the only real painting."

This explains the motivation of the frequent references to the new 'language' or 'symbolism' of the cubists, for instance when Kahnweiler

Fig. 9.   Kandinsky, Study for a 'Last Judgement' (1913).

speaks of the "new language" of the cubists[41] or when Raynal refers to their "new representation"[42] or when Cooper speaks of their using "a comprehensive system of spatial notation".[43] Here we can also see more clearly in what sense cubist art is abstract. It is not abstract because it is non-representational, but in the sense in which a symbolic notation is more abstract than a purely pictorial one.

It would be an interesting task to try to say more about the languages cubists used. For instance, the verbal allusions Picasso and Braque included in their pictures can be studied with profit.[44]

There are also interesting theoretical problems about the whole enterprise. A nonnaturalistic mode of representation can be shared by a school, by a tradition, or even by a whole culture. It may also be the invention of an individual artist. But how free is he in choosing his language? Cubists emphasized the freedom of choice here and especially the resulting relativity of representational conventions. This feature of the cubist 'philosophy' and its reasons are summed up very well by Robert Rosenblum who writes: "The inevitable conclusion is that a work of art presents a complex interchange between artifice and reality. A picture depends upon external reality, but the Cubist means of recording this reality – unlike the means devised by the Renaissance – are not absolute but relative. One pictorial language is no more 'real' than another...".[45] Yet it is far from obvious that this relativity is absolute. Are there limits to what a painter can do on his own and yet be understood by others? It is clear that in the apparent freedom which an artist enjoys in choosing his own language we have one of the reasons why cubism has in practice led artists toward greater and greater abstraction. It is also clear that in this direction we soon run into the aesthetic counterpart of Wittgenstein's famous problem of the impossibility of completely private languages.[46] We shall not examine either problem here, however.

It may nevertheless be in order to point out that whatever freedom of the choice of one's representational notation the cubists postulated, it is enough to disprove a line of philosophical interpretation of cubism that earlier enjoyed some currency. When cubists renounced the appearances of objects for conceptual reality, some of their early interpreters compared this move to the idealistic philosophy of Immanuel Kant.[47] This is misleading, for the representational freedom which the cubists asserted goes much beyond the innate forms of sense-perception which Kant emphasized and which are grounded not in artistic choice but in immutable human nature.

It is useful here to stick closer to the aims and methods of the original cubists. They did much more than just create new pictorial languages, new systems of "ideational notation".[48] They were fully aware of what they were doing in creating new representational possibilities and in fact called attention to the very problem of the interrelation, not to say interplay, of art and reality in painting. Only they did this by artistic and not by theoretical means. In their work, they illustrated strikingly certain aspects of the 'dialectic' of artistic representation. For this reason, one can say of their art with a much greater justification than Novotny of Cézanne's paintings that it is "gemalte Erkenntniskritik".[49]

If one allows oneself full freedom in varying the representational relationship between language and reality or between pictures and reality, one will come up with surprising results. In logic, a technique sometimes used in model theory is a nice instance of this. It was apparently first used by Leon Henkin in his important completeness proofs around 1950,[50] and has been frequently employed since. It consists in interpreting (for certain technical purposes) certain sets of formulae as literally speaking of themselves, as being the very reality they speak about. This idea of making as it were a chunk of language into an independent reality of its own has a neat counterpart in the artistic repertoire of the cubists and their followers. For that is precisely what the technique of collage amounts to: you insert an actual object, a chunk of reality, into your picture. Thus the so-called model sets and other sets of formulae one can use in the Henkin technique are precisely logicians' collages, we may perhaps say.

Again the intentions of the cubists have often been misrepresented. The collage technique is not a new trick calculated to create an illusion of reality, but as Braque said in his 'Thoughts on Art' of 1917,[51] "precisely the opposite". This technique is not intended to improve illusionistic representation, but to confound it. For how could you confuse more thoroughly the interrelations of art and reality than by incorporating a real object into your painting or drawing?

Indeed, what the cubists did was even more ambivalent than this. The very first collage in the history of modern art, Picasso's 'Still Life with Cane Chair' of 1912 (illustration 10) is enough to show this. There Picasso

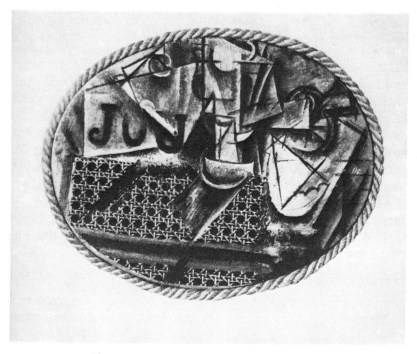

Fig. 10.   Picasso, Still Life with Cane Chair (1911).

represents the bottom of the chair, not by painting it, but by pasting a real object on the canvas. However, the irony is heightened by the fact that this 'real' object is itself 'false': it is not a piece of real caning but only a ready-made piece of wax cloth made to look like caning. The nice self-irony of this trick illustrates strikingly cubists' emphasis on the relativity of all representation.

Similar examples are easily found *ad libitum.* For instance, for a while Braque used in his collages pieces of paper made to look like wood. And a great deal of Picasso's art involves playful and ironic superimposal of reality and representation. For instance, we do not enjoy the intended effect (or shock) of Picasso's famous 'Bull's Head' (illustration 11) unless we see in it *both* a bull's head *and* the saddle and handlebar of a discarded bicycle.

There are thus several important connections between the problems of representation in modern art and modern philosophy, several of them worth further inquiry. The similarity between the two is further heightened by a similarity in the spirit in which some of the best artists and best philosophers and logicians have approached their task. This similarity is brought out by a formulation Picasso once gave to his criticism of his predecessors.[52] He mocked the pre-cubist painters by saying: "What would you say of a mathematician who wrote down a string of figures giving no solution to a problem and said: 'You see this group of sevens and eights side by side – how pretty! Isn't it delicious!' That is what the painters whose pictures are hanging in the Louvre have done. And, moreover, they have a very restricted number of signs. To make an arm they do this [describing a circle in the air] – and to draw a leg they do the same thing. And what is left? Nothing but charm. The charm of a prostitute."

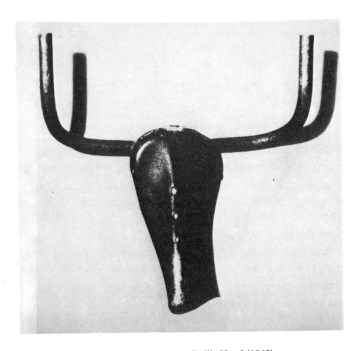

Fig. 11.   Picasso, Bull's Head (1943).

The spirit of problem-solving, the sense of addressing oneself to specific tasks instead of lofty ideals which is reflected by Picasso's words is shared by much of the best modern philosophy.

NOTES

[1] 'The Cubist Epoch', *The New Yorker*, 8 May, 1971, p. 102ff.

[2] Douglas Cooper, *The Cubist Epoch*, Phaidon Press, London, 1971.

[3] In discussion with Daniel-Henry Kahnweiler on 22 June, 1946, as reported in 'Voice of the Artist III', *The Observer*, 8 December, 1957.

[4] Discussion with Kahnweiler, 12 February, 1935, reported in *loc. cit.* It is interesting to see how Picasso later produced his interesting variations on that very painting by Velasquez.

[5] See D.-H. Kahnweiler, *Juan Gris*, Revised Edition, Abrams, New York, n.d., pp. 202–203.

[6] John Golding, *Cubism: A History and an Analysis 1907–1914*, Faber and Faber, London, 1959.

[7] Edward F. Fry, *Cubism*, Thames and Hudson, London, 1966.

[8] Maurice Raynal, 'Conception et vision', *Gil Blas*, Paris, 28 August, 1912; partly translated in Fry, *op. cit.*, pp. 94–96.

[9] Cooper, *op. cit.*, pp. 12–13, 107–111.

[10] Gottlob Frege, 'Über Sinn und Bedeutung', *Zeitschrift für Philosophie und philosophische Kritik* **100** (1892) 25–50.

[11] See H. Spiegelberg, *The Phenomenological Movement*, Martinus Nijhoff, The Hague, 1960, III, C, 3.

[12] See especially *Ideen zu einer reinen Phänomenologie* (1913), sec. 124. (Husserliana ed., pp. 303–307.)

[13] Dagfinn Føllesdal, *Husserl und Frege*, Aschehoug, Oslo, 1958; 'An Introduction to Phenomenology for Analytic Philosophers', in *Contemporary Philosophy in Scandinavia*, R. E. Olson and A. M. Paul (eds.), The Johns Hopkins Press, Baltimore, 1972, pp. 417–429.

[14] Gertrude Stein's story, recounted by Janet Flanner in *The New Yorker*, 6 October, 1956, p. 78.

[15] Note 8 above.

[16] At one point Husserl even made the claim that "no ordinary 'realist' has ever been as realistic and as concrete as I, the so-called phenomenological 'idealist'" (letter quoted in Iso Kern, *Husserl und Kant*, Nijhoff, The Hague, 1964, note to p. 276).

[17] Ernst Mach, *The Analysis of Sensations*, Dover Publications, New York, 1959.

[18] Ortega y Gasset, 'Sobre el punto de vista en las artes', 1924, translated in Ortega y Gasset, *The Dehumanization of Art and Other Writings on Art and Culture*, New York, 1956.

[19] Guy Habasque, 'Cubisme et phénoménologie', *Revue d'Esthétique*, Paris, 1949, pp. 151–161. Cf. also Guy Habasque, *Cubism*, Albert Skira, 1959.

[20] See Ronald McIntyre and David Smith, 'Intentionality via Intensions', *Journal of Philosophy* **68** (1971) 541–561.

[21] An Interview with Gelett Burgess, reported in 'The Wild Men of Paris', *The Architectural Record*, New York, May 1910, especially p. 405 (partially reprinted in Fry, *op. cit.*, p. 53).

[22] Dagfinn Føllesdal, 'Phenomenology', *The Handbook of Perception*, Vol. 1, E. C. Carte-

rette and M. P. Friedman (eds.), Academic Press, New York, 1974. I have relied on Prof. Føllesdal's article in several important ways in the present essay.

²³ Fry, *op. cit.*, pp. 16–17 and 54.

²⁴ Jacques Rivière, 'Sur les tendences actuelles de la peinture', *Revue d'Europe et d'Amérique*, Paris, 1 March, 1912, pp. 384–406. Partly translated in Fry, *op. cit.*, pp. 75–81.

²⁵ The character of noemata as abstract entities is shown very well in Dagfinn Føllesdal, 'Husserl's Notion of Noema', *Journal of Philosophy* **66** (1969) 680–687.

²⁶ *Ideen*, the Husserliana-edition, pp. 224–225.

²⁷ Its main architects include Richard Montague, Saul Kripke, and David Kaplan. It grew from the semantics of modal logics developed by Stig Kanger, Jaakko Hintikka, and Saul Kripke. On the development and nature of possible-worlds semantics, see also Jaakko Hintikka, 'Carnap's Semantics in Retrospect', *Synthese* **25** (1972–73) 372–397, reprinted above as Chapter 5 of this volume.

²⁸ Frege, *op. cit.*, p. 26.

²⁹ Albert Gleizes and Jean Metzinger, *Du Cubisme*, Paris, 1912. Notice also that the emphasis on 'essences' goes nicely together with the analogy with phenomenology, one of whose methods was in so many words called '*Wesensschau*'.

³⁰ Daniel-Henry Kahnweiler, *Der Weg zum Kubismus*, Munich, 1920, pp. 33–34.

³¹ Cf. R. J. Hirst, 'Primary and Secondary Qualities', in the *Encyclopedia of Philosophy*, Paul Edwards (ed.), Macmillan and the Free Press, New York, 1967, Vol. 6, pp. 455–457.

³² Cf., for instance, Saul Kripke's recent writings for a dissenting view.

³³ See Jaakko Hintikka, 'On the Logic of Perception', reprinted as Ch. 8 of Hintikka, *Models for Modalities*, D. Reidel, Dordrecht, 1969; 'Knowledge by Acquaintance – Individuation by Acquaintance', in *Bertrand Russell* (Modern Studies in Philosophy), David Pears (ed.), Doubleday, Garden City, N.J., 1972, pp. 52–79.

³⁴ Jean van Heijenoort, 'Logic as Calculus and Logic as Language', *Synthese* **17** (1967) 324–330.

³⁵ This is shown vividly by Quine's frequent use of the metaphor of language as a ship at sea which we cannot abandon and which we can only rebuild carefully plank by plank.

³⁶ Thus the *deep* idea underlying logicians' concept of a formal calculus is not that such a calculus is an uninterpreted formal game, but rather that it can be *freely* interpreted.

³⁷ It is also not accidental that for as prolific a logician as Quine he has contributed very little to model theory.

³⁸ In 1957 Picasso in fact produced a whole series of variations on Velasquez' theme. The differences between them illustrate strikingly some of the different ways in which Picasso projected Velasquez' picture into his own schemes of representation.

³⁹ Discussion on 22 June, 1946, reported in *op. cit.* (note 3 above).

⁴⁰ By a curious coincidence, Kandinsky had anticipated Picasso's ironical recipe and produced almost nonfigurative 'last judgements' already in 1911. See Will Grohmann's Classified Catalogue in his book on Kandinsky (Abrams, New York), items 666, 757, and 663, and Fig. 9.

⁴¹ Daniel-Henry Kahnweiler, *Der Weg zum Kubismus*, Munich, 1920, p. 34.

⁴² Maurice Raynal, *Quelques intentions du cubisme*, Paris, 1919, excerpts translated in Fry, *op. cit.* (note 7 above), pp. 151–153.

⁴³ *Op. cit.*, p. 49.

⁴⁴ Cf. Robert Rosenblum, 'Picasso and the Typography of Cubism', in *Picasso 1881–1973*, Roland Penrose and John Golding (eds.), Paul Elek Ltd., London, 1973, pp. 49–75.

⁴⁵ Robert Rosenblum, *Cubism and Twentieth-Century Art*, Abrams, New York, n.d., p. 58.

⁴⁶ Cf. Ludwig Wittgenstein, *Philosophische Untersuchungen*, Blackwell's, Oxford, 1953,

especially pp. 243ff., and *Wittgenstein and the Problem of Other Minds*, Harold Morick (ed.), McGraw-Hill, New York, 1967.

[47] Cf., e.g., Christopher Gray, *Cubist Aesthetic Theories*, The Johns Hopkins Press, Baltimore, 1953, pp. 45–46, 65–67, 143–145 and *passim*.

[48] Maurice Raynal, *op. cit.* (note 42 above).

[49] Fritz Novotny, quoted in Christopher Gray, *Cubist Aesthetic Theories*, The Johns Hopkins Press, Baltimore, 1953, p. 47 (note 16).

[50] Leon Henkin, 'The Completeness of the First-Order Functional Calculus', *Journal of Symbolic Logic* **14** (1949) 159–166; 'Completeness in the Theory of Types', *Journal of Symbolic Logic* **15** (1950) 81–91; both reprinted in *The Philosophy of Mathematics*, Jaakko Hintikka (ed.), Oxford University Press, London, 1969.

[51] 'Pensées et réflexions sur la peinture', *Nord-Sud*, Paris, December 1917; translated in Fry, *op. cit.*, pp. 147–148.

[52] Discussions with Kahnweiler, 22 June, 1946, reported in *loc. cit.* (note 3 above).

Grateful acknowledgement is made to those persons and institutions who so graciously extended the permissions necessary to print the illustrations contained in Chapter 11 of this book.

INDEX OF NAMES

INDEX OF SUBJECTS

SYNTHESE LIBRARY

Monographs on Epistemology, Logic, Methodology,
Philosophy of Science, Sociology of Science and of Knowledge, and on the
Mathematical Methods of Social and Behavioral Sciences

Managing Editor:
JAAKKO HINTIKKA (Academy of Finland and Stanford University)

Editors:
ROBERT S. COHEN (Boston University)
DONALD DAVIDSON (The Rockefeller University and Princeton University)
GABRIËL NUCHELMANS (University of Leyden)
WESLEY C. SALMON (University of Arizona)

1. J. M. BOCHEŃSKI, *A Precis of Mathematical Logic.* 1959, X + 100 pp.
2. P. L. GUIRAUD, *Problèmes et méthodes de la statistique linguistique.* 1960, VI + 146 pp.
3. HANS FREUDENTHAL (ed.), *The Concept and the Role of the Model in Mathematics and Natural and Social Sciences, Proceedings of a Colloquium held at Utrecht, The Netherlands, January 1960.* 1961, VI + 194 pp.
4. EVERT W. BETH, *Formal Methods. An Introduction to Symbolic Logic and the Study of Effective Operations in Arithmetic and Logic.* 1962, XIV + 170 pp.
5. B. H. KAZEMIER and D. VUYSJE (eds.), *Logic and Language. Studies dedicated to Professor Rudolf Carnap on the Occasion of his Seventieth Birthday.* 1962, VI + 256 pp.
6. MARX W. WARTOFSKY (ed.), *Proceedings of the Boston Colloquium for the Philosophy of Science, 1961–1962*, Boston Studies in the Philosophy of Science (ed. by Robert S. Cohen and Marx W. Wartofsky), Volume I. 1973, VIII + 212 pp.
7. A. A. ZINOV'EV, *Philosophical Problems of Many-Valued Logic.* 1963, XIV + 155 pp.
8. GEORGES GURVITCH, *The Spectrum of Social Time.* 1964, XXVI + 152 pp.
9. PAUL LORENZEN, *Formal Logic.* 1965, VIII + 123 pp.
10. ROBERT S. COHEN and MARX W. WARTOFSKY (eds.), *In Honor of Philipp Frank*, Boston Studies in the Philosophy of Science (ed. by Robert S. Cohen and Marx W. Wartofsky), Volume II. 1965, XXXIV + 475 pp.
11. EVERT W. BETH, *Mathematical Thought. An Introduction to the Philosophy of Mathematics.* 1965, XII + 208 pp.
12. EVERT W. BETH and JEAN PIAGET, *Mathematical Epistemology and Psychology.* 1966, XII + 326 pp.
13. GUIDO KÜNG, *Ontology and the Logistic Analysis of Language. An Enquiry into the Contemporary Views on Universals.* 1967, XI + 210 pp.
14. ROBERT S. COHEN and MARX W. WARTOFSKY (eds.), *Proceedings of the Boston Colloquium for the Philosophy of Science 1964–1966, in Memory of Norwood Russell Hanson*, Boston Studies in the Philosophy of Science (ed. by Robert S. Cohen and Marx W. Wartofsky), Volume III. 1967, XLIX + 489 pp.

15. C. D. BROAD, *Induction, Probability, and Causation. Selected Papers.* 1968, XI + 296 pp.
16. GÜNTHER PATZIG, *Aristotle's Theory of the Syllogism. A Logical-Philosophical Study of Book A of the Prior Analytics.* 1968, XVII + 215 pp.
17. NICHOLAS RESCHER, *Topics in Philosophical Logic.* 1968, XIV + 347 pp.
18. ROBERT S. COHEN and MARX W. WARTOFSKY (eds.), *Proceedings of the Boston Colloquium for the Philosophy of Science 1966–1968*, Boston Studies in the Philosophy of Science (ed. by Robert S. Cohen and Marx W. Wartofsky), Volume IV. 1969, VIII + 537 pp.
19. ROBERT S. COHEN and MARX W. WARTOFSKY (eds.), *Proceedings of the Boston Colloquium for the Philosophy of Science 1966–1968*, Boston Studies in the Philosophy of Science (ed. by Robert S. Cohen and Marx W. Wartofsky), Volume V. 1969, VIII + 482 pp.
20. J. W. DAVIS, D. J. HOCKNEY, and W. K. WILSON (eds.), *Philosophical Logic.* 1969, VIII + 277 pp.
21. D. DAVIDSON and J. HINTIKKA (eds.), *Words and Objections: Essays on the Work of W. V. Quine.* 1969, VIII + 366 pp.
22. PATRICK SUPPES, *Studies in the Methodology and Foundations of Science. Selected Papers from 1911 to 1969*, XII + 473 pp.
23. JAAKKO HINTIKKA, *Models for Modalities. Selected Essays.* 1969, IX + 220 pp.
24. NICHOLAS RESCHER *et al.* (eds.), *Essays in Honor of Carl G. Hempel. A Tribute on the Occasion of his Sixty-Fifth Birthday.* 1969, VII + 272 pp.
25. P. V. TAVANEC (ed.), *Problems of the Logic of Scientific Knowledge.* 1969, XII + 429 pp.
26. MARSHALL SWAIN (ed.), *Induction, Acceptance, and Rational Belief.* 1970, VII + 232 pp.
27. ROBERT S. COHEN and RAYMOND J. SEEGER (eds.), *Ernst Mach; Physicist and Philosopher*, Boston Studies in the Philosophy of Science (ed. by Robert S. Cohen and Marx W. Wartofsky), Volume VI. 1970, VIII + 295 pp.
28. JAAKKO HINTIKKA and PATRICK SUPPES, *Information and Inference.* 1970, X + 336 pp.
29. KAREL LAMBERT, *Philosophical Problems in Logic. Some Recent Developments.* 1970, VII + 176 pp.
30. ROLF A. EBERLE, *Nominalistic Systems.* 1970, IX + 217 pp.
31. PAUL WEINGARTNER and GERHARD ZECHA (eds.), *Induction, Physics, and Ethics, Proceedings and Discussions of the 1968 Salzburg Colloquium in the Philosophy of Science.* 1970, X + 382 pp.
32. EVERT W. BETH, *Aspects of Modern Logic.* 1970, XI + 176 pp.
33. RISTO HILPINEN (ed.), *Deontic Logic: Introductory and Systematic Readings.* 1971, VII + 182 pp.
34. JEAN-LOUIS KRIVINE, *Introduction to Axiomatic Set Theory.* 1971, VII + 98 pp.
35. JOSEPH D. SNEED, *The Logical Structure of Mathematical Physics.* 1971, XV + 311 pp.
36. CARL R. KORDIG, *The Justification of Scientific Change.* 1971, XIV + 119 pp.
37. MILIČ ČAPEK, *Bergson and Modern Physics*, Boston Studies in the Philosophy of Science (ed. by Robert S. Cohen and Marx W. Wartofsky), Volume VII. 1971, XV + 414 pp.
38. NORWOOD RUSSELL HANSON, *What I do not Believe, and other Essays*, (ed. by Stephen Toulmin and Harry Woolf), 1971, XII + 390 pp.
39. ROGER C. BUCK and ROBERT S. COHEN (eds.), *PSA 1970. In Memory of Rudolf Carnap*, Boston Studies in the Philosophy of Science (ed. by Robert S. Cohen and Marx W. Wartofsky), Volume VIII. 1971, LXVI + 615 pp. Also available as a paperback.
40. DONALD DAVIDSON and GILBERT HARMAN (eds.), *Semantics of Natural Language.* 1972, X + 769 pp. Also available as a paperback.

41. YEHOSHUA BAR-HILLEL (ed.), *Pragmatics of Natural Languages*. 1971, VII + 231 pp.
42. SÖREN STENLUND, *Combinators, λ-Terms and Proof Theory*. 1972, 184 pp.
43. MARTIN STRAUSS, *Modern Physics and Its Philosophy. Selected Papers in the Logic, History, and Philosophy of Science*. 1972, X + 297 pp.
44. MARIO BUNGE, *Method, Model and Matter*. 1973, VII + 196 pp.
45. MARIO BUNGE, *Philosophy of Physics*. 1973, IX + 248 pp.
46. A. A. ZINOV'EV, *Foundations of the Logical Theory of Scientific Knowledge (Complex Logic)*, Boston Studies in the Philosophy of Science (ed. by Robert S. Cohen and Marx W. Wartofsky), Volume IX. Revised and enlarged English edition with an appendix, by G. A. Smirnov, E. A. Sidorenka, A. M. Fedina, and L. A. Bobrova 1973, XXII + 301 pp. Also available as a paperback.
47. LADISLAV TONDL, *Scientific Procedures*, Boston Studies in the Philosophy of Science (ed. by Robert S. Cohen and Marx W. Wartofsky), Volume X. 1973, XII + 268 pp. Also available as a paperback.
48. NORWOOD RUSSELL HANSON, *Constellations and Conjectures*, (ed. by Willard C. Humphreys, Jr.), 1973, X + 282 pp.
49. K. J. J. HINTIKKA, J. M. E. MORAVCSIK, and P. SUPPES (eds.), *Approaches to Natural Language. Proceedings of the 1970 Stanford Workshop on Grammar and Semantics*. 1973, VIII + 526 pp. Also available as a paperback.
50. MARIO BUNGE (ed.), *Exact Philosophy – Problems, Tools, and Goals*. 1973, X + 214 pp.
51. RADU J. BOGDAN and ILKKA NIINILUOTO (eds.), *Logic, Language, and Probability*. A selection of papers contributed to Sections IV, VI, and XI of the Fourth International Congress for Logic, Methodology, and Philosophy of Science, Bucharest, September 1971. 1973, X + 323 pp.
52. GLENN PEARCE and PATRICK MAYNARD (eds.), *Conceptual Chance*. 1973, XII + 282 pp.
53. ILKKA NIINILUOTO and RAIMO TUOMELA, *Theoretical Concepts and Hypothetico-Inductive Inference*. 1973, VII + 264 pp.
54. ROLAND FRAÏSSÉ, *Course of Mathematical Logic* – Volume 1: *Relation and Logical Formula*. 1973, XVI + 186 pp. Also available as a paperback.
55. ADOLF GRÜNBAUM, *Philosophical Problems of Space and Time*. Second, enlarged edition, Boston Studies in the Philosophy of Science (ed. by Robert S. Cohen and Marx W. Wartofsky), Volume XII. 1973, XXIII + 884 pp. Also available as a paperback.
56. PATRICK SUPPES (ed.), *Space, Time, and Geometry*. 1973, XI + 424 pp.
57. HANS KELSEN, *Essays in Legal and Moral Philosophy*, selected and introduced by Ota Weinberger. 1973, XXVIII + 300 pp.
58. R. J. SEEGER and ROBERT S. COHEN (eds.), *Philosophical Foundations of Science. Proceedings of an AAAS Program, 1969*. Boston Studies in the Philosophy of Science (ed. by Robert S. Cohen and Marx W. Wartofsky), Volume XI. 1974, X + 545 pp. Also available as paperback.
59. ROBERT S. COHEN and MARX W. WARTOFSKY (eds.), *Logical and Epistemological Studies in Contemporary Physics*, Boston Studies in the Philosophy of Science (ed. by Robert S. Cohen and Marx W. Wartofsky), Volume XIII. 1973, VIII + 462 pp. Also available as paperback.
60. ROBERT S. COHEN and MARX W. WARTOFSKY (eds.), *Methodological and Historical Essays in the Natural and Social Sciences. Proceedings of the Boston Colloquium for the Philosophy of Science, 1969–1972*, Boston Studies in the Philosophy of Science (ed. by Robert S. Cohen and Marx W. Wartofsky), Volume XIV. 1974, VIII + 405 pp. Also available as paperback.
61. ROBERT S. COHEN, J. J. STACHEL and MARX W. WARTOFSKY (eds.), *For Dirk Struik*.

Scientific, Historical and Political Essays in Honor of Dirk J. Struik, Boston Studies in the Philosophy of Science (ed. by Robert S. Cohen and Marx W. Wartofsky), Volume XV. 1974, XXVII + 652 pp. Also available as paperback.

62. KAZIMIERZ AJDUKIEWICZ, *Pragmatic Logic*, transl. from the Polish by Olgierd Wojtasiewicz. 1974, XV + 460 pp.

63. SÖREN STENLUND (ed.), *Logical Theory and Semantic Analysis. Essays Dedicated to Stig Kanger on His Fiftieth Birthday*. 1974, V + 217 pp.

64. KENNETH F. SCHAFFNER and ROBERT S. COHEN (eds.), *Proceedings of the 1972 Biennial Meeting, Philosophy of Science Association*, Boston Studies in the Philosophy of Science (ed. by Robert S. Cohen and Marx W. Wartofsky), Volume XX. 1974, IX + 444 pp. Also available as paperback.

65. HENRY E. KYBURG, JR., *The Logical Foundations of Statistical Inference*. 1974, IX + 421 pp.

66. MARJORIE GRENE, *The Understanding of Nature: Essays in the Philosophy of Biology*, Boston Studies in the Philosophy of Science (ed. by Robert S. Cohen and Marx W. Wartofsky), Volume XXIII. 1974, XII + 360 pp. Also available as paperback.

67. JAN M. BROEKMAN, *Structuralism: Moscow, Prague, Paris*. 1974, IX + 117 pp.

68. NORMAN GESCHWIND, *Selected Papers on Language and the Brain*, Boston Studies in the Philosophy of Science (ed. by Robert S. Cohen and Marx W. Wartofsky), Volume XVI. 1974, XII + 549 pp. Also available as paperback.

69. ROLAND FRAÏSSÉ, *Course of Mathematical Logic – Volume II: Model Theory*. 1974, XIX + 192 pp.

70. ANDRZEJ GRZEGORCZYK, *An Outline of Mathematical Logic. Fundamental Results and Notions Explained with All Details*. 1974, X + 596 pp.

71. FRANZ VON KUTSCHERA, *Philosophy of Language*. 1975, VII + 305 pp.

75. JAAKKO HINTIKKA and UNTO REMES, *The Method of Analysis. Its Geometrical Origin and Its General Significance*. Boston Studies in the Philosophy of Science (ed. by Robert S. Cohen and Marx W. Wartofsky), Volume XXV. 1974, XVIII + 144 pp. Also available as paperback.

76. JOHN EMERY MURDOCH and EDITH DUDLEY SYLLA, *The Cultural Context of Medieval Learning. Proceedings of the First International Colloquium on Philosophy, Science, and Theology in the Middle Ages – September 1973*. Boston Studies in the Philosophy of Science (ed. by Robert S. Cohen and Marx W. Wartofsky), Volume XXVI. 1975, X + 566 pp. Also available as paperback.

77. STEFAN AMSTERDAMSKI, *Between Experience and Metaphysics. Philosophical Problems of the Evolution of Science*. Boston Studies in the Philosophy of Science (ed. by Robert S. Cohen and Marx W. Wartofsky), Volume XXXV. 1975, XVIII + 193 pp. Also available as paperback.

80. JOSEPH AGASSI, *Science in Flux*. Boston Studies in the Philosophy of Science (ed. by Robert S. Cohen and Marx W. Wartofsky), Volume XXVIII. 1975, XXVI + 553 pp. Also available as paperback.

SYNTHESE HISTORICAL LIBRARY

Texts and Studies
in the History of Logic and Philosophy

Editors:

N. KRETZMANN (Cornell University)
G. NUCHELMANS (University of Leyden)
L. M. DE RIJK (University of Leyden)

1. M. T. BEONIO-BROCCHIERI FUMAGALLI, *The Logic of Abelard.* Translated from the Italian. 1969, IX + 101 pp.

2. GOTTFRIED WILHELM LEIBNITZ, *Philosophical Papers and Letters.* A selection translated and edited, with an introduction, by Leroy E. Loemker. 1969, XII + 736 pp.

3. ERNST MALLY, *Logische Schriften*, ed. by Karl Wolf and Paul Weingartner. 1971, X + 340 pp.

4. LEWIS WHITE BECK (ed.), *Proceedings of the Third International Kant Congress.* 1972, XI + 718 pp.

5. BERNARD BOLZANO, *Theory of Science*, ed. by Jan Berg. 1973, XV + 398 pp.

6. J. M. E. MORAVCSIK (ed.), *Patterns in Plato's Thought. Papers arising out of the 1971 West Coast Greek Philosophy Conference.* 1973, VIII + 212 pp.

7. NABIL SHEHABY, *The Propositional Logic of Avicenna: A Translation from al-Shifā: al-Qiyās*, with Introduction, Commentary and Glossary. 1973, XIII + 296 pp.

8. DESMOND PAUL HENRY, *Commentary on De Grammatico: The Historical-Logical Dimensions of a Dialogue of St. Anselm's.* 1974, IX + 345 pp.

9. JOHN CORCORAN, *Ancient Logic and Its Modern Interpretations.* 1974, X + 208 pp.

10. E. M. BARTH, *The Logic of the Articles in Traditional Philosophy.* 1974, XXVII + 533 pp.

11. JAAKKO HINTIKKA, *Knowledge and the Known. Historical Perspectives in Epistemology.* 1974, XII + 243 pp.

12. E. J. ASHWORTH, *Language and Logic in the Post-Medieval Period.* 1974, XIII + 304 pp.

13. ARISTOTLE, *The Nicomachean Ethics.* Translated with Commentaries and Glossary by Hypocrates G. Apostle. 1975, XXI + 372 pp.

14. R. M. DANCY, *Sense and Contradiction: A Study in Aristotle*. 1975, XII + 184 pp.

15. WILBUR RICHARD KNORR, *The Evolution of the Euclidean Elements. A Study of the Theory of Incommensurable Magnitudes and Its Significance for Early Greek Geometry.* 1975, IX + 374 pp.

16. AUGUSTINE, *De Dialectica*. Translated with the Introduction and Notes by B. Darrell Jackson. 1975, XI + 151 pp.